Architecting Cloud SaaS Software – Solutions or Products

Engineering Multi-tenanted Distributed Architecture Software

International & Alumni Relations
INDIAN INSTITUTE OF TECHNOLOGY MADRAS
Chennai 600 036

+91 44 2257 8070 +91 44 2257 4926
oaa@iitm.ac.in oir@iitm.ac.in

Prof. R. Nagarajan
Dean, I & AR

+91 94440 08390
deaniar@iitm.ac.in

Being an "aspiring author and perspiring Professor myself", I can well appreciate the effort that Shri Prithviraj has put into this book. IIT Madras alumni do everything well, and this book is another case in point. While I'm not a subject matter expert in "Cloud SaaS software", I can still glean that is an extraordinarily well-organized book that lays out the material clearly and crisply. Shri Prithviraj's varied experience in the IT industry, as well as his academic training at IISc and at IITM, are evident in the way he has effortlessly communicated the nuances. Writing well may only be a journey to an end, but the journey here is to be savored.... I wish the book a great reception in the target industry and by all its practitioners.

R. Nagarajan

May 12, 2015

Architecting Cloud SaaS Software – Solutions or Products

Engineering Multi-tenanted Distributed Architecture Software

Sankaran Prithviraj

Pearson

I dedicate this book to all professors at IISC, Bangalore and at IIT Madras, for shaping my mental ability to have a successful career, life and ability even to write this book.

Editor—Acquisitions: S. Shankari

Senior Editor—Production: C. Purushothaman

ISBN 978-93-325-3760-6

First Impression
Current Impression, 2026

Published by Pearson India Education Services Pvt. Ltd, CIN: U72200TN2005PTC057128.

Head Office: 1st Floor, Berger Tower, Plot No. C-001A/2, Sector 16B, Noida - 201 301, Uttar Pradesh, India.

Registered Office: 6th Floor, Tower A, Unit A and B, International Tech Park, CapitaLand Chennai,

200 Feet Radial Road,Zamin Pallavaram, Old Pallavaram Chennai – 600117, Tamil Nadu, India

Website: in.pearson.com; Email: companysecretary.india@pearson.com

Digitally printed in India by Trinity Academy for Corporate Training Ltd, New Delhi in the year of 2026.

Contents

Preface

In *Architecting Cloud SaaS Software: Solutions or Products,* I have presented specific engineering insights that are required to architect and engineer cloud SaaS. By this, I imply that I have included new and emerging engineering knowledge relating to cloud SaaS architecture apart from the ones used for architecting hitherto conventional software. The book focuses on this additional information, which is only the beginning of a foray to the exciting field of cloud computing. It compiles the approaches used to create software solutions (and products) that can run as multi-tenanted single instance software in cloud platforms. Thus, it shall be a useful text to anyone who wants to become a specialist in this niche area of architecting cloud SaaS.

It is common knowledge that the need to execute software on public, private or hybrid clouds created a necessity to architect software differently. However, the important question is whether the additional knowledge required to architect this class of software is essential for all software professionals or only for those who specialize in developing cloud SaaS software. The answer to this question lies in the answer to another intriguing poser: how long will cloud technology last? In other words, if the cloud is going to stay here forever, there is little option for any IT professional to skip acquiring this knowledge. Cloud pervades the industry in one form or another; hence, this knowledge becomes indispensible. Infrastructure as a Service (IaaS) is one of the first cloud based value providing solutions that most companies acquire; IaaS may be implemented within the boundary of an enterprise, though many companies may be less than willing to use public or hybrid clouds for their regular business-processing needs. Hence, even regular business solutions need to be provided on IaaS platform (within the enterprise boundary) and need to be multi-tenanted because of the various advantages it provides. Thus, the concepts covered in this book will only get further refined and enhanced, and continue to be relevant for the future. Forthcoming software will not be written ignoring specific characteristics such as multi-tenancy for hosting them in cloud platforms. The theory and ideas discussed in the book will go a long way to help those who wish to have a sustained career in the IT field.

This book has been written from a practical perspective with case studies being used to explain most of the concepts for the benefit of IT professionals who engineer, architect or design cloud SaaS. Technical leads, architects, designers, software engineers and software developers also stand to benefit from this book. Those who are into Marketing can read Chapters 1, 3 and 4 as these will be of immediate use to them and help them to understand and use accurately the taxonomy associated with cloud computing. Project managers and practice heads can recommend this book for their engineering team. They too shall benefit by reading Chapter 1 to use the taxonomies of this field very accurately. Chapter 3 introduces more taxonomies; this chapter is recommended to all. The architecting project methodology discussed in chapter 2, will prove to be useful since it helps to adopt and monitor architecting projects, although that is not the focus of the contents of this book.

Chapter 4 describes, step by step, the procedure for conventional software to be architected for IaaS cloud platform – be it public or private. Thus the chapter is useful to all those who are currently providing software solutions on the IaaS platform irrespective of whether or not they are keen to develop a skill in multi-tenanted cloud compatible SaaS software.

Professionals in marketing, project managers and non-hands on CxOs, who want to know more beyond introductory material on cloud computing found in Chapter 1, can read Chapter 5 on Characteristics of Cloud SaaS Software and Chapter 6 on Cloud Compatibility Measure. These chapters reveal the difference between conventional software and the cloud compatible one. They also provide measures to monitor the extent to which the software being developed in your projects is cloud compatible. These parameters by which one can define, measure and monitor 'cloud compatibility' are unique and not found in any other book of my knowledge. Thus, the chapters of this book will be useful to:

a. the sales and marketing team to identify pre-sale solutions
b. project managers and tech leads to monitor the compatibility of their end product architecture to the Cloud.

There are many knowledge barriers for aspiring professionals who want to enter into this field of architecting cloud SaaS. The subject requires advanced knowledge from at least three different fields: architecting software, architecting methodology such as The Open Group Architecture Framework (TOGAF) and a strong design and engineering knowledge of distributed computing. A typical engineer who designs object-oriented software can comfortably read this book. The book has useful references that will help the reader to get over difficulties, if any, in understanding some of the concepts. Those who seriously practice architecting cloud SaaS can consider employing TOGAF as architecting methodology. Chapter 2 gives a method of tailoring TOGAF, the general purpose architecting methodology, to suit to the specific purpose of architecting cloud compatible SaaS. I recommend reading Chapter 2 in the second pass rather than the first one. Knowing TOGAF will be an advantage in getting the best out of this chapter.

Along with Chapter 4, Chapters 7, 8 and 9 forms a set and it is the core of this book. As suggested by the title of these chapters, they cover the principles that govern the architecture of cloud-compatible SaaS solutions or products, using currently available non- or semi- cloud-compatible products. While customers look for highly cloud-compatible solutions, it is disappointing when component software that needs to be used for solution is not cloud compatible. That is the reality faced by today's practising engineers in real-life architecting projects. Keeping this reality in mind, Chapters 7, 8 and 9 have been written to provide direct help to the practising engineers. The topics covered in these chapters should come in handy in their projects.

Chapter 10 reviews one of the standards for architecture of the cloud platform. Although this chapter can be read in the second pass, the theory covered here is used in explaining concepts in other chapters. Tailoring generic standards to the specific purpose of architecting cloud SaaS is from the practice point of view and another original contribution in this book.

Users are concerned not so much about the challenges in cloud compatible SaaS development and the solutions the technology offers, as they are about the security aspects of cloud computing. I do not think that a chapter on security can provide all the answers. As security in cloud is a vast and specialized field, it needs elaborate treatment in a separate book. Chapter 11 is just a preliminary and does not intend to cover any aspect in depth.

The illustration given below suggests an effective method to read this book quickly and profit from it in each pass. Each horizontal listing of chapters gives one logical group of chapters. In each pass, readers can read the set of chapters in that level. Traverse from top to bottom in that order, one level at a time.

Recommended reading sequence for software professionals

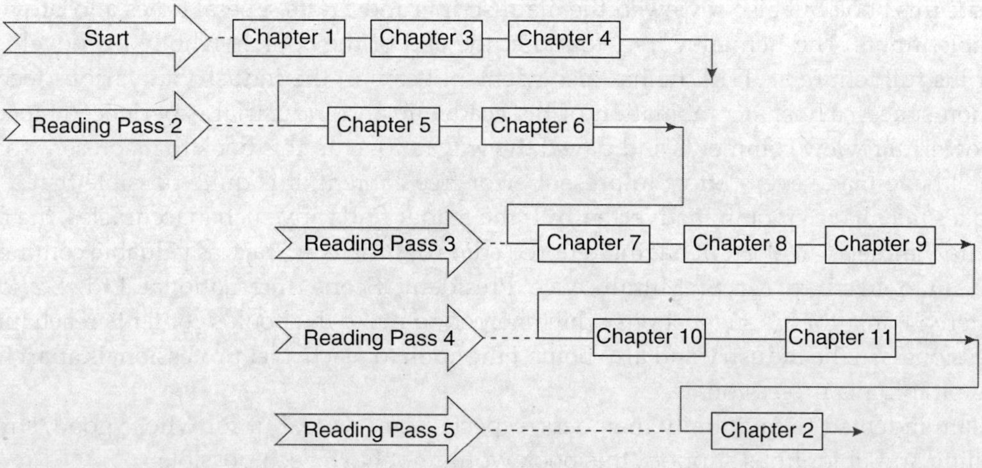

In the following table, I have given my recommendation on who can read what chapters to gain maximum benefit.

Chapter number	Software professionals, architects, designers and engineers	Tech leads and project managers	Sales and marketing and customer-facing people	Non-hands on CxOs
1	✓	✓	✓	✓
2	✓			
3	✓	✓	✓	✓
4	✓	✓	(optional)	
5	✓	✓	✓	✓
6	✓	✓	✓	✓
7	✓			
8	✓			
9	✓			
10	✓	(optional)		
11	✓		✓	✓

In a rapidly growing field such as cloud computing, it is a great challenge for any author including me to keep the contents of the book in sync with current developments. I am sure that the contents of this book will serve as a sound basis to understand later-day developments in the field. I wish all readers the best to succeed in this exciting field of cloud computing.

Acknowledgements

I thank Prof. R. Nagarajan, retired, formerly professor of Computer Science, IIT Madras, Chennai, without whose help this book could not have been conceived. A mere 'Thank you' appears to be far too less a term than what I would like to convey. He not only encouraged me to write this book but also reviewed the manuscripts and drafts several times and provided valuable inputs. The 'semantic tree' found at the end of the book is wholly his novel idea. After his full tenure at IITM, he has also spent 14 years in the industry at various techno-solution spaces. Thus, a combination of his academic and industrial experience helped in his powerful review comments and paved the way to tone up this book to its present shape. While I have made every effort to present error-free content, it is quite possible that a few mistakes may have crept in inadvertently. If the reader finds any such inaccuracies, the fault is entirely mine as an effect of having ignored some of Prof. Nagarajan's valuable comments.

I am obliged to Mr S. Murali, Vice President, Scope International Ltd, Standard Chartered Bank, for his suggestions which helped to make the book's contents reach junior professionals in the industry and also helped the book to reach .Net professionals apart from its intent for Java professionals.

I am indebted to my family members, especially my wife, but for whose good, strong, unfailing and ubiquitous support, this book would not have been possible.

Thanks are also to the new generation gadgets and apps, which lessened the writing burden. Text-to-voice for proof-reading, voice-to-text for dictating the manuscript are definitely worth mentioning. These gadgets helped, in no small measure, to mitigate this arduous task of writing two hundred pages of technical content and reviewing them several times.

Last but not the least, I am grateful to all those who have helped me in several ways to make this book possible.

Sankaran Prithviraj

Why This Book

Development of future software is set to take a decisive turn for the better with progressive advances in software engineering practices, new sets of architectural principles and design practices that help to build a cloud compatible SaaS. Such development is only to be expected irrespective of whether or not cloud computing technology has come to stay or firms adopt the cloud technology. Such an approach to build new generation software is essential not only to find solutions to known problems such as scaling but also to reap its advantages in easier and cost-effective maintenance, on-the-fly maintenance, upgrades of the software, economies of scale, etc.

Before cloud computing could arrive, software architecture appeared to have reached a dead-end with respect to architecture templates, architecture blue prints, domain architectures and a well-developed methodology to architect software. However, arrival of the cloud computing paradigm and availability of software as a service for architectures such as single-instance multi-tenancy demanded a new set of software behaviour, quality and requirements, and called for a lot of new thinking for architecting and designing it. This additional knowledge is available only in scattered literature and familiar to just a few practicing architects.

Cloud computing is therefore at the core of this additional knowledge in the frontier area of several fields such as service-oriented architecture. It is being applied to entire software and architecture development methodologies, paving a completely new way of provisioning user interfaces, reports and databases. It provided a means of getting rid of scaling problems through auto-scaling techniques, etc. Thus, it has to be compounded with new security measures in service-oriented architected (SOA) software. The advanced concepts in each of these fields need to be understood before getting into how these advances blend and become useful in architecting cloud SaaS.

Literature in the subject is rife with accounts of the advancements made in each of fields individually. However, it is silent about how these headways can be used for architecting cloud SaaS. More importantly, the order in which one needs to apply the concepts to build a multi-tenanted, highly scalable, flexible and easy-to-maintain cloud SaaS software is not known.

This book is first of its kind to bring such information under a single cover and to provide sequenced instructions to the architect step by step so as to enable him build any cloud compatible SaaS.

The top management personnel of software firms can benefit from this book as it gives them adequate foundation in the concept of cloud compatible SaaS to which they would otherwise have limited exposure, as sponsors of IT projects. Encouraging the team to develop cloud SaaS compatible software can bring potential cost benefits to the company.

A popular question raised about SaaS is whether a company or firm has to itself adopt cloud computing first before getting into the business of building cloud compatible SaaS. The simple answer to this is 'No'. A more complex answer and justification of why it need not be so forms the contents of this book.

Project managers can use the points provided in the book to guide their customers and team to the right deliverable – a cloud-compatible software that defines, measures, monitors and steers to a desirable end-product.

Architects, aspiring designers and developers will find in this book a ready reckoner that is indispensible for use in their chosen fields.

About the Author

Sankaran Prithviraj, in his current role as independent technology strategist, provides thought leadership, advises CxOs on technology selection and use as strategic tool for business, and innovates new solutions using emerging technologies such as cloud computing, mobile computing, analytics, and enterprise architecture. He provides novel, technical solutions for verticals such as banking, government, telecom and media. In an illustrious career spanning over thirty years in the IT industry, he has not only worked on all the technologies as they emerged but also climbed the corporate ladder by serving several companies both in India as well as in the USA catering to the needs of a worldwide clientele for IT-enabled business solutions. He established and headed Center of Excellence for several technologies and served in the Chief Technology Officer's office besides conducting research in industrial R&D labs. He ventured his own company and hived off portions of the business after several years of running it successfully.

Based on his experience in delivering solutions, Prithviraj has published several papers on cloud computing and enterprise architecture, and enterprise mobile computing in international forums such as The Open Group Architecture Forum (TOGAF) and Enterprise Architecture Practitioners Conference. He is a regular among the conference speakers in his subject area and a member in noted panel discussions. He has also served as a member in the standing committee of world body for architecture, TOGAF. An alumnus of IISc Bangalore and IIT Madras where he earned his bachelor's and master's degrees in engineering respectively, his education covers four branches of engineering – metallurgy, aeronautics, production technology and computer science. He can be reached at ArcCloudSaaS@yahoo.in.

Chapter 1

Introduction

This chapter explains the title of this book and also introduces various basics that are necessary to understand concepts and body of knowledge dealt with in this book.

The acronym SaaS stands for software as a service. The concept of providing SaaS is not new. Although it has been less popular in the past several decades, software has been provided as a service by various means. The most popular one was a hosted model in 1990s. It has evolved over a period of time and now software can be deployed and provided from 'cloud'. However, this is a service provider's viewpoint. From service consumers' viewpoint, customers enjoy these services through public Internet, using thin clients such as Web browsers on desktops or mobile devices.

1.1 SaaS Deployed and Provided from Cloud Environment

Cloud computing reference architecture document proposed by IBM™ to The Open Group Architecture Framework (TOGAF) has the following definition and explanation:

The capability provided to the consumer is to use the provider's applications running on a cloud infrastructure and accessible from various client devices through a thin client interface such as a Web browser (e.g., web-based email). The consumer does not manage or control the underlying cloud infrastructure, network, servers, operating systems, storage, or even individual application capabilities, with the possible exception of limited user-specific application configuration settings[24].

SaaS is also referred to as applications as a service because SaaS is essentially about providing applications as a service (as opposed to software in general). This also includes content services (e.g. video-on-demand) and higher value network services (e.g. VoIP) as typically encountered in communication service provider scenarios[37].

"Software-as-a-Service (SaaS)[37] *shares the distinction of being both a business model and an application delivery model. SaaS enables customers to utilize an application on a pay-as-you-go basis and eliminates the need to install and run the application on the customer's own hardware".*

Using above statements, we can settle for a simpler definition: SaaS can be roughly defined as software deployed on cloud, provided from or through cloud and also being consumed by accessing these services through cloud. The cloud here refers to the Internet.

SaaS through cloud has:

(i) A new method to provide software, which has otherwise been provided in compact disk or memory stick.
(ii) A new business model for software providers on a 'pay-per-use' mode rather than one-time buying of license for each copy being used.
(iii) SaaS has begun to open a new market segment for software; otherwise is confined to use by large enterprises with heavy IT use.

Architecting a solution or software that would address these paradigms has resulted in a whole new body of knowledge in itself. Before looking at concepts to architect SaaS for the cloud, it is important to understand these three areas.

From software provider's perspective, SaaS (deployed and provided through cloud) supports many customers from a single instance. This new ability of serving many customers from single instance of software is referred to as 'multi-tenancy'. This demands a new architecting approach for tackling requirements such as multi-tenant customization and extensibility, data scaling and isolation.

Challenges such as 'scaling' have disappeared due to new technique that cloud brings in, namely 'auto-scaling'. 'Scaling' refers to an attribute of a software that it can accommodate more number of users when deployed and running in production, actually even unexpected or unplanned number of users, without requiring to modify or re-write the software.

Architecting for 'auto-scaling' comes with its own challenges:

(a) The scalability issue has been addressed differently, before cloud computing could arrive, through the following technique: scaled either vertically (by more processors or main memories) or horizontally (by adding additional servers working in parallel).
(b) But cloud computing made automatic allocation of additional processing powers on the fly, while the instance is running and serving in the production, without bringing down servers or waiting for procurement lead times. This is in nutshell 'auto-scaling'.

Customers pay as they use it, in contrast to buying a copy of a software through a license agreement. In this sense, business model for providing SaaS through cloud has also changed.

Such a change lowered the cost of software, which otherwise remained as costly investment, and affordable only by large enterprises. With pay-per-use model, even small enterprises with very thin IT budgets can consume these services. Hence, these – named 'long tail'[5] – become a new market segment for SaaS providers.

1.2 Software Solution

A software solution refers to certain business capabilities (or helps in achieving certain business capabilities) that are possible because of an intended software.

By 'cloud software solutions or products', this book consistently refers to the 'line-of-business services' offered to enterprises of all sizes. 'Line-of-business services' are often large, customizable business software solutions aimed at facilitating business processes such as customer relationship management, enterprise resources planning system, enterprise content management system, costing, accounting and finance. In cloud SaaS, these services are typically sold to customers on a subscription basis[5].

Architecting software solutions has two different connotations in software system integrators industry, and these are as follows:

(i) First is in pre-sales situation for obtaining sponsors' acceptance.
(ii) Second is after the project is fully approved and given a go-ahead.

Before obtaining a formal approval to develop a solution, software solution is architected to provide an idea of what the intended solution would be with minimal essential details of the solution.

After obtaining formal approval and sponsorship to develop solution, a detailed architecture will be created. This is the (second) context in which contents of this book provide a body of knowledge required for architecting, especially for cloud SaaS software solutions or products.

A general method of architecting software solutions can be found in enterprise architecture benchmarks promoted by TOGAF[4]. This general method is also applicable to architecting SaaS solutions or products in the cloud.

This generic method has been customized and adopted by the author in various cloud-related projects. The customization attracts a special interest when architecting solutions for a variety of companies, small or medium enterprises (SMEs) in particular. Chapter 2 in this book elaborates these points.

Technical aspects of solution architecting have grown by leaps and bounds in the past two decades, but the growth rate appeared to have slowed down till cloud computing emerged to take centre stage. Architects have developed reference architectures, blue prints, domain architectures, architectural patterns, etc. Thus, templated architecture and best practices in architecture have been well documented, for reducing challenges to solution architects.

Architects need to customize these ideal architectures to provide a solution to their specific business need. But architecting SaaS for cloud demanded many new concepts to evolve to support many new attributes (or characteristics of software) such as multi-tenant customization and extensibility, metering, auto-scaling, data scaling and isolation. Thus, SaaS through cloud (or cloud SaaS as it is used in this book) expanded the field of architecting software. This book mainly covers this additional knowledge.

The primary role of solution architects' is to provide a software system that addresses business requirements as solution[4]. Architects conceive solution in their mind before communicating the same to others. A typical civil engineering architect will construct a physical model of the envisaged building to communicate what he/she conceived in his or her mind as solution. However, for software solution architects constructing physical model is not always possible. However, software solution architects can communicate their envisaged system through a series of views of the envisaged system.

Reference [6] is an international level to describe software architecture and possible views of that can be used to describe an architecture.

1.3 'Software Architecting' is Different from 'Software Designing'

Architecting software solution, as found in the title of this book, means designing software solution. This book uses a newly coined term, 'architecting', to bring to the attention of readers that architects do a lot of things different from software 'designers'.

Architecting = developing architecture

The English language provides a verb 'design' for the actions of architects. Unfortunately, the same verb is also used for actions of designers. Therefore, the use of the verb 'designing' leaves an inherent ambiguity of who is 'subject' of the verb – architect or designer? To eliminate this ambiguity, this book proposes to use two different verbs: architecting and designing to unambiguously refer to actions being carried out by architect and designer, respectively.

In computer, software development life cycle, role and deliverable of architects are totally different from that of designers.

Knowledge required to architect software products or solutions is now vast, and requires a deep specialization, different from that of designing software. Designing is the next step to architecting, and architecting is the first step which conceives the solution and provides its detail at a very high level (top level).

Architecting is a process by which architects visualize and arrive at a set of 'building blocks' that will make up the software solution. Visualizing and specifying interactions and connections between these 'building blocks' are also a deliverable and part of architecting work.

Specifying an architecture of a solution by its constituting architecture building blocks (ABBs) and their interaction is considered as one of many possible views of the solution. For guidelines on other possible views, readers are referred to Ref. [6].

1.4 TOGAF, ABBs, SBBs and Building Blocks

Building blocks that make up an architecture, referred to as ABB, are a collection of systems' functionalities that the software will eventually provide[4]. Subsequently, each ABB will be implemented as one or more (functional) module(s) of that software (product or solution).

ABB is a basic term defined and explained in the global enterprise architecture levels promoted by TOGAF[4]. The guidelines have defined and explained many such terms and benchmarked the language for architects to consistently communicate among themselves. This book adopts, follows and uses the language, acronyms, taxonomy and vocabulary that have been idealized and promoted by TOGAF.

Solution Building Blocks (SBBs)

The software modules (or software products) that realize ABB are said to be solution building blocks (SBBs), as per TOGAF's definition[4]. One or many software modules or products will realize one or more ABBs

There are several ways of developing or implementing software solutions.

As most readers may know, a bespoke solution or tailor-made solution is most popularly also known as 'custom-built solution'. A software, built specifically to serve a single enterprise usage, is what is alternatively referred to as a custom solution. The cost of such a solution is pretty high.

Only a few organizations can afford such a solution. Although such an approach is required to meet certain highly specific business objectives, software-developing vendors realized that the cost of such an approach is also high. They then began to build generic software that can be customized with less effort and cost to meet individual corporations need. Such a generic solution is built once, and copies are sold to many client enterprises. The term 'COTS', commercial off-the-shelf products, is used to refer to these software products.

Community of software professionals felt that the cost of COTS is exorbitantly high. Hence, out of interest and voluntary effort, software professionals began to develop products parallel to each and almost every possible COTS products. This community of software professionals even made source code of these products available to customers. Hence, these are also referred to 'open-source' products. Therefore, we have two kinds of products: one is referred to as COTS and the other is referred to as 'open source'. In general, the cost of 'open-source' software products is less than that of COTS.

To provide a complete solution, architects may have to choose one or more software products – be it open source or COTS. In addition to these, some more software modules need to be custom-developed to cover functionalities that are not covered by the selected software products.

A bunch of functionalities in COTS or open-source products or custom developed code meeting functionalities of one or some of ABBs is referred to as SBBs as per TOGAF's terminology[4].

Software products that become part of any cloud SaaS solution also need to possess certain special characteristics. This book describes these characteristics as part of what is defined as 'cloud compatibility' in Chapter 5.

For architecting cloud SaaS solution, all components that make-up a solution, namely, be it COTS or open-source products or custom module (in nutshell all SBBs) should also be desirably '100 per cent cloud compatible'.

In reality, many of the available software products are not yet absolutely cloud compatible. Some of them are partially cloud compatible and some of them are fully not cloud compatible. Hence, architects need to face a situation to architect solutions with a various combinations of cloud compatible or non-compatible.

This book shows how to engineer (architect) software solutions that can serve as cloud SaaS from the cloud computing environment and accessible through the cloud:

(i) Using perfectly cloud compatible software products.
(ii) Using semi-cloud compatible software products – (Chapter 7 is devoted to this topic).
(iii) Using software products that are not cloud compatible – (Chapter 8 is devoted for this topic).
(iv) In addition, this book also shows how to engineer completely cloud compatible software products – (Chapter 9 is devoted for this topic).

Readers can figure out from the knowledge gained through this book, how to re-engineer and re-architect existing non-cloud compatible products into a cloud compatible one.

If software products become cloud compatible, then architecting a solution will become much easier, natural and cheaper too. This drives home a point: that there is a need to have an engineering method to take cloud not compatible software products and re-engineer them to make them more cloud compatible products. Information found in Chapter 9 can be used for this purpose of re-engineering an existing product to make it more cloud compatible.

Some of the principles discussed in Chapter 9 can also be used to engineer (architect) even 'custom code' that may be necessary to complete any solution so that the resultant solution will be a good cloud compatible SaaS solution.

1.5 Cloud SaaS – An Evolution and SaaS Business Models

This section will review how cloud SaaS has evolved over a period of time. As and when the technology has been developing and getting adopted, the associated business model also has been undergoing a change.

Business model refers how service providers have been charging their customers for their services. Business models vary from model to model as explained here. This is also intermingled with what kind of organizations that can afford those prices.

This section will also review various business models in chronological order of evolution from 'mainframe leasing' days to now in cloud SaaS time.

1.5.1 Mainframe Leasing Model

In 1960s and 1970, mainframes were leased out rather than being sold. The common argument given by many mainframe manufacturers of those times was that the intellectual property cost was so high that the mainframe computing machines could not be sold because of prohibiting high cost, and hence it could not be bought. Therefore, it could only be leased out.

(i) Leasing customers paid a fee for the time of CPU, memory, storage and other peripheral devices utilized on a monthly basis. Cost per time for each of these units varied with CPU time being the highest. (Today most of public cloud infrastructure as a service uses a similar pricing model for charging their customers who are using their hardware platform.)
(ii) The use of their infrastructure software such as compilers, editors, etc. were charged on pay-as-per-use basis in proportion to the time used.
(iii) Mainframe providers (leasers) provided for a fee professional service to develop 'custom software' to meet the business requirements that it should serve. However, this software could not be utilized by other organizations as these are custom developed to serve one organization's specific requirements. The cost of professional services was also on 'pay-per-use' model though that term 'pay-per-use' was absent then.
(iv) Also professionals' costs needed to be paid to maintain the 'custom software'. In reality, this was an on-going expense as long as the software was in use.

The above elements of cost structure predominantly exist even today in the SaaS-through-cloud pricing model.

Cloud SaaS model reduces costs in each of those components mentioned earlier; this is possible because costs are shared among all customers[5]. Uses a term called 'economy of scale' to denote cost reduction on sharing among customers in the cloud model.

1.5.2 Conventional, On-Premise Installed Model

Many readers may be familiar with a traditional practice of buying software and installing it in their machines on-premise before using it.

In this scenario, software-manufacturing (or publishing) companies provide a copy of software in a suitable media such as a compact disk. Software is sold as a product and bought by customers as a product. Once customers buy software (solutions) as a product, they have every right to do whatever they want with the product (of course as permitted by the license). Please note the use of word 'product' (and not yet 'service').

1.5.3 Hosted Model of 1990s

By this time, software products began to emerge. Instead of custom developing same or similar application solution for each customer, vendors realized one software product could be developed and a copy can be sold to each customer enterprise. Such an attempt helped reduce software solution development cost.

Since these products provided a facility for customization, the cost of item 3 in sub-section 1.5.1 came down.

Thus, two cost elements were low compared with costs in 'mainframe leasing model'.

Hosted model providers implement these solutions in a data centre (which is away from the enterprises' boundaries) in hardware (and infrastructure software) dedicated for each of their customers. Therefore, this cost element came straight on customers for whom these are dedicated to.

Installation, customization of solution and subsequent maintenance are part of providers' responsibility. Some of the providers are optimally using this team of professionals across customers and that brings the cost down compared with dedicated team.

Some of the hosted solution service providers optimized cost of maintenance professionals by optimally sharing those resources across customers. This is the third cost element, which is lower compared to 'mainframe leasing model' (see sub-section 1.5.1) where the professional resources were also dedicated.

This was a very significant step in SaaS evolution. This was the first time that customers could get their SaaS. They did not have to go into the technical details of implementing or customizing or maintaining their dedicated solution. Thus, client enterprises transferred IT responsibilities to the hosted service provider. (Most of these aspects are retained in modern-day cloud SaaS providers, and cloud SaaS consumers enjoy the same).

In this scenario, customers need not worry about the following key parameters: (1) customers need not have their own hardware on which (SaaS and infrastructure) software need to be installed. (2) They need not worry about tasks related to installation, maintenance and upgrades of software.

Customers will pay a fee for use of the hosted software. In this model, customers do not see even the computer centre wherein the software is implemented. They just make use of the software to get a useful output for their business.

For example, if the software is for payroll processing, customers will get their employees' pay cheques printed out. It is equivalent to having an accountant get the payroll processed and write pay cheques for employees. Therefore, the accountant provided the service of calculating pay amount and writing pay cheques.

Here, software is provided as a service and customers can consume it as a service. Customers pay for the service used to that extent. They do not own unlike in buying software products where they at least own copies of software products they bought.

The advantages of this model are listed below:

1. For the first time, customers got a complete solution for their IT need. Hardware, software and maintenance required including managing IT environment was completely outsourced (from service consumers' viewpoint).
2. In this model, facility is dedicated to each customer, although it is outside customers' premises.
3. Since it is dedicated, it is expected to have data security and privacy.
4. Client enterprises clearly know the total cost of utilizing these services.
5. Each client can ask for their own customization of software and solutions to meet their business needs.

The disadvantage of this model is that similar to the 'mainframe leasing model', the cost of providing service is high in this model too (compared to the cloud SaaS model), since the facility is dedicated to each customer (and not shared across all customers as in cloud SaaS model).

1.5.4 Cloud Model: (SaaS Provided from Cloud Environment)

Software can be provided as a service from cloud environment too. This book focuses only on such a situation.

SaaS provided from cloud has a lot of additional advantages over the other models described. It can be considered as logical improvement over the 'hosted model'.

Infrastructure hardware and software is not dedicated to each customer. It is one single shared infrastructure across all customers. Unutilized hardware capacity is effectively put into use for other customers' demand who may be using the same. Similarly, all other resources such as network cost, data centre cost and hardware maintenance professional's costs are also shared among all customers, and hence the operation cost is optimized for its use, which is the essence of 'economy of scale'.

Customers are charged on a pay-per-use basis. This opened a new market of small time users whose total market size is bigger than dedicated solutions' consumers[34], which is explained later.

Enterprises can customize SaaS solution. (On one single copy per every customer, customers can customize their own copy.) Thus, the advantage of customizable products is provided in cloud SaaS model too. But the task of customization is left to the customers in cloud SaaS model unlike the other models. Many organizations would also like to use off-the-shelf services of the solution rather than customizing it heavily. SMEs prefer this for both convenience and cost saving. Some of the small time users do not customize them at all.

Software upgrades and system maintenance are done by cloud SaaS providers, and the professional services required for maintenance are shared across all users. This way the cost comes down to each customer (compared to other models).

1.6 SaaS Provided from Cloud Environment vs Hosted Model

The following section compares and contrasts 'hosted model' to 'cloud model' of providing Software as a Service.

Service providers' view	Cloud SaaS model	Hosted model of 1990s
Service provider to service consumer relation	One service provider provides one single copy of solution software as service, but many customers use the same instance.	One service provider; For each customer, a dedicated facility – hardware or software or solution copy – is provided.
Location of providing service	SaaS can be provided within enterprise boundary or outside enterprise.	SaaS can be provided typically from providers own data centre outside enterprise boundary.
Infrastructure hardware as per deployment architecture.	Deployment architecture is horizontally scalable or scale out to support any number of customers. Infrastructure is transparent to customers, and its cost is shared among all customers and rolled into price of service. Therefore, the cost comes down.	One set of hardware corresponding to deployment architecture is provided for each customer separately.
Infrastructure software such as O/S, app servers, Web servers, etc.	One license will serve and support all customers. Infrastructure is transparent to customers, and its cost is shared among all customers and rolled into price of service. Therefore, the cost comes down.	

(*Continued*)

Service providers' view	Cloud SaaS model	Hosted model of 1990s
Application software or solution software	There is only one installed copy (one instance) of the software solution that simultaneously serves many customers.	In hosted model, for each customer, one copy of the software is installed; this means that if there are 100 customers who are availing the software as a service, then there will be 100 copies running in the service provider's data centre.
Customer data	It depends on the data model: it can either be in a dedicated database or may lie along with other customers' data in the same database.	It is a dedicated database, and hence there is complete isolation of one customer's data from others.
Software upgrade procedure.	In the cloud model, since there is only one version running, it will be upgraded, and it is so easy. Hence, the cost of maintaining the software is low. However, running version will not be stopped for the purpose of upgrade.	In the hosted model, every one of the several installed software will be separately upgraded.
Business model	Consumers pay a price in proportion to their usage of the software services.	This is a fixed monthly fees, and this is not in proportion to the usage of the software.
Who owns the software?	Customers do not own anything in providers' boundary.	Since dedicated facility is mostly built using customers' money, it belongs to them.
Who is responsible for the functionalities or business capabilities that the solution addresses?	Cloud SaaS provider or the software product vendor.	Provider is not responsible at all.
Who is responsible for managing facilities? – h/w, s/w, version upgrades, bug fixing in software.	It is the responsibility of the service provider.	The service provider will apply patches, upgrade software, etc., but for a fee.
Service consumers' viewpoint		
Customizing software	Customers are responsible for customizing.	Customers are responsible for customizing.
Managing user accounts	Customers are responsible for managing user accounts and providing access rights.	Customers are responsible for managing user accounts and providing access rights.

1.7 Enterprise Models for SaaS Consumption

When the software product is provided for on-premise (or a hosted model of 1990s), the implications to the vendor are different as compared to cloud SaaS service providers. Solution architects need to understand the group or class of industries to which the solution is provided as service.

In mainframe times, only a few enterprises could afford to use these technology-based solutions. Productizing software made many enterprises affordable to buy these products. Cloud SaaS opens many more possibilities such as SMEs or very small time to afford IT consumers also to consume these services. The same is explained further.

This section discusses three types of enterprises: First is large enterprises; second is a group of enterprises or a community of enterprises comprising a large number of very SMEs; and third is referred as 'long tail' pointing to very large number of small time users of these services.

Understanding these three types of consuming enterprises is essential for architecting solution to them (be it cloud SaaS or otherwise too).

1.7.1 Modelling Enterprises (for the Sake of Providing Solutions)

While architecting cloud SaaS solutions or products, architects need to reflect the characteristics of enterprises nature in the solution or product.

Any enterprise characteristics can be described through an enterprise model referred to as an enterprise architecture[9, 35].

Zaachman's model of enterprise architecture is given in Ref. [35].

The diagram in Ref. [35] indicates that enterprises can differ from one another by at least 36 parameters.

For example, enterprises might have organized themselves based on type of products or services they offer to their customers. Some enterprises may organize themselves based on the countries, regions and continents on which they operate. Some enterprises may have a predominant organization structure based on their internal functions such as main product or service delivery department, HR department, legal department and other support departments.

The above paragraph indicates that there are at least two possible values for one parameter, namely, organization structure. If we assume 10 possibilities for each of the 36 parameters, then the total numbers of combinations available is 36 to the power of 10. This analysis indicates that there are a wide range of enterprise models possible, and they exist out in the world.

Business rules, business processes, organizational structure, etc., of an enterprise may need to reflect in the software to be able to use solution software correctly.

Obviously, entertaining all these 36 power 10 (36^{10}) variations in a single software is not practical.

1.7.2 Bigger Enterprises and Verticals

Enterprises being grouped segment wise, such as Telco's (telecommunication service providers) or retail or health care, reduces solution complexity to a major extent due to likely similarities among enterprises in the same segment. Software products are being developed, which are industry- and solution-specific ones. As discussed earlier, the cost of development decreases if the solution software is industry segment specific, but the product vendors need to make their money by selling copies of the solution software.

Sometimes, a single software (product or solution) alone may not address all the business requirements of an enterprise even though the enterprise is within the industry segment for which the product is aimed at. Hence, software solutions are being developed using software products bound with a few custom-specific codes too. Or the software product is customized as the software product would allow matching the practices of individual enterprises.

Hence, industry-specific software solutions need to address only a limited number of possible variations in the 36 parameters modelling enterprises.

Typically, the cost of these solutions can be afforded only by a few large enterprises that have larger IT budgets and referred to as 'addressable market' in Figure 1.1[5].

1.7.3 Small- and Medium-sized Enterprises

As cloud SaaS solutions could bring down the cost of providing these solutions, the same solution can also be used by other industry segments whose IT budgets are relatively lower. SMEs are one such example.

Cloud SaaS solutions are built also to serve a community of SMEs such as textile manufacturers or automobile spare parts manufacturers (this is quite true for Ref. [1]). In the North and South Carolina States of the United States, there are about 300–400 small or medium wooden furniture manufacturers whose typical revenue will be of the order of 10 million US dollars or less. Each enterprise in this community may not have a very elaborate enterprise architecture as discussed in the earlier section. Enterprises in SME segments are simple and have simplest possible enterprises architecture, but never have a documented one. However, some small enterprise would like to differentiate itself from the remaining competitors in the community.

Individual enterprises may be trivially simpler, but a community of them may demand a wide range of possibilities in enterprises model to be accommodated in the SaaS cloud solutions.

In reality, there is need to architect a software that will accommodate all the possibilities of enterprises variations as mentioned in the type 'larger enterprises' if the software is also meant for SMEs.

1.7.4 Long Tail

This can be considered as a special case too. These are a large number of enterprises that consume lower amount of IT services and products. Their total revenue may be small enough to prevent them to go for any dedicated on-premise implementation of any line-of-business software solutions. The IT budgets that they can afford may be very small compared to big enterprises that can afford to have dedicated custom solutions to run within their enterprise boundaries. It may be even smaller than the SMEs segment. Probably, they will not even have any specified IT budget. They can preferably use it one time or as and when required and pay only for it rather than having any upfront capital investment or captive IT facility serving them dedicatedly.

Although they are small time users, they may have a very similar need among themselves unlike SMEs of special class discussed earlier, and also they may essentially from the same vertical such as Telco's, or retail or manufacturing, etc.

As cloud SaaS solutions can support the business model of pay-per-use, these small time IT consumers can also use cloud SaaS solutions.

As discussed in Ref. [36], there are a large number of such small time users out in the market.

Also Ref. [34] indicates the size of such market is enormous.

The success of Amazon™ (the online book seller) helps in confirming the same. Conventional bookstores need to have enough space to store book titles that customers are most likely to buy. In this model, the space of the store will put a limitation to the number of titles it can store on-display. But Amazon™ has a catalogue, and books need not be stored in any one single physical place. It can be kept even in publishers'/printers' place or warehouse. On getting the order, Amazon™ can give instruction to ship the book from the publishers'/printers' warehouse to customers' address. This way all books in print can be in the catalogue, and there is no inventory holding cost for Amazon™.

Similarly, titles less popular that are bought by one-off users are large in number, and this is the one that contributes to a large percentage of sales.

The customers who buy low volume of products but who are large in number out there in the market are referred to as 'long tail'. This market segment is also known by the same name as 'long tail'.

Reference [5] explains how this is applicable to software products market. Figures 1.1 and 1.2 show revenue per customer on the y-axis and the number of customers who can spend that much on the x-axis.

In mainframe leasing model or conventional on-premise installed model or 1990s hosted model, the cost of providing service was so high (as indicated by dotted line that runs parallel to x-axis in Figure 1.1). Hence, 'addressable market' that could avail these services was limited to a few number of larger enterprises. Consequently, the 'addressable market' size was relatively smaller. The non-addressable market includes 'long tail'.

Compare cost of services indicated by dotted lines in Figures 1.1 and 1.2. Due to economy of scale in cloud SaaS model, the cost has got lowered as in Figure 1.2. Hence previous non-addressable market could now become addressable.

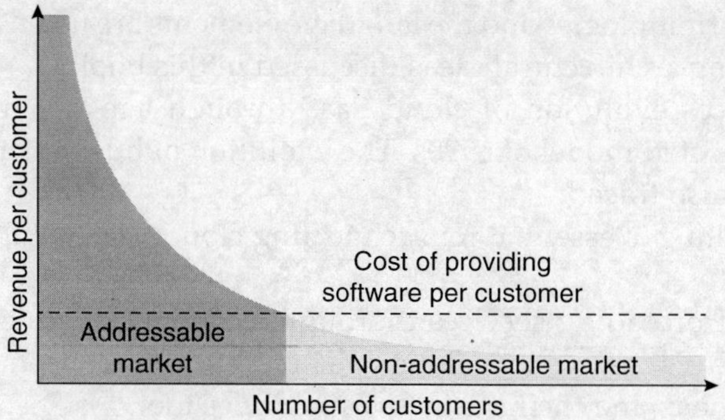

Figure 1.1 Non-addressable market due to higher cost-of-providing software [5]

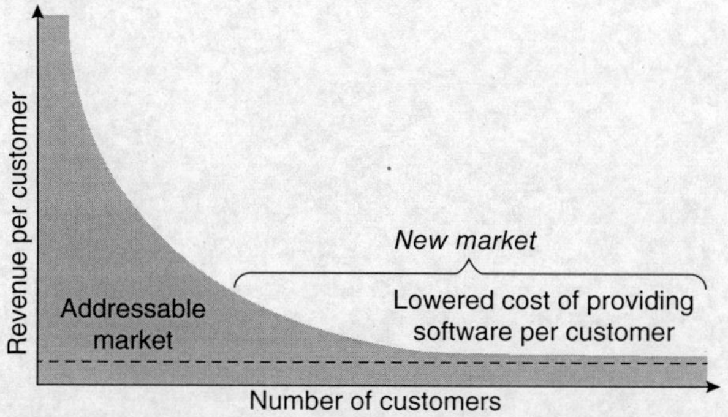

Figure 1.2 New market opened by lower cost of cloud SaaS [5]

This is an untapped new market for cloud SaaS solution providers. This is a huge market, and hence business potential is huge. Cloud SaaS solution is a successful attempt to bring down the cost of providing software services, and hence it addresses this long-tail market.

1.8 Summary

- This chapter introduces and explains the title of this book.
- It also provides context for the subject matter covered in this book.
- SaaS is roughly defined as software deployed on cloud, provided from or through cloud and also being consumed by accessing these services through cloud.
- Most commonly and loosely used terms such as 'software solution' are explained to carry the same meaning throughout this book.

- TOGAF's basic terminologies and the language elements are taken as the base language for communicating architectural ideas discussed in this book.
- This chapter traces evolution of cloud SaaS through ages from mainframe leasing model through hosted model of 1990s. The evolution of business models of providing these services is also traced.
- Enterprise modelling is essential for architecting cloud SaaS solution, and the same is introduced.
- Lowering cost of providing services thorough 'economy of scale' by cloud SaaS has made even to SMEs, as well as 'long tail' of small time users afford information technology for enhancing their business capabilities too.

Chapter 2
Architecting Methods for Cloud SaaS Software – Solutions or Products

2.1 Introduction

Architecting or 'architecture development' is still a mixture of art and science. The 'science' or to say more precisely the 'engineering aspect' is addressed throughout this book in various chapters.

The effort required to develop architecture is large. Various teams will work on different segments of the architecture development project. Yet, a robust method is also essential to coordinate the work among team members and get desired work product, namely, the solution architecture.

Architects need to communicate during the development of architecture as well as post development and throughout the life cycle of realization of the architecture. The communication can be in the form of architectural diagrams or views, but it is very much essential to maintain consistency in communication.

Software architects around the globe have similar needs. The open group fulfilled such needs through a global architecture model The Open Group Architecture Framework (TOGAF) Version 9.1. The architecture development method (ADM) in TOGAF Version 9.1 gives a complete and comprehensive methodology for architecture development. In addition, TOGAF has benchmarked the language, acronyms, vocabulary and taxonomy that are commonly required for architects to exchange and communicate their ideas.

The International Standards Organization (ISO)[6] has idealized views of the architecture that are necessary to communicate the architecture to various stakeholders.

Thus, we have the basic method of developing architecture from world principle body – TOGAF.

This book presents the following practical use of this generic methodology:

(i) TOGAF ADM is the overall architecting methodology that one can put in place for all projects requiring architecture development for cloud Software as a Service (SaaS) solutions or products. TOGAF itself is a framework, and hence any enterprise can adopt it. Its applicability is not limited because of the technology or other reasons.

(ii) Most of the cloud SaaS solutions will be service-oriented architecture (SOA) based; TOGAF also provides elaborate guidelines on how to use TOGAF with SOA. Reference [28] is in particular useful as it is 'using TOGAF to define and govern SOAs'.

(iii) A typical cloud SaaS solution is no longer a 'point solution' that will be used by a single enterprise. Therefore, the solution architects have to re-orient themselves. They have to bear in mind single instance of cloud SaaS solution or product that will be simultaneously used by multiple enterprises. Therefore, TOGAF's ADM should be adopted for this purpose.

(iv) There are two special classes of potential customers for cloud SaaS product: a. small- or medium-sized enterprises (SMEs), b. 'long tail'. It will be a new experience for most of the architects to adopt ADM for giving solution to these two segments. This section provides one approach that can be used for SMEs.

(v) In this 'agile' era, many a times architects need to architect cloud SaaS solutions even before requirement gathering begins! This chapter will touch upon how to architect under agile situation where the requirements are not available.
(vi) Detailed steps to architect for a specific product (or solution) are discussed in Chapter 9.

Reading and understanding TOGAF and its ADM is advisable for better appreciation of the contents of this chapter; and also the content of this chapter is a pre-requisite for reading Chapters 7 through 9.

Based on experiences in various projects, an overall process that can govern the architecture development project for SMEs is summarized in the following Figure 2.1[19]:

The process has three major stages: (1) before applying TOGAF ADM steps, (2) using TOGAF ADM and develop architecture and (3) post-architecture developments work such as mapping architectural building blocks (ABBs) to solution building blocks (SBBs) etc.

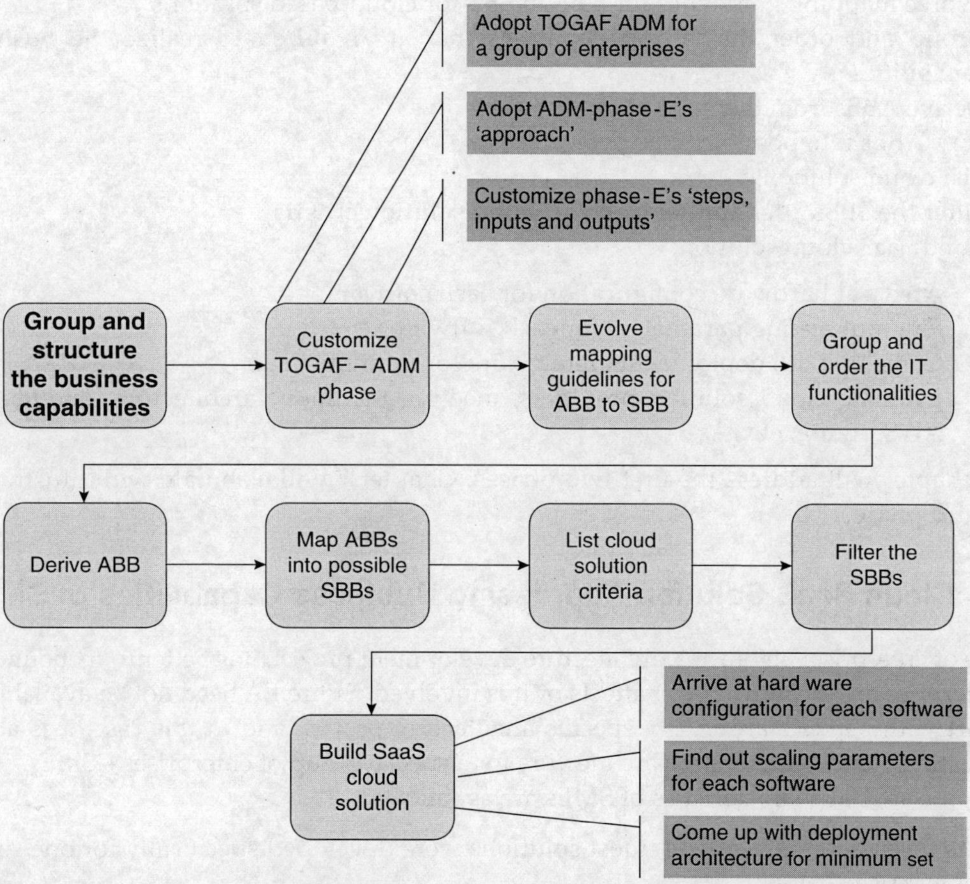

Figure 2.1 TOGAF- and ADM-based process for cloud SaaS architecture development project

The three stages in the above are as illustrated below:

Stage 1

1. Group and structure the required business capabilities

Stage 2

2. Customize TOGAF ADM phase for this specific use:
   - Adopt TOGAF ADM for a group of enterprises.
   - Adopt ADM phase E's 'approach' for a group of enterprises.
   - Customize phase E's 'steps, inputs and outputs'.

Stage 3

3. Evolve mapping guidelines for ABB to SBB for cloud-based solutions.
4. Group and order the IT functionalities that are required to realize the business capabilities.
5. Derive ABBs from there.
6. Map ABBs into possible SBBs.
7. List cloud solution criteria.
8. Filter the SBBs after applying above 'cloud solution criteria'.
9. Build SaaS cloud solution:
   - Arrive at hardware configuration for each software.
   - Find out scaling parameters for each software.
   - Come up with deployment architecture for minimum set.
   - Evaluate cloud solution providers, meeting the above architecture. (cloud O/S AWS, Azure, etc.)

This chapter will address the first two phases; Chapter 7 will elaborate with illustration the third phase.

2.2 Cloud SaaS Solution Addressing Business Capabilities of SMEs

Scope of enterprise: Before any architecture development project, it is better to fix boundary of enterprise architecture (EA) it affects or it is involved. Entire EA need not be available[2, 3] to start with before starting any specific architecture project; and in this case, it is about developing cloud SaaS solution architecture for a special group of enterprises – SMEs.

Some special characteristics of SMEs are as follows:

(i) As discussed in Chapter 1, most solutions were developed specifically for one single enterprise.

(ii) Later trend of coming up with software products tried to generalize the requirements across similar industries and address them.

SMEs do not fall under any of the above two categories. They can be grouped under one vertical segment such as textile industry or automobile spare parts industries or leather manufacturing industry. But within the segment, individual enterprises may not produce or offer similar services. Most often, they provide complimentary services such as one company may produce yarn, another company may dye them or third company may only weave or knit. Thus, all enterprises within the community may collectively have the capability of producing a class of end-products; and in this case, vests or pants or shirts. But in most of the cases, one is not a customer or vendor for another within the same community. Thus, none of them have same business capabilities.

Thus, what is the 'scope of enterprise' that will use this cloud SaaS solution? – If it is SMEs, it is not one single enterprise or a sub-part of an enterprise; it is a community of enterprises; but solution should be common to all enterprises in the community.

In addition, these enterprises, being small, they individually would not have EA models developed for themselves.

Size and complexity of each enterprise in the community may affect EA model to be assumed within cloud SaaS solution software.

Most enterprises within the community are smaller and less complex in business operations; but that naturally allows them to adopt common sharable community cloud SaaS capabilities.

For such a situation, it is better to adapt one important recommendation of TOGAF; that is to develop first, a strategic (enterprise) architecture that gives a summary of formal description of the enterprise. Then, identify and recognize particular segments of enterprise to which a business capability is demanded. Cloud SaaS solution will address that capability (e.g. enterprise resource planning (ERP) or human resources management (HRM)).

Enterprise architects could then develop segment architectures (which can define the scope of enterprise for the current architecture project). In each segment, one or more specific business capabilities can be achieved through cloud SaaS solutions. Scope of enterprise will comprise all these segments.

2.3 Adopting TOGAF's ADM Phases for Cloud SaaS Solution

This section gives an example of how to adapt TOGAF ADM when developing cloud SaaS solutions for SMEs. This is not intended as a self-standing description; and should be read in conjunction with activities and other details found in each phase of TOGAF ADM Version 9.1[4]. The adaption discussed here is based on a couple of real-life experience.

2.3.1 Phases – Preliminary Phase to Phase A–D

2.3.1.1 Preliminary Phase

The preliminary phase is where architecture capability should be adapted to support cloud computing reference architecture (CCRA) (e.g. draft proposal from IBM™) and

SOA reference architecture. Key outputs of this phase are (architecture, governing or organization) principles, organizational structure, governance and initial content of the architecture repository[4].

Architecture principles will come from two reference architectures mentioned above. A few more will come due nature of 'enterprise segment' that the solution aims to address. For example, one architecture principle can be *'complete shield of information not to be revealed to any other member enterprise within SME community'*. This will be segment specific such as textile or retail or leather manufacturing, sometime stipulated by main stakeholders of the community of SMEs.

2.3.1.2 Phase A: Architecture Vision

Business vision is normally obtained in the context in which business is asking to develop cloud SaaS solutions.

For example, when Indian economy was opened to international economy, all Indian enterprises have to compete in global market with internationally repute enterprises whose business capabilities have matured a lot.

Therefore, one of the communities of Indian SMEs enterprises set a business vision to empower these SMEs to have business capabilities to be on par with big enterprises and compete equally with them in the international market place[1].

Some example business capabilities are international-level ERP and management, financial management and transparency, and HRM. Such specific business vision is essential.

A consortium of small or medium banks in Europe set a business vision of keeping their operating cost as low as possible, by commonly sharing all possible computing resources for conducting their 'new customers account-opening operations'.

2.3.1.3 Phase B: Business Architecture

Building Business Capabilities for a Group of Enterprises

In tune with the business vision, cloud SaaS solution should aim to build and provide required business capabilities.

This section explains how it is different to build a solution for group of enterprises (SMEs in particular) and the challenges involved in it.

The first challenge is that the cost of solution will restrict from providing 'all capabilities' that a large enterprise can afford to. But there is no way to escape from providing 'all capabilities'. Any given enterprise in a community may need or use only a small subset of entire business capabilities; but the cloud SaaS solution needs to provide all capabilities. This is because sum total of individual company's requirements will add up to 'all capabilities', and sometimes it may even exceed that. Therefore, cloud SaaS solution architects need to plan for providing 'all capabilities'; but it can plan to implement them in parts as per the demand for each part comes up.

In a way, they need to think like product architects to provide a complete solution that can compete in the market community.

The second challenge emerges from the fact that existing capabilities of each enterprise in this group may vary vastly. Therefore, any assumption on 'as-is' capability of any enterprise within the community may be erroneous.

The third challenge was in grouping the demanded capabilities.

A possible solution to this third challenge is explained below:

(i) One way is to group them in an order-of-maturity from small or medium enterprises. As the enterprises grow and matures to provide higher level services, they may need higher level business capabilities.

(ii) The second way is to group all the required capabilities of small enterprises or medium enterprises into a separate bucket. For each enterprise, the capabilities required can be further divided into two sub-categories:

   (a) Very specific to an enterprise
   (b) Common to most of similar enterprises in the community

(iii) The third way is to group them in terms of similar products or services produced by enterprises irrespective of their size – small or medium; and then group them as per point (ii), then within that group as per point (i).

The given list of requirements has to be analysed in the above three ways before finalizing one model.

At a minimum, the above-mentioned ways of grouping capabilities are essential to identify the correct set of ABBs. The grouping is also to plan to allow customization features of business capabilities.

The above is a simplified application of what is discussed in Chapter 20 of TOGAF ADM Version 9.1[4].

2.3.1.4 Phase C: Information Systems Architectures

This phase consists of two sub-phases: Development of data architecture and applications architecture[4].

Cloud SaaS solutions need a special attention and development effort for data architecture. This is discussed in Chapters 5 and 9.

Chapters 7 and 8 give prime importance to explain application architecture. The finer details that need to be taken care of in architecting cloud SaaS solutions are discussed in Chapter 9.

2.3.1.5 Phase D: Technology Architecture

The technology architecture defines the software and hardware infrastructure that are needed to support the cloud SaaS solution. This is covered in Chapters 4, 7, 8 and 9.

The starting point is CCRA which is discussed in Chapter 10. Chapter 9 indicates how to make use of the CCRA.

2.3.2 Phase E: Opportunities and Solutions

2.3.2.1 Phase E for a Group of Enterprises

Adopting TOGAF's ADM Phase E for architecting cloud SaaS solutions for a group of enterprises (SMEs) can be explained in three paragraphs:

(i) Adapting TOGAF ADM Phase E 'approach'.
(ii) What are all applicable 'steps, inputs and outputs' of phase E in this context.
(iii) Discussion about ABB to SBB mapping guidelines for cloud-based solutions in brief. This step is elaborately discussed in Chapter 7, and hence not discussed here.

2.3.2.2 Adopting TOGAF ADM Phase E's 'Approach'

The following figure[19] summarizes three important points:

(i) 'Standard approach' column summarizes essential points in TOGAF grades 'approach' that we could not adopt without modifications.
(ii) The second column summarizes key factors that influence adaption of the basic approach. These factors are specific to SMEs. In reality, there may be many more.
(iii) 'Adopted approach' column summarizes resultant modified points.

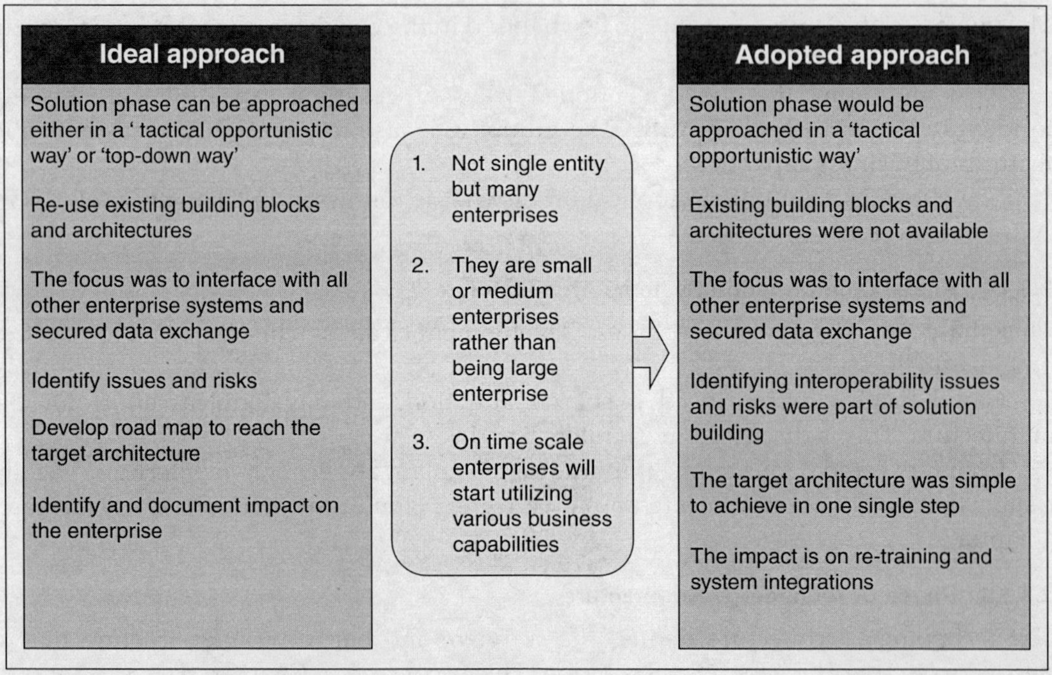

(Existing building blocks and EA may not be available.)

(The steps and procedures mentioned here can also be adopted for re-architecting even (home grown b-spoke or custom) enterprises systems to make them fully cloud compatible SaaS software and host them on IaaS platforms.)

The above figure can give some idea of adopting the 'approach'; but that is not the end of it. Although the above is an extract from real-life project, individual project teams may need to do a lot of work in this area for their specific projects.

2.3.2.3 Customizing Phase E's 'Steps, Inputs and Outputs'

The following table[4] highlights some of the mostly used 'steps, inputs and outputs' in cloud SaaS architecting projects.

Objective	Steps	Inputs	Outputs
To review the target business objectives and capabilities, consolidate the gaps from phases B–D and then organize groups of building blocks to address these capabilities.	Determine/confirm key corporate change attributes.	Product information	Statement of architecture work, updated if necessary
To review and confirm the enterprise's current parameters for and ability to absorb change	Determine business constraints for implementation.	**Request for architecture work**	Architecture vision updated if necessary
To derive a series of transition architecture that delivers continuous business value (e.g. capability increments) through the exploitation of opportunities to realize the building blocks	Review and consolidate gap analysis results from phases B–D	**capability assessment**	Draft architecture definition document, including content updates for:
To generate and gain consensus on an outline implementation and migration strategy	**Review IT requirements from functional perspective**.	Communications Plan	Identification of requirements
	Consolidate and reconcile interoperability requirements*.	**Planning methodologies**	**Interoperability and coexistence requirements**
	Refine and validate dependencies.	**Organization model for enterprise architecture**	**Implementation and migration strategy**

(Continued)

Objective	Steps	Inputs	Outputs
	Confirm readiness and risk for business transformation.	Tailored architecture framework	Inclusion of project list and project charters
	Formulate high-level implementation and migration strategy.	**Statement of architecture work**	Draft architecture requirements specification updated if necessary
	Identify and group major work packages.	**Architecture vision**	**Capability assessment including content updates for**
	Identify transition architectures.	Architecture repository	**Enterprise architecture maturity profile**
	Create portfolio and project charters and update the architectures.	Draft architecture definition document	**Transformation readiness report**
		Draft architecture requirements specification	**Transition architectures including the following:**
		Change requests for existing programs and projects	**Consolidated gaps, solutions and dependencies assessment, risk register, impact analysis – project list, dependency analysis report, implementation factor assessment and deduction matrix**
			implementation and migration plan (outline)

*At this stage, architect would also need to review of non-functional requirements/parameters to meet the functional specifications. But TOGAF will not give these finer detailed steps.

The following are simple explanations of the above table:

(i) If the customer segment is SMEs, except two steps (which are highlighted in **bold** in Column 2 of the table above); all others cannot be directly executed. This is mainly because customer is a 'group of enterprises' and not a single enterprise. Some of these omitted steps have two components. One is very specific to an enterprise and the other is common across all enterprises in the community. The common ones were collected and carefully examined before providing solution in a separate sub-project.

(ii) For example, the prescribed step 'Determine/confirm key corporate change attributes' had to be deferred until a particular enterprise subscribes to a sub-set of the solution. The 'change attributes' need to be decided for that enterprise based on the chosen services.

(iii) Similarly, all required *inputs* will not be available at all or at the beginning of the project. Examples of the ones available are highlighted in Column 3.

(iv) However, it is up to the architect to come up with all possible and necessary *outputs*; these are highlighted in Column 4.

2.3.3 Remaining Phases in ADM

2.3.3.1 Phase F: Migration Planning, Phase G: Implementation Governance and Phase H: Architecture Change Management

Most of the steps are very much like any other architecture project. However, a few factors already discussed such as the following:

(i) multiple tenants using same single instance of software or

(ii) nature of the customers group – may be 'long tail' or SMEs or other verticals

will have some or other impact in these phases; but, they become mostly project specific, if any. Therefore, it is not discussed here.

That brings to an end of our discussion on adapting ADM for architecting cloud SaaS solution.

2.4 Agile Architecting Method

This additional architecting method[17] summarized here will be of definite relevance and use to the readers.

The project situation: requirement gathering has inherent difficulties in cloud SaaS project

(i) For most (cloud SaaS) product development projects functional specifications will not be given by a single person or by a single enterprise; neither anyone will sign off functional specification document. For architects moving from traditional enterprise projects experience, this itself will be quite a shocking experience.

(ii) Even for conventional software product development company, finding functional specification is not going to be easy. They have to synthesis functional specification from many enterprises in the same industry segment. But many product vendors have got used to this and successfully got over this hurdle to develop industry-specific solutions or products.

(iii) For cloud SaaS solutions, the ambiguity in freezing functional specs is much larger than what is discussed earlier:

(a) Most of the time, business could adjust functional requirements based on how customers are using/consuming cloud SaaS services. This should come either from use of previous similar solutions, or it will be known after cloud SaaS solution is launched and customers begin to use the same.

(b) If customer segment is SMEs or 'long tail', the average literacy levels of users may affect usage pattern and participation from them in terms of expressing their feedback or desires for modifications of cloud SaaS solutions.

(c) Very rarely organized communities of enterprises could spell out their requirements more clearly up front by employing professional bodies to collect their requirements and specify to service provider. But, if cloud SaaS providers have to collect the requirements on their own initiative, then requirement gathering is a difficult proposition as individual enterprises will not spare their time or effort to provide the same.

All these will demand a strong team that has deeper knowledge across industry, domain, vertical and a thorough understanding of the domain problem for which solution is sought, to spell out the 'requirements' in the final cloud SaaS solution.

In addition, architects should be ready to accommodate changes in functionalities and capabilities post launch of the service based on user feedback.

Such a situation alarms since the architecture needs to be flexible to take those changes.

At the first place, it is better and desirable to come up with a 'flexible architecture' – if anything called 'flexible architecture' – to accommodate such challenging requirements that may come as a surprise after launch.

In addition to the above situation of 'where to go for' functional and non-functional requirements, agile methodology expects the coding to start from day one of the project start. Where is the time for collecting requirements, freezing it and then start architecting and then designing, etc., as in waterfall method of software development life cycle (SDLC)? In the conventional SDLC method, architecting starts after requirements are frozen.

These challenges are more common in cloud SaaS development projects.

Therefore, architecting has to happen in parallel to requirements gathering. May be the architecture will serve as input for even collecting requirements!; this could be a practical approach. This implies that cloud SaaS software architecture should be ready and available even before requirements gathering is initiated.

We will see how to architect under these project situations. Let us review an ADM for this situation.

Reference [17] discusses the same method with an illustration. Chapter 10 makes use of this knowledge and also gives finer details of this method.

Method

There are two starting points for developing architecture under the above-mentioned condition:

1. Start collecting requirements and identifying ABBs for the solution.
2. Start architecting by employing knowledge from TOGAF.

2.4.1 Requirements Collection and Identification of ABBs

There are two main streams of activities that one may follow the other: They are as follows:

(i) Requirements collection for cloud SaaS software.
(ii) Domain knowledge and identification or recognition of ABBs.

Some of the domain knowledge and problem for which the cloud SaaS solution is being applied, will help identify or recognize a bunch of requirements. For example, one can recognize that we need a product catalogue or tax calculating engine if we are attempting e-commerce-related solution.

From the ecosystems in which solution is going to exist, architects can visualize another bunch of requirements; for example, interfacing-module requirements can be identified for information exchange, assuming the solution need to work closely with other enterprise systems.

Identify the common services/components of the intended application software at early stage of cycle, which is less prone to change. However, all common services required to build and provide SaaS will be default from or available in CCRA as Chapter 10 explains.

On elaborating problem statement and also from architects knowledge and experience, architects can visualize a few more ABBs. For example, an ordering system will naturally have customer-specific pricing algorithm. It may even warrant an e-commerce module.

All the above steps may not result in any specific frozen requirements; but it will help in recognizing a need for a module or bunch of requirements that can appear as ABBs.

2.4.2 Architecting by Employing Techniques from TOGAF

TOGAF ADM and the body of knowledge centred on TOGAF gives a lot of clues to recognize or identify architectural components; this is very handy to develop architecture in this situation where requirements are not available before architecting.

Reasonably, detail level of architecture can be developed by following steps discussed below:

(i) Applying principles of EA continuum[30]
(ii) Trying to utilize domain architectures available in open literatures
(iii) Using EA
(iv) Utilising CCRA
(v) Deriving Architectural components from SOA reference architecture
(vi) Adapting multi-tier distributed architecture
(vii) Finalizing technical environment of the solution
(viii) Identifying SBBs

These steps need to be executed more or less in the same sequence as they appear above. However, these steps can be carried out in parallel to 'requirements gathering and ABB identification steps'.

(i) Applying principles of enterprise architecture continuum

The enterprise continuum enables organization of reusable architecture artefacts and solution assets

Enterprise continuum can be imagined as a repository of all architectural assets[29, 30]. These include architecture descriptions, models, building blocks, patterns, viewpoints and other artefacts that exist both within the enterprise and in the IT industry at large, which the enterprise would like to have them available for themselves for the development of architectures[30].

The architecture continuum (Figure 2.2) illustrates how architectures are developed and evolved across a continuum ranging from foundation architectures, through common systems architectures, and industry architectures, and to an enterprise's own organization-specific architectures (In our case, it can mean the cloud SaaS solution architecture).

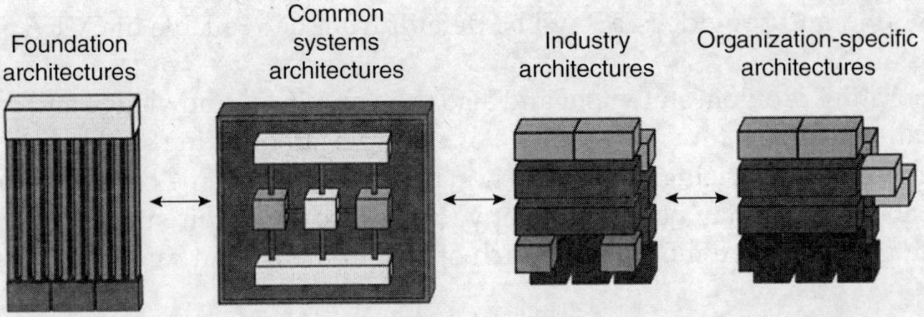

Figure 2.2 Architecture continuum. Reproduced from Ref. [30] with permission

Enterprise needs and business requirements are addressed in increasing detail from left to right. Architects will typically look to find re-usable architectural elements towards left of the continuum. When elements are not found, requirements for the missing elements are passed to the left of the continuum for incorporation. Those implementing architectures within their own organizations can use the same continuum models specialized for their business.

Notes: *That means there may be many re-usable architectural components available in the repository either within or outside enterprises. Identifying them is essential. Marking those that are not existing becomes part of the new requirements. This is also a good way of checking completeness of requirements!*

"The TOGAF ADM describes the process of developing an enterprise-specific architecture and an enterprise-specific solution(s) that confirm to that architecture by adopting and adapting (where appropriate) generic architectures and solutions (left to right in the continuum classification). In a similar way, specific architectures and solutions that prove to be credible and effective will be generalized for re-use (right to left in the continuum classification)".

Clippings from TOGAF on architecture continuum[30] only assures that any solution architecture does not exist in isolation. It is a point in a continuum space of architecture. This only conveys to practising architects that he or she need not (re)invent most of the architectural components that are necessary for a specific project; most of the pieces will be available somewhere there.

In any given architecture development project, only the missing components for which requirements are raised may have to be developed; and other components need to be taken from internal (to enterprise) or external repository of components, and they have to be tweaked, if necessary, and adapted for the specific project.

The first step is identifying the point in space as to where the solution lies. This will naturally follow collecting all reusable existing architectural components relevant to the project on hand.

In addition, during the same time, it is advisable to collect architectural components of adjoining pieces of the solution too. These will let architects know about interface requirements and the required components in the solution architecture.

Architects need to look for these components both from within (SaaS providers as well as customers or the specific industry) enterprise as well from outside enterprise.

It is worth investing time and effort to locate these components from various repositories, and that is one of the ways of bringing best practice and matured and tested components into the solution architecture.

This is the first source of information for an architect to begin developing architecture, even before requirements are ready.

(ii) Trying to utilize domain architectures

Domain architectures are those that may be available outside enterprises. Architectures within enterprises are interpolation to *domain architecture* as detailed in EA continuum discussed earlier in this section.

There are domain-specific architectures such as NGOSS for telecom. Similar ones are available for retail industry.

These domain architectures are again another quite useful source to pick necessary architectural components for the project. Domain architectures also help in specifying where the specific cloud SaaS architecture that is being developed fits in the continuum.

The solution's position in domain architecture will give some more top-level descriptions about requirements from domain perspective.

In addition, the *domain architecture* can explain about possible grades that are available to which this intended specific solution needs to fit in.

Therefore, examining respective domain architectures, where cloud SaaS solution fits in, will help in identifying some more relevant architecture components for the solution.

(iii) Using enterprise architecture

Here, EA can refer to two different repositories:
EA repository of

(a) Cloud SaaS provider
(b) Cloud SaaS consumers or customers

Providers EA repository may contain many architecture components that can be reused for the specific project: such as architectural principles, reusable components, guidance for architecture practice, etc.

Customers in long tail or SMEs segment may not even have any EA practice or repositories established. Therefore, architects cannot expect any reusable component from them.

Sometimes, big enterprises (consumers) EA repository may have useful reusable components. Unfortunately, it may or may not be available for providers for the purpose of their use.

If any of these architectural components are available in open source or published media, then that can also serve the purpose. Architectures from SaaS consumers will give enough clues, specifications and functional requirements to guide architectural components such as those for interfacing with customer systems.

In addition, it will give a good direction on the usefulness of the solution – the missing piece in the puzzle of enterprises capabilities too. That verifies demand for this service.

(iv) Utilizing CCRA

(a) Chapter 10 gives a quick review of CCRA that is proposed by IBM™ and under review by TOGAF.
(b) CCRA gives default architecture for any cloud SaaS software.
(c) This is a good starting point for most of the architecture projects.
(d) Architects need to start with this default generic architecture and need to work on it to obtain specific solution architecture.

1. Review all architecture components in the reference architecture.
    - Retain those that are essential for a specific project.
    - Identify those components that need to be modified to adapt to the specific project.
2. Find SBBs for default and necessary common services that are finalized for specific solution.
3. Fill functional layer with services that the final cloud SaaS solution needs to offer to customers.

(v) Deriving architectural components from SOA reference architecture

(a) A good knowledge of SOA is essential for all cloud SaaS solution architects.
(b) TOGAF provides SOA reference architecture.
(c) Since cloud SaaS is basically (software as) a service, SOA knowledge is inevitable.
(d) SOA RA will give additional architecture principles and other architecture components necessary for completing cloud SaaS solution.
(e) On adapting CCRA, automatically one is into SOA. CCRA is a super set of SOA RA by including those that are essential for cloud computing. However, being aware of the fact that CCRA is a super set of SOA RA will help in not missing any architectural components.
(f) All these need to be added to the architecture asset repository.

Chapter 9 discuss this in further detail.

(vi) Adapting multi-tier architecture

Multi-tier architecture or n-tier architecture is a generalization of three-tier architecture.

The multi-tier architecture style guides and provides place holders for identified ABBs on its various tiers. Multi-tier architecture is a fundamental to provide a cloud SaaS solution. Chapter 10 provides tier-wise details relevant to cloud SaaS software architecture.

(vii) Technical environment of solution

Technology choice and platform will also give a lot of necessary ABBs and components for the architecture. For example, if it is decided to support mobile devices apart from desktop clients, there is a need for corresponding module on the Web tier.

(viii) Identify SBBs

Last but one step in architecting is to identify SBBs.

This involves identifying third-party products, plugins and specific engines that are matching and helpful to realize ABBs.

For some of the benchmark components such as BSS or OSS, there may be basic COTS or open sources available in the market.

SBBs corresponding to business functionalities addressed specifically by the solution need to wait until all functional requirements are frozen. In that sense, mapping those ABBs to SBBs need to wait until requirements are almost finalized. Chapter 7 provides special techniques that can be adapted for mapping ABBs to ABB in cloud SaaS solution projects.

Concluding remarks in the method:

The above steps in this particular track give specific architecture and its components.

These steps work like a funnel. It all starts with a very generic and high-level architecture; then, it becomes more specific architecture for a given cloud SaaS solution as the architects take the architecture through these steps from *a–h*.

ABBs that come out of requirements analysis also get mapped into this skeleton architecture.

Requirements that are being gathered, during and also after development of architecture, will be mapped onto envisaged individual-specific ABBs.

If any existing or identified ABBs cannot accommodate any new incoming requirement, then new ABBs can be created.

The software architecture at this stage can also be used for collecting remaining details of requirements.

Architecture principles, identified other architecture components, envisaged building blocks and recognized ecosystem – all the above will give enough of information for architects to figure out connections required to connect the building blocks and components in the architecture.

Thus, the architecture at this stage will have enough details. The nitty-gritty details of functional requirements will not alter this first good draft Architecture.

This Architecture needs to be reviewed when details of non-functional requirements arrive. Most of the time non-functional requirements are estimates for cloud SaaS solutions based on the experience of the Architects team.

2.5 Summary

- This chapter points out that TOGAF ADM can be a core method that can be put in place for any cloud SaaS architecture development project.
- This chapter provides two architecting methods that are adapted from ADM for two specific situations:
  - One is for cloud SaaS architecture development projects for a community of enterprises of small- or medium-sized enterprises. Therefore, the first section of this chapter shows how to adapt TOGAF's ADM for developing cloud SaaS solutions or products for SMEs.
  - The second one describes how to develop architecture under agile conditions such as in cases where even the requirement is not ready.
- Although these two may outwardly appear to be special cases, these methods along with TOGAF's ADM will help architects to figure out one for their organization as well as to their specific project.

Chapter 3

How Do Hypervisors Work? How Does IaaS Function?

3.1 Introduction

It is essential to understand infrastructure as a service (IaaS) as a pre-requisite to understanding the remaining concepts in this book. This introductory chapter is oriented to give a conceptual view of how hypervisors work and how IaaS function. This conceptual understanding is what is required for (solution) architects for the following:

(i) Architecting software solutions (not as SaaS) for IaaS (Chapter 4).
(ii) Architecting cloud Software as a Service (SaaS) software with non- or semi-cloud compatible products (Chapters 7 and 8).
(iii) Architecting cloud compatible cloud SaaS product (Chapter 9) to launch on using public or private IaaS.
(iv) Architects, it covers the pre-requisite knowledge for deploying solutions on IaaS.

Definition

At its simplest level, IaaS is a system by which hardware servers (to deploy any software solution) can be provided as a service and accessed from a public Internet.

Amazon Web Services™ and Microsoft Azure™ are great examples of such IaaS sites. Users can create an account on these sites and then proceed to specify the type of hardware that they require. This specification can include the number of core CPUs required, main memory required and also secondary storage required. Most public IaaS providers offer pre-configured sizes in terms of the number of cores, processor speeds and the main memory amount. The bundle of CPUs and memory sizes are very often made available in idealized configurations, referred to as 'small', 'medium' or 'large'. Users can request one or more 'instance/s' of any of these sizes and are charged on a monthly basis as per the usage of CPU time and memory or secondary storage usage sizes.

Note: *Users can also specify their entire organizational requirement, based on their intended infrastructure deployment architecture.*

Therefore, sitting in front of a Web browser, users can allocate some machine instances as, for example, a load balancer and simply attach a few other instances as parallel machines under the load balancer.

Users (not end users but typically those who allocate hardware resources to project teams in infrastructure support teams of enterprises) can also specify (which) operating systems to run on each of those instances, as well as other infrastructure software – such as application server or RDBMS – that need to run on each instance. Finally, users can load the application software on this server or hardware machine and run it.

3.2 Hardware Virtualization

Having understood the typical user experience and services that users can get from IaaS, we will now turn to the other side to see how service providers can provide these infrastructures as a service.

Through the use of IaaS, most users such as those that handle HTTP or HTTPS requests that are initiated through Web browsers.

This is true both when servers are accessed in a LAN environment or through public Internet.

Just as how files are organized in a file system, hardware servers in data centres are organized hierarchically, and given a virtual name or address. At each node of the hierarchy, a table is maintained to map the virtual name or address to a physical name or address of the hardware server. A request (such as http or https) from any Web client is addressed to a particular server using its virtual name. The table at each node helps in decoding and directing the request to physical location of the specific server. For example, if the virtual name is 'www.google.com', it will be decoded to map to an HTTP server which, in this case, is http://www.google.com.

Such an arrangement gives freedom to locate the physical hardware server and access it from anywhere in the network. If the network is the combination of LAN and public Internet, given access rights, clients from anywhere through the public network can access any of the other servers within the LAN.

In addition, if one physical hardware server is down, the table can be altered to point to another physically good working hardware server that is physically located elsewhere and having different physical address. Thus, the time required to correct fault of a hardware does not affect system availability to users.

Similarly, any hardware server upgrades or software upgrades that are running in the hardware server can be done with least impact on availability of the servers to users. This is done normally by doing upgrades and maintenance on a parallel similar server on the LAN/network, and by finally changing the physical address to point out this new updated server.

This is the basic first step or simplest model explaining hardware virtualization.

3.3 Auto-Provisioning

Let us examine the next logical step in this virtualization.

If one could automate the above functionalities, then the resultant would be referred to as 'auto-provisioning'.

Below is a scenario to explain this feature.

Assume there are approximately 1,000 hardware servers connected on a LAN.

(i) Users send an http request from their thin client to one designated http server in the LAN.
(ii) Users typically send a request to allocate one instance of small, medium or large server (see Section 3.1.1 definition for description of 'small', 'medium' or 'large' server).
(iii) A software program running in the http server processing the request looks up a table and identifies one free hardware server.

(iv) The software program looks up a pre-designated table for locating any free hardware server.

(v) Passes on the virtual address of the same to the requesting client.

(vi) This software need to perform other functions too:

(a) Track usage of this hardware.

(b) Raise a bill to the user on every month according to the usage.

(c) When the user relinquishes the hardware after their need, the software also should mark the hardware free and stop billing.

(vii) User gets the virtual address and carries on the necessary usages on it until they inform to relinquish.

The above describes an ideal normal flow. This process of automating the provisioning of hardware server is referred to as 'auto-provisioning'.

3.4 Data Centre Rack Systems

Conventionally, servers are arranged in independent casings. Servers under a typical hypervisor need not necessarily be in this arrangement.

A typical IaaS provider will need to have 1,000s of servers under one data centre, and every moment one or several of servers will be allocated or released.

A convenient form is to have rack systems. For instance, assume a rack full of CPUs with several printed circuit board (PCB). Each board can contain only two, four or eight core CPUs; and in this way, several boards can be inserted one below the other in the rack.

Similarly, a separate rack can contain several PCB boards and each board can contain only memory chips.

The ability of the 'hypervisor' software is to slice and dice the CPUs in the CPU rack and combine them with specified amount of main memory, available in the memory rack. Thus, it can create one instance of a server with the specified number of CPUs and main memory. Thus, one instance can act like a virtual machine. This is normally referred to as 'bare metal' in cloud computing parlance.

Users can specify the operating system they want to load onto the bare metal. Users can also specify a certain quantity of secondary storage memory to attach to the virtual machine. Normally, secondary storage is available as a SAN – which is a huge contiguous memory from which a specified portion will be allocated to the virtual machine or user can configure it to serve as a backup memory for the entire set of machine instances.

From the above description, it is now clear that

(i) Hypervisor will be closer to the bare metal than the operating system itself.

(ii) Hypervisor will have the power to terminate an operating system, whereas an operating system running in hypervisor cannot terminate the hypervisor. This indicates that hypervisor is the fundamental software in IaaS. Many operating systems and many instances of same operating system can be simultaneously running in one hypervisor instance.

(iii) It will also have the power to dismantle a particular machine instance and return CPUs and memory of the instance/s to their respective common free pool.

(vi) The term 'hypervisor' is used in this book to refer to a class of software that has the core functions discussed in this chapter. It is very similar to use of the term 'operating system' to refer to a class of software. There are many hypervisors available in the market both commercial and open-source products. Hypervisor is key software to create and provide IaaS. Readers can refer to[24] for other software components required to formulate and offer a complete IaaS. Such a discussion is out of scope for this book.

There are many hypervisors now available. Some of them are freeware and a few are commercial off-the-shelf (COTS) products.

3.5 Scaling through Software Architecture or Hardware

Over the past decade, we have constantly been working towards architecting highly scalable software systems. 'Scaling' here refers to the ability of the system to accommodate more users (or) scaling to process more data volumes (or) where more computational power is required, and it is typically achieved by a combination of both software and hardware.

Scaling is specifically achieved by two important aspects of the software architecture:

1. By software architecture
2. By deployment architecture

How a software is architected influences the scalability of the resultant software. Software architecture also dictates/determines deployment architecture. This in turn determines the feasibility of adding processing power or memory to specific heavily-used modules.

The software architecture and hence also the deployment architecture should be amenable for adding more processing powers as and when more users (or) data load (or) computational power are demanding the system.

3.6 Motivation or Need for Scalable Architecture

When architecting a system, it is difficult to predict how many concurrent users will try to access the system during peak usage.

That means system has to be architected for handling maximum number of concurrent users or logged in users. Therefore, at the start of deploying the solution itself, the number of servers that have to be procured is for maximum number or peak load of users.

The obvious disadvantage of this design is that the amount of hardware resources allocated will be too large or sub-optimally used in off-peak times. The risks in this design are as follows:

(i) Peak load envisaged may or may not be happening in post-implemented production situation.
(ii) It may take more time, for example, such as 3 months or 6 months or 8 months to reach the envisaged peak usage and hence experience peak load; and hence experience peak usage at later time from launch than sooner.

Hence,

(i) Capital investment required for implementing the system will be too large.
(ii) The capital investment is not properly utilized.
(iii) Thus, initially calculated ROI would not match with actual ROI.
(iv) Therefore, the break-even period becomes unpredictable.
(v) This uncertainty comes into play because of the inability to accurately estimate the peak load and the time to reach the peak load.

There are possible alternative scenarios too:

(a) Actual peak load may be much higher than that estimated peak load.
(b) As the system usage becomes more and more popular, more and more users may join to use the system.
(c) To set up a near scalable environment for testing a system, whose usage has increased enormously, is also a major concern'.

In this scenario to handle unanticipated additional peak load, one need to add additional hardware. There is a minimum lead time for procuring the servers and installing them. Usually in bigger organizations, it is of the order of 3–4 months even in the best optimized procurement cycles. During this time, users will feel slow response, and hence will get frustrated and may leave using the system.

3.7 Scalable Architecture (of Software)

Now let us see how software architecture helps achieve high scalability. To achieve higher scalability, the architecture needs to be multi-layered[1] and multi-tiered[2] and also highly modularized into components.

Note: [1]*What is layer? Layer defines the application to break up into logical structure such as presentation (UI), the business logic (processing) and data access (to access the data).*
[2]*What is tier? While layer is logical, tier defines how these layers will run whether in the same physical server (or) different servers.*

To achieve scalability, the components of cloud SaaS software, namely layers, tiers or components, will be distributed over networked servers; one or more servers will provide computing power to each component or tier or layer. As discussed in Chapter 10, software architecture consists of two main elements:

(i) It is distributed architecture; it is on a multi-tiered architecture style. An example is popular three-tier model – Web tier, business tier and data tier.
(ii) Each tier may consist of one or more components, for example
  (a) business tier may have components such as bpm, business rules engine, etc.
  (b) data tier may have further more components: data access object, database management system and data storage.

Such a software architecture will have a convenient corresponding deployment architecture: Generally, as a rule of thumb, each tier will be supported by one set of hardware servers.

If there are more than one significant components in any tier, then each of the significant components is housed in a separate hardware server. For example, business rules engine is a component in business tier and as a part of 'design' one or a cluster of servers can be allocated for business rules engine alone.

By assigning one or more servers to each tier or each significant component, we can provide adequate processing power that is required to handle appropriate number of concurrent users. There exists an equation connecting between the processing power and memory of servers to the number of users (requests) it can handle. If more number of users come, then additional units of server need to be added at that point – the component or tier – which becomes bottleneck in completing turnaround of users' requests.

Let us take a scenario to explain it further:

(i) Let us assume an architecture for a hypothetical software as given in Figure 3.1.
(ii) An http request coming from user client: Various tiers and components in the software will come into play to process the request.
(iii) Figure 3.2 gives a sample sequence of tiers and components that will come into play for satisfying the request. (Sequence diagram of UML is the most appropriate way of describing this. For some common understanding, a non-ideal notation is used here.) Each tier or component will process its own part and return a value; that is why there is an arrow that is travelling back to the Web tier.
(iv) Let us assume that one hardware server is provided to support each one of the tiers or for each one of the major components in any tier.
(v) For simplicity sake and discussion required for this chapter, we have assumed same configuration for all the servers.
(vi) Let the server configuration be 1.7 Ghz quad core processor with 8 GB of main memory.
(vii) Some of the tiers or components may require more processing power since they may perform CPU bound operations, for example business tier components. How many concurrent users can be accommodated in a given server configuration is normally done as part of 'capacity calculation': This is not a very precise engineering calculation. There is not any unique satisfactory method available for it. Every senior architect in the field develops her or his own method and follows it. For most of the projects, some of the following suggestions may be useful:

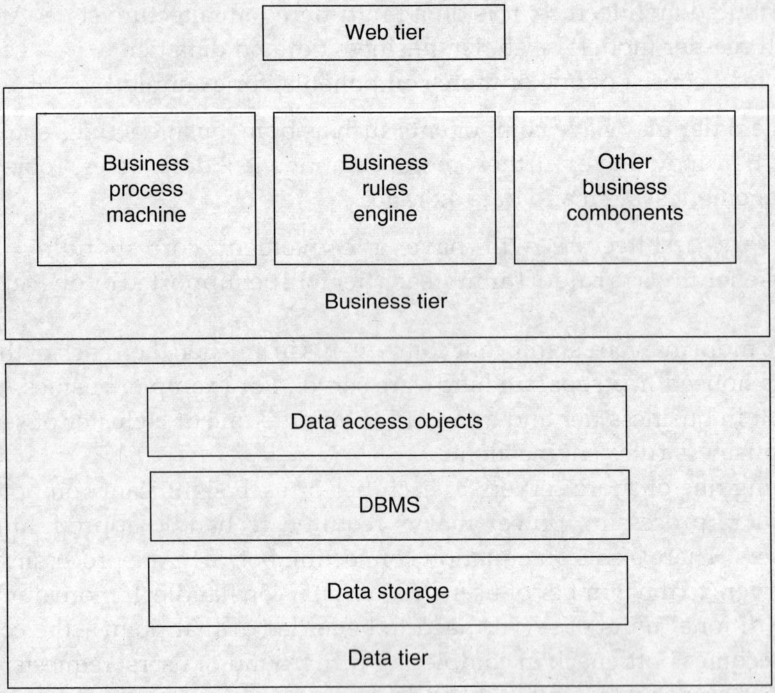

Figure 3.1 Various components in 3-tier architecture

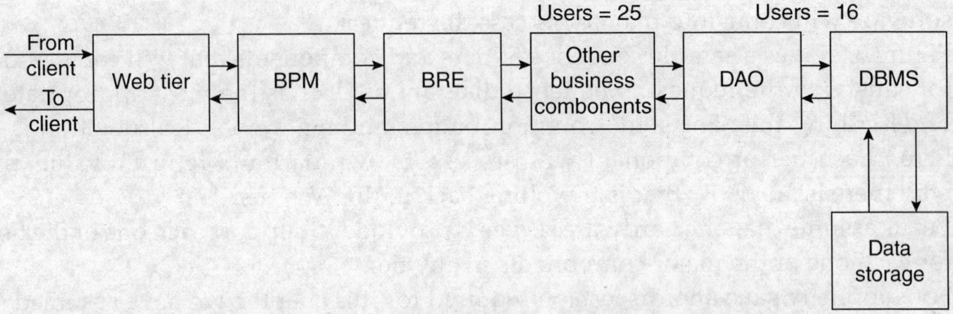

Figure 3.2 'Sequence diagram' of a system

(a) A load test can be used to practically find out how many number of users a server can accommodate without the response time being adversely affected.

(b) Sometimes, a stress test (i.e. loading the system progressively with more and more number of users) is conducted from all angles (UI, data access) for testing to determine correct deployment solution.

(c) One can calculate the number of Java objects that have to be processed by the CPU for processing the request at each module in the pipeline. From there, one can calculate how many number of users can be processed 'concurrently'. Similar method is available for .Net objects too.

(d) Some software product vendors provide 'calculators' for arriving at deployment architecture; for this calculation, inputs are number of concurrent users and simultaneous logged-in users.

(viii) Using one of the above or any empirical methods that will help in arriving at how many number of maximum users can be accommodated in a given configuration of the server at every stage. An example of the number of users at every server is mentioned in the diagram.

(ix) Some of the tiers may perform memory intensive operations. Example for this is data tier. For every connection to DataBase in connection pool, about 512 MB of memory is required. Therefore, in 8 GB machine there could be a possibility of accommodating $8 \times 2 = 16$ connections.

(x) Therefore, data tier cannot accommodate more than 16 concurrent users in this example solution deployment architecture.

(xi) That component or tier that can process lowest number of concurrent users may mostly be bottleneck and determines the total number of concurrent users the entire system can handle.

(xii) If we provide necessary processing power and required memory to that lowest processing component, then the bottleneck will move to the next slower processing component or tier. By that, we mean thus:

In this example,

(a) Only data tier alone can process not more than 16 user requests at any point of time.

(b) If we add one more server to data tier of the same configuration, then the processing capability gets doubled to 32 current users.

(c) Now from 16 to 32 users, the data tier will not be bottleneck. But after 25 concurrent users, component aa will become the bottleneck; unless and until the processing ability at this component aa is not increased, the whole system throughput cannot be increased to handle more than 25 concurrent users (without users experiencing a dramatic drop in response time).

Thus, the multi-tier, highly componentized software that can be on a distributed hardware servers – each hardware server supporting one or more tier/s or software components – are said to have architected for scalability or said to have scalable architecture.

Horizontal Scaling vs Vertical Scaling

In actual production situation, when there is a need to processes more users (requests) at any component or tier (as demanded in the above situation). There are two ways of adding additional computing power as described below:

1. Vertical scaling
2. Horizontal scaling

Vertical scaling means the processing power can be improved in the same server. For example, in the previous scenario, we have assumed quad core with 1.7 Ghz processor. To achieve scaling, we can replace this with higher speed processor, such as 2.3 Ghz still can with quad core processor.

Horizontal scaling means adding one or more servers of the same CPU with same processor speed and memory size. Therefore, two or more servers will work in parallel. In practice, this is usually even extended to make three servers work in parallel. (Why only up to three and why not more such as four or five is left as exercise to readers). All the two or three servers will have the same software – be they module or tier.

How to coordinate among these many servers to make them appear as if additional computing power is provided to process more number of user (requests) needs a coordinator; or technically, it is called 'load balancer'.

A bunch of servers serving same module is referred to as cluster. It is also referred as a node since it runs only one component of the entire software. In addition, it may be referred to as node because all the three or so servers may sit on the same node of the network of servers.

3.8 Concept of Load Balancer

To ensure proper coordination between two or more machines, working in parallel, supporting the same component (or tier or module) in a software, a new additional component by name 'load balancer' is needed.

Figure 3.3 pictorially explains a function of a load balancer that has three server instances among whose the load is balanced. Here, the load balancer is a typical hardware (bare metal) machine. The combination of all servers under one load balancer is said to be 'cluster'. Network load balancers (NLBs) can be software also in which case they will be installed in all the servers under one cluster.

As the name indicates, load balancer keeps monitoring workloads at each of the servers connected to it.

The workload is nothing but object codes that are queuing in front of the CPU for getting processed or serviced by CPU.

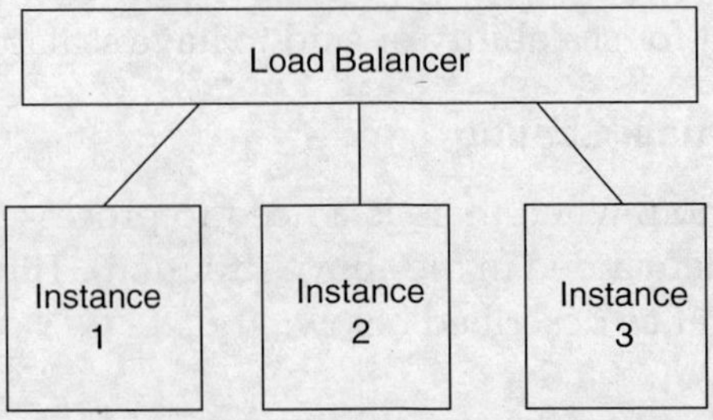

Figure 3.3 Schematic of 'Load Balancer'

Load balancer moves workloads between the servers that are relatively free.

Therefore, load balancers constantly keep monitoring workloads or queues in front of CPU as well as free CPU or memory available at each of the servers (which are connected to the load balancer). Load balancers in a cluster keep communicating the workload and free/busy of CPU + memory information among themselves and later move the objects among the servers in the same clusters to get the processing 'attention'.

Load balancer can be another physical hardware, or it can be purely only software too. Sometimes, software load balancers are also referred to as NLBs.

One copy of NLB will be installed in each of the servers that are expected to work in parallel. Obviously, the server being hardware it would have been connected by high-speed LAN environment.

The load balancer (Microsoft™ uses the acronym 'NLB'; and NLB is also Microsoft's software and not a physical hardware) normally supports both algorithmic and deterministic approach to manage or distribute the load among the servers under one cluster.

The above explained how a load balancer works and also explained how it helps in scaling.

The functionalities of load balancer are also moved into hypervisor.

3.9 Auto-Scaling

Let us examine how to achieve high scalability using hypervisors and the modern rack systems described above. This knowledge is essential as an introduction to understand auto-scaling.

By combining two major functionalities – auto-provisioning and load balancing – we can expect hypervisors to do automated scaling function. This is explained as below:

(i) Assume a script can run in hypervisor.
(ii) The script has two parts:
   (a) One is called 'cloud watch'
   (b) Second part does the following:
      1. Ask for required server through auto-provisioning feature of hypervisor and
      2. Load required software + load software component or tier to which it goes as additional server to handle.
   (c) About 'cloud watch' pattern: one can specify to 'cloud watch' to observe certain happening phenomenon such as keep monitoring and counting <number of users <at a tier>> and can specify to trigger <some actions> on <a condition such as greater than x number of users in this tier> <do something>.

For example, keep monitoring the number of logged-in users newly arriving at web tier;

If the number of logged-in users increases beyond 1,000, then add one more server to web tier.

(d) The trigger is used to carry out actions such as auto-provision another server instance using step (c).

(e) Now change the server to be monitored (such as next would be bottlenecking server) and go back to step (c).

(iii) Thus, the above algorithm will ensure that servers are automatically provisioned as and when the number of users keep increasing.

(iv) (Obviously, there is an assumption that there are enough number of servers available for making this happen).

(v) The above script can be made much more comprehensive by writing a separate loop for de-provisioning as and when the number of users come down.

(vi) The de-provisioning loop will keep removing servers as and when the number of users come down in the right (reverse) order.

Since it is a script,

(i) It can be modified any time.

(ii) It can be parameterized.

(iii) It can be written for any deployment architecture.

(iv) 'Cloud watch' can 'watch' the key items that architect wants it to 'watch' for taking some specific action.

Thus, through this kind of scripts, complete scaling required can be automated.

3.10 Summary of Capabilities of Hypervisors

(i) Hypervisor can create virtual machines (which is referred as an instance of server) to specification by combining CPUs and memories from rack systems.

(ii) Server instances can be requested remotely through cloud and Web browsers and hypervisor can provision it.

(iii) It can also load required software such as operating system and specified other software too.

(iv) Server instances can be automated to provision to specification.

(v) The functionalities of load balancer are also included in the hypervisor.

(vi) Using cloud watch capabilities, auto-scaling is possible.

(vii) De-provisioning is also possible.

(viii) In commercial public IaaS, other operational and business support systems such as to monitor the usage of servers and raising bill according to the usage is also available.

3.11 A Simple Model of Infrastructure as a Service (IaaS)

The following description will give an idea on how IaaS is organized from service providers' perspective. This model will help in architecting solutions for IaaS as discussed in Chapter 4; it will also help in subsequent cloud SaaS solutions being discussed in rest of the chapters.

(i) Assuming availability of rack systems of CPUs and memories; also availability of SAN.
(ii) All these 'bare metal' is under hypervisor.
(iii) The user can interact with hypervisor using their Web browser for provisioning requests; auto-provisioning is possible by hypervisor.
(iv) A billing system takes care of prepare bills for every user as per the usage of hardware.

3.12 Example Case Situations

Example 1

Start-ups and uncertainty and unpredictability for system usage consider a situation such as for the first time an application such as Facebook™ has to be launched. The creator of Facebook™ is completely uncertain how this will be welcomed in that open market. Implying that it is impossible to predict how many number of logged-in users or concurrent users will be there for this system. It is also impossible to predict the peak or turf loads for this system*.

(i) If we assume any number and it is likely to go wrong
(ii) If one predicts a large number of users and procures a large amount of hardware, then a huge capital investment is required; and this is not practical.
(iii) If a small amount of hardware is used, thinking it is first-time launch or announcement to the public, then
    (a) The use of the site and services becomes so popular; and if a large number of users land on in that site to avail the services, then the hardware would not be in a position to support that many users, and hence the performance will fall down drastically.
    (b) This will frustrate the users and likely that they may stop using this or may go to alternative competitive sites and services.
(iv) Public IaaS will provide complete 'elasticity' of the hardware that are required for this situation.
    (a) It will do an auto-scaling and hence will also provide automatically additional computing power necessary to handle new spurt up users.
    (b) If the users come down, the system also will be de-provisioning and de-allocate the hardware and shrink it to minimum required level.

---

*Disclaimer: The author does not say that Facebook™ used this technique in any way.

(c) The charges for using hardware are directly proportional to the duration of the time for which they are used.
(d) No initial investment. All 'pay as you go'.

Thus, opting for public IaaS matches this kind of requirement perfectly in many ways:

1. Initial investment for starting it can be kept as minimum as possible. Since the use of public IaaS is only on pay-per-use model, there is no investment for hardware servers.
2. Public IaaS can be assumed to have an infinite computing resources. We can assume the hardware can automatically scale-up to meet any peak-demand.
3. Additional expenses and hence pay-out to IaaS for additional usage of hardware service is in proportion to income due to additional users.

Thus, opting public IaaS is good solution for this kind of start-up situation.

Example 2

Seasonal peak demands in North America or Europe during Christmas season

There are many systems that are deployed for sales promotion. Similarly, in India during Diwali festival time, a lot of sales promotion systems are put in place.

Such systems are typically used for 2 or 3 months. During the time, system will be in peak use. After that, the system may not be having any use, or it may be at the lowest use just to keep maintaining till next season.

Investing to buy hardware for such systems will unnecessarily eat away corporate IT budget.

Use of IaaS is appropriate.

Example 3

Sports event or event management

Federation of International Football Association (FIFA) kind of organizations conduct sports events such as FIFA's World Cup once in 4 years. They also conduct other events such as European champion of regional or local championships. Thus, on the whole, they are busy throughout the year.

FIFA maintains websites for each of the events. Each website becomes very busy a few months before the start of the event. That means, the site users will be large, and it will be increasing as the date to event increases. After the event, the users will come down drastically.

A typical event such as FIFA's World Cup may past for 40 days. Even during the event time depending on which team wins at a particular stage such as second round or pre-quarter final, number of visitors to site may peak.

For such highly fluctuating load of users, dynamic-auto scaling through IaaS is an ideal solution.

3.13 Summary

- This chapter introduced the architectural attribute 'scalable'.
- It has discussed two traditional means of achieving scalability through 'horizontal scaling' or 'vertical scaling'.
- This chapter also discusses how software needs to be architected, help as well achieve scalability.
- In this context, this chapter also discusses how IaaS supports 'auto-scaling' and handles fluctuating incoming loads and also optimally utilizes the hardware in proportion to load.
- The role of load balancers and software load balancers are introduced.
- A summary of functionalities of hypervisor will be useful for architecting solutions for IaaS.
- Use cases presented here will be useful for concretizing readers understanding on these areas.
- In this context where 'hypervisors' fit in and make up IaaS is also described.
- Thus, the knowledge of how hypervisors work and how IaaS function are good prerequisites for architecting solutions discussed in Chapters 4, 7, 8 and 9.
- The simple model of IaaS discussed here will be very useful for solution architects.

Chapter 4

Architecting Software Solutions for Public IaaS Cloud (without SaaS)

4.1 Introduction

How to architect software or solutions (leave alone 'cloud') itself is an interesting topic for discussions. References [21, 22] discuss methods of architecting software. This knowledge is essential and fundamental to architecting solutions or products. These details are not repeated here; and conveniently, it is assumed that readers will be familiar with the contents in those references Such an assumption is essential to focus on the intent of this book.

Reference [20] discusses how the cloud pushed the frontiers of architecting software or solutions. Chapter 3 discusses elaborately the conceptual view of Infrastructure as a Service (IaaS) that is good enough for an architect. In future, all softwares will be deployed only on IaaS.

This chapter illustrates how to architect software for IaaS. This is simple and straightforward. Although the complexity of knowledge required for this is low, this information of how to architect solution for deployment in cloud IaaS is provided in this chapter. Many novice solutions architects expressed need for this simple information.

Primarily, solution software will be deployed in public (or private) IaaS. Irrespective of the fact whether solution software need or need not serve multiple tenants as in cloud software as a service (SaaS) solution, the architect needs to follow steps mentioned here for deploying solution software on IaaS.

In future, all softwares will be deployed only on IaaS – be it private or public, be it for single tenant as dedicated system or for multiple tenants as in cloud SaaS. Therefore, learning to architect solutions to deploy on IaaS is inevitably the first major step.

The steps involved in the method discussed in this chapter to architect these solutions will anyhow be required to architect cloud SaaS solutions that will be discussed in Chapters 7, 8 and 9. This method is illustrated through a case study.

4.2 The Method in Brief

Reference [17] discusses how to architect solutions when there are no requirements available upfront from customers. Chapter 2 has a relevant extract of the same.

References [32, 33] explain the context, usefulness and applicability of the solutions used as case study in this chapter.

Proceed from requirements until you (architect) complete architecting solution as usual. There is no big change in steps until this point is reached or this deliverable is made ready in solution architecting project. Reference [4] will be of some use in detailing steps involved in this part of architecting. References [21, 22] are absolutely very good resources for architecting solutions. Chapter 9 will be useful if the solution is cloud SaaS solution. (The case study presented here enumerates some of these steps too.)

At the end of solutioning phase, architects would have identified solution building blocks (SBBs). Some SBBs may be software product/s, and some SBBs may require custom development.

Architecting for IaaS starts with deployment architecture development and its implementation structure. To be ready for this step, the architect needs to analyse all SBBs thoroughly and come up with implementation hardware and other infrastructure software requirements for each of them.

4.2.1 Identifying Minimum Deployment Hardware Configuration for each SBB

(i) Each SBB will have, in itself, many tiers: Web tier, business tier, data tier, etc. For each tier, the architect needs to collect the minimum deployment hardware configuration and deployment architecture.

(ii) In addition, it is essential to collect information on minimum online and concurrent users for the specified minimum deployment configuration for each of the modules of every SBB. This in turn will be used to determine minimum deployment architecture configuration to be prescribed or arrived at for each of the building blocks.

(iii) For deploying each product, respective product vendor would have specified minimum configuration of infrastructures required to deploy for each of the tiers.

(iv) Some product vendors give hardware requirement calculators; this can be used by architects to calculate the configuration of the hardware required for each tier of the product for a prescribed minimum login users and concurrent users.

(v) Sometimes, product vendors would specify directly the number of users their recommended minimum-hardware configuration can handle.

(vi) Most of the product vendors provide calculators to arrive at final deployment hardware configuration for peak loads – this is of no use for cloud SaaS solution; the architect needs to look for minimum configuration and also the number of users the minimum configuration can entertain with agreeable user-response time.

(vii) Architects should avoid very trivial configuration of putting in a single box of minimum configuration all the tiers and infrastructure software required for any COTS or software products. One minimum configuration for each – scalable – tier and one each for every single-infrastructure product.

(viii) For custom-built modules, architects need to specify deployment architecture for each of the tiers. This is again minimum configuration, and architects need to document minimum number of users for the minimum configuration.

(ix) The basic reason for specifying the above steps is to apply scalability algorithms for each of the tiers or modules of the SBBs involved at a fine granular level of each tier or module of each SBB.

4.2.2 Calculating IaaS Infrastructure Configuration

(i) Map each (minimum configuration) unit hardware into ideal instances in the catalogue of IaaS infrastructure service provider.

(ii) Select necessary support services and also note down their one-time, initial, annual or recurring cost. Most of the time, these costs are not pay-per-use types.

(iii) For selecting an IaaS service provider from a list of probable service providers (assuming that their technical capabilities will meet the requirement for the solution), the above steps need to be repeated for every vendor being evaluated. These costs, along with pay-per-use costs, will help in deciding the final public IaaS vendor. There may be many more criteria such as legal protection to the cloud SaaS software and customer data that the IaaS provider may offer. Such facilities may also play a part in selecting the vendor. (Discussion of legal aspects to select public IaaS provider is out of scope for this book.)

After finalizing IaaS service provider,

(iv) Arrive at scaling algorithm when implemented in the target IaaS platform. This will help the solution to scale-up on demand as well as scale down during off-peak demands. (Chapter 7 illustrates with a case study how to arrive at scaling algorithm).

These steps are the only difference in specifying IaaS as part of solution from conventional deployment architecture calculations.

Now we will study how these steps are applied through a case study.

4.3 Digital Communication Platform

For various perspectives of this case study, please refer to Refs. [32, 33]. The following is a case discussed in detail.

System Requirements

Customer wants to have a digital communication platform. This may comprise a website (content management system) that is mobile-enabled with social media interaction for the following three phases of a sports event:

(i) Pre-event
(ii) During the event
(iii) Post-event

(a) The 'digital communication platform' will have website accessible by desktop clients, mobile clients and will have ubiquitous access.

(b) It will have two gateways to open free popular social media: One is to publish about the events in those media and the other is to collect what people are talking in those media about the event to take corrective action.

(c) Conventional push technologies such as email and SMS will be required.
(d) The user community will be general public, sports fans, participating athletics, event officials, media persons and many more types. The platform will also provide as many of the features on mobile clients too.
(e) Apart from fans, there are other important stakeholders such as athletes, coaches, media partners, fan clubs, retail advertisers, etc., whose needs must be catered to before, during and after the event.
(f) It should also provide many means to promote the event.

Website

(i) Requirements from athletics associations: the website should follow certain statutory principles prescribed by governing sporting bodies in that geographic region.
(ii) Mobile site content should be accessible via iOS and android mobile devices. (Other operating systems are of lesser priority.)
(iii) Leverage in advance software engineering practices in the areas of mobile and cloud computing for the event.
(iv) Syndication and aggregation of news feeds and support for Web services.
(v) Support for special features, graphics and contents as per guidelines provided by the customer.
(vi) Web stats: It is imperative that each customer department be able to effectively review, analyse and audit the usage of their extranet. Administrators and Web masters should also be able to review how various extranets and intranets are being used and increase content effectiveness.
(vii) Time visitor traffic and their flow through the site.
(viii) Search engine optimized (SEO) design of website in a way that it will appear higher in search engine rankings.
(ix) Search functionality: Search is the core functionality in any website/portal implementation.
(x) Live streaming and post-event streaming of events videos.
(xi) High-quality hardware platform and state-of-the-art hosting infrastructure that is highly scalable and available to be provided by vendor.

Mobile Apps

(i) Requirement of mobile apps for ticketing, photo gallery and video streaming for the event.
(ii) Accessibility of calendar and news page through mobile apps.
(iii) Accessibility of accreditation documents (PDFs) through mobile apps.
(iv) Live video streaming (of any such events) should be viewable through mobile app.
(v) Accessibility to stadium or venue information through mobile apps.
(vi) Rating of the contents of site through mobile apps.

Social Media

(i) Increased buzz about the event in the relevant public domain, leading to increased ticket/merchandise sales.
(ii) Creation of long-term relationship with the fans that can be leveraged for post-event activities and brand-building.
(iii) By providing timely information over internet. Increase patronage of fans who are not physically present during the event (because of timely information provided to them through the games website).
(iv) Creation of referenceable information database that can be re-used for similar events conducted by the customer.

Social media solution is suggested in three innovative buckets:

(a) *Collaboration platform* – This platform is within the customer official event site (where different users can engage on discussion forums, blogs, community discussions, photo sharing, etc.).
(b) *Listening platform* – This platform would allow for the customer to listen to social messages that are of relevance.
(c) *Broadcasting platform* – This platform will serve the following two purposes:
  1. To act on insights generated by listening platform selectively in wallpost/tweet on a particular social profile that might be 'detracting' the customer brand.
  2. To proactively reach out to audiences through targeted communications on events, merchandise, calendar, giveaways, etc.

4.4 Approach to Realization

Functional Architecture

Following is the solution in nutshell for the customer to support the sports event.

Proposed functional architecture description: The following explains the functional architecture of the solution using Figure 4.1.

(i) It has various functional modules: user management, content management server (CMS), event management (including ticketing), media management, doc management, Web analytics, messaging, social media, general (widgets management, accreditation).
(ii) The platform has a website for desktop clients, and it also includes a mobile access to the same.
(iii) Web content management (w)CMS server serves as the heart of the solution. This has both Web content database and a separate mobile content database.
(iv) To this a listening platform, such as Radian6, is attached which fetches the customers' comments from the open social media such as Facebook™ or Twitter™.
(v) Analytics functionalities are available – say custom-built sentiment analytics as well cloud service based – and helps analyse the comments of the customers and infer the overall feedback from sports enthusiasts and fans. Each stakeholder department can get analytics of their interest area.

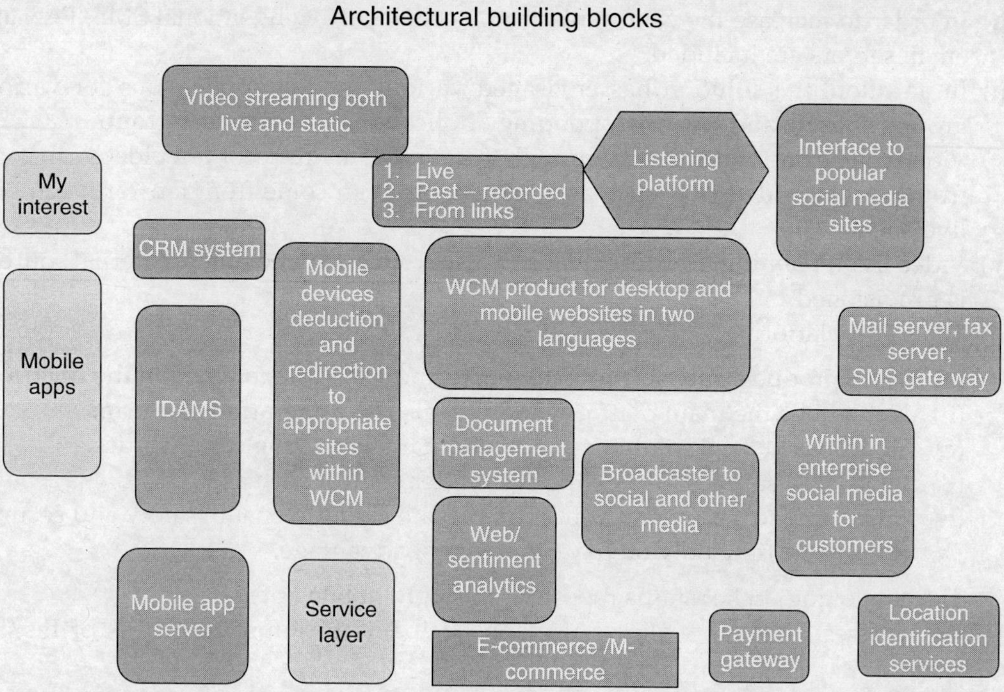

Figure 4.1 Functional architecture with architectural building blocks derived from grouped requirements of the solution

(vi) In addition, the solution provides a separate and exclusively created 'enterprise social media' for customers to chat, blog or comment or, in general, express themselves or exchange views and points among various stakeholders of this event. This can be organized to provide customer-helping-customer both during post- and pre-events. Also at the back-end, analytics can be run on this to understand the sentiments that are running about the event.

(vii) Broadcaster service is (unlike RSS feed) to make regular announcements by the events organizers in popular pre-configured social media.

(viii) Of course e-commerce server delivers requests from both desktop clients and mobile clients. Hence, it scales up with specific functionalities to serve as mobile-commerce (m-commerce) too.

(ix) Payment gateway is a component that must already exist in any e-commerce solution.

(x) Please notice that there are specific technical software components for deducting mobile devices when the site is accessed from a mobile device. In addition, one can entertain dedicated mobile apps through a separate server.

(xi) Please notice location services that will add 'spice' to mobile contents in the form of location-aware content delivery.

(xii) In order to increase the communication mechanism – conventional SMS, FAX and email servers are included.

(xiii) In addition, the solution has envisaged various mobile applications for various groups of users and has corresponding applications for each user group.

(xiv) Video can be one of the inputs through this platform. Pre-recorded videos can come from popular video sites such as YouTube, or it can come from fans or it can be a live one too.

(xv) Video live streaming, from archival and also from open free public external sources, is provisioned.

(xvi) Tools and platform

- (a) COTS products such as (w)CMS server and CMS as explained in the diagram;
- (b) .Net will be the main platform and will also be integration platform;
- (c) Cloud-based SaaS solutions such as Radian6 and Google™ analytics;
- (d) Some open sources to keep the cost under control such as WURFL;
- (e) Entire infrastructure platform is on private cloud to ensure safety and security at the same time only on pay-per-use cost advantage.

(xvii) Ticket booking/ticket status reporting through mobile apps.

(xviii) 'My interest' feature – allows users/participants to jump into areas of his/her interest.

Customization

(xix) Private secured cloud-based IaaS solution – cost effective, pay-as-you-go model and highly scalable hardware infrastructure.

Integration of Subsystems

(xx) Communication including instant messaging (IM) via Smartphone (provide this feature through mobile app).

(xxi) Event promotion through broadcaster/event manager/Web channel.

(xxii) Live video streaming, Recording/Past Events Video streaming, links to open sources of video.

(xxiii) Web Content Management Systems ((w)CMS) server supports multiple file formats and also allows metadata associated with these various file formats to be uploaded into (w)CMS server. (w)CMS server will need to be integrated with a video streaming server for rendering multimedia content. Graphical/animation can be easily shown from (w)CMS server in mainly three ways – through a (w)CMS server data factory Web service (basic Web service), by calling (w)CMS server pages directly that output XML/HTML data to read/render and by outputting the data directly on the page integration with social media.

(xxiv) Integrated with many popular public social media.

(xxv) Solution also provides exclusive enterprise social media within the digital communication platform for various user groups to collaborate.

(xxvi) Easily configurable workflow for approving contents/approving contents that need to be published in social media.

Integration with External Systems

(xxvii) Listening platform is cloud-based (Radian 6), and hence is very cost effective and follows pay-as-you-go model.

(xxviii) All data communication in the form of restful services enables seamless integration between cloud, mobile apps and partner's (other vendors and stakeholders home grown) apps or systems.

4.5 Realization of the Envisaged Solution Architecture

Table 4.1 summarizes various software products (or technologies such as .Net) and meets the functional modules mentioned in previous section. (The grouping of functional capabilities can be roughly considered as architectural building blocks (ABB).)

Table 4.1 Indicates realization of envisaged architecture by indicating what functional group will be realized by (finalized or selected) software products

Features	Realization mechanism	Product stack
Single sign on	Application server	(w)CMS server security extensions
Personalization	Application server	(w)CMS server
Authentication and authorization	Application server	(w)CMS server security extensions
Policy management	Application server	(w)CMS server
Report generation	Application server	(w)CMS server
Session management	Application server	IIS
State management	Application server	.Net
Transaction management	Application server	IIS
Reporting service	Application server	(w)CMS server, (w)CMS server logging services
Mail framework	Application server	(w)CMS server, .Net
Events and notification framework	Application server	(w)CMS server
Integration with database	Data access layer	OLE DB
Workflow	(w)CMS server workflow engine	(w)CMS server

Note: In the above illustration, the Web server and app server are assumed to be in the same physical box.

The recommended (w)CMS Server solution comes bundled with (w)CMS Trace/Google™ analytics. The (w)CMS Server-based framework is also compatible with other Web analytics and reporting tools such as Web trends, Surf Aid and Hitbox. Raw data related to website usage and tracking is saved in log files, a bespoke reporting module can be built to review and analyse the usage of various intranets and extranets.

The use of (w)CMS Server Relate+, which offers a rich set of features (such as blogs, discussions, forums, bulletin boards, etc.), is necessary for creating social media and collaboration platform.

Figure 4.2 gives a pictorial view of the solution products finalized, and tabulated in Table 4.1, for each of the modules. (Reference [6] is international grade, which provides guidelines to what are all views of architecture can be provided. However, the architecture views provided, in this chapter or in the entire book, are not checked for its compliance with the benchmarks.)

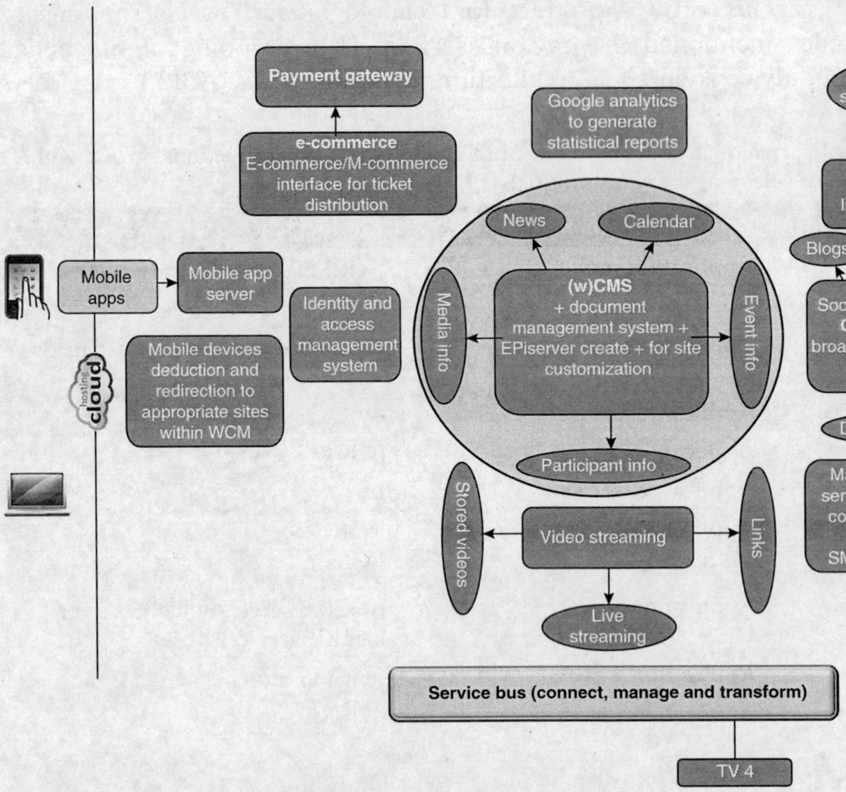

Figure 4.2 Mapping SBBs into ABBs: selection of software solution products that can match ABBs

4.6 Architectural Considerations

Description: Refer Figure 4.3 also for physical deployment architecture.

(i) The above view depicts the physical view of the proposed system.

(ii) The users will be screened through the protocol firewall.

(iii) Based on some of the non-functional requirements regarding number of concurrent users and active users, the recommended practice is to deploy all these servers as clusters in a federated environment. The server capacity may be for forecasted peak loads.

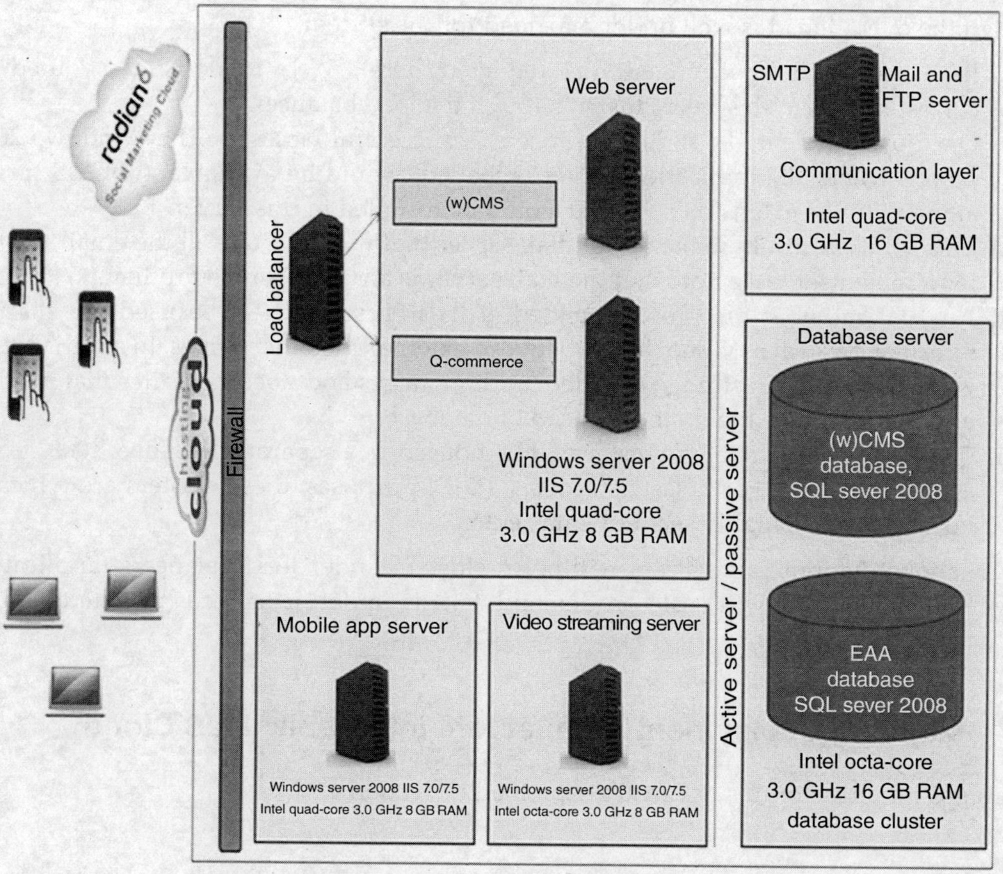

Figure 4.3 Physical deployment architecture

(For cloud IaaS, it is recommended to obtain the details of minimum configuration and the number of users or load it can handle; then as and when the load increases through an auto-scaling algorithm, additional servers will be automatically provisioned. See Chapter 7 for an illustrated explanation of this.)

For solutions such as sports events, which last for a few days, or maximum a few weeks, the organizers prefer using maximum estimated load as default hardware size.

For events such as this, it is better to go for maximum load approach; after the event, the load will drastically drop down, and hence it can be brought to highly shrinked architecture to save the cost. The same is illustrated here too. See the spreadsheet 'capacity' for it.

Auto-scaling is essential when the load surges beyond the estimated maximum load. Also some of the modules may face high load, depends on the features used by users, even though the overall load is well under max load for the system.

(iv) In a federated environment (as depicted here), Web requests are routed to corresponding Web server cluster through the load balancer.

(v) Once user-credential validation process is successful, access to the Windows 2008 server, where IIS application server is loaded, would be available. (w)CMS server along with the extension software would be installed in this server.

(vi) This solution would make use of mail server that will facilitate all the email-related requirements. Please note that the mail server is an open-source product.

(vii) An FTP server is also recommended. This FTP server will be used for sharing information such as video/audio between external customer drives. In addition, this would be useful in storage of video/audio, images and document files that need to be archived in the file system instead of database.

(viii) The SQL server database cluster will be housed in a separate Windows 2008 server across a firewall. For disaster-recovery (D-R) purposes, these clusters are typically housed inside a highly secured data centre.

In the above diagram, all servers will be in clusters under load balancers (application servers and database) will scale on demand as it is undervirtualized (private cloud or public IaaS) environment.

4.7 Mapping Deployment Architecture into Public IaaS Cloud

The steps required for this is already explained in Section 4.2.

Disclaimers

(i) The cost indicated are tentative and illustrative but does not reflect the actual cost taken from AWS.

(ii) AWS itself provides a cost calculator.

AWS costing for printing

Server	Purpose	Instance type	Months	Amount / Month	Budget / Server	One time	Per Hour	Monthly	Data I/O / GB	Data volume / GB	Data per month	Cloud Watch / Month	Load Balancer / GB	Data volume / GB2	ELB / Month	EBS (Storage) / GB	Data volume / GB3	Storage / Month	Bronze support
Web Server	Production	Extra Large	6	1121	6729		0.96	691	0.138	1024	141	35	0.028	1024	29	0.220	1024	225	
Web Server	Production	Extra Large	6	1121	6729		0.96	691	0.138	1024	141	35	0.028	1024	29	0.220	1024	225	
Database Server	Production	Extra Large	6	1553	9321		1.56	1123	0.138	1024	141	35	0.028	1024	29	0.220	1024	225	
Database Server	Production	Extra Large	6	1553	9321		1.56	1123	0.138	1024	141	35	0.028	1024	29	0.220	1024	225	
App Server	Production	Extra Large	6	1121	6729		0.96	691	0.138	1024	141	35	0.028	1024	29	0.220	1024	225	
App Server	Production	Extra Large	6	1121	6729		0.96	691	0.138	1024	141	35	0.028	1024	29	0.220	1024	225	
Web Server (Staging)	Staging	Extra Large	7	924	6467		0.96	691	0.138	512	71	35	0.028	512	14	0.220	512	113	
Database Server (Staging)	Staging	Extra Large	7	1356	9491		1.56	1123	0.138	512	71	35	0.028	512	14	0.220	512	113	
App Server (Staging)	Staging	Extra Large	7	924	6467		0.96	691	0.138	512	71	35	0.028	512	14	0.220	512	113	
Database Server (Staging)	Staging	Extra Large	7	1356	9491		1.56	1123	0.138	512	71	35	0.028	512	14	0.220	512	113	
ADFS	Development	Large	21	420	8829	600	0.33	238	0.138	256	35	35	0.028	256	7	0.220	256	56	49
Web	Development	Large	21	420	8829	600	0.33	238	0.138	256	35	35	0.028	256	7	0.220	256	56	49
App	Development	Large	21	420	8829	600	0.33	238	0.138	256	35	35	0.028	256	7	0.220	256	56	49
DB	Development	Large	21	528	11097	2600	0.48	346	0.138	256	35	35	0.028	256	7	0.220	256	56	49
Gen	Development	Large	21	420	8829	600	0.33	238	0.138	256	35	35	0.028	256	7	0.220	256	56	49
S3 for Archival Storage (RRS)	Archival		30	1091	32717											0.213	5120	1091	49
Additional instance for redundency	Production	Extra Large	9	1121	10089													0	49
Live site migration	Existing site	Extra Large	7	1553	10874													0	49

(continued)

AWS costing for printing (Continued)

Server	Purpose	Instance type	Months	Amount / Month	Budget / Server	One time	Per Hour	Monthly	Data I/O / GB	Data volume / GB	Data per month	Cloud Watch / Month	Load Balancer / GB	Data volume / GB2	ELB / Month	EBS (Storage) / GB	Data volume / GB3	Storage / Month	Bronze support
Spike data trafic (10 times for 6 months) (Optional)	Production		60	141	8479													0	
Hardware VPN connection (Optional)	Development		21	36	756		0.05	36										0	
Total			296	18305	186798	5000		9972			1307	525			265			3174	
Support at 10%			3	1830.4528	5491.3584														
					192289.8064														
provision for contigency				10%	19228.98064														
Proffessional Services Provision			21	3550	74550														
Grand Total					286068.787														

The pricing includes:
Virtual Private Cloud
Load balancer for Production, Staging and Development
dev for 21 months
prod for 6 months
one time cost for dev is based on 36 months
windows server included for all the instances
SQL Server standard edition included for DB servers
5 Elastic IP for publishing the production servers
20 volumes with 200 GB for each volume
1 TB data trafic
AMI backups can be taken
RTO of 1 hour and RPO of 8 hrs can be achieved
Pricing and Instances based on DC at Europe (Ireland)
Lesser RTO and RPO can achieved having additional instances at US / Sing DC
Annual Uptime Percentage of at least 99.95% during the Service Year.
Bronze support - web ticketing and support during customers local working hours
Platinum support for Production run with 5 mts turn around time and dedicated account manager
Redundancy servers included
ELB / High availability restricted to Europe region

(iii) AWS of Amazon™ is used as an illustration; AWS is taken up as illustration as it also supports Windows and .Net in their IaaS infrastructure. Since the terms such as 'large', 'medium' referring to ideal server sizes are very pertinent to AWS.

Explanations for the spreadsheets:

First sheet to be studied is titled as 'topology': This explains how a virtual private cloud is created within public IaaS; and the same is accessed from a remote developer LAN for developing and dumping the developed or maintained code into the IaaS.

The diagram did not show how users would access the system; it is through cloud from their devices.

Second sheet to be studied is titled 'availability': This indicates for how long the individual servers are required for the project.

(a) Some of the servers are required for development purposes; therefore, they need to be available well ahead of the event date.
(b) Some of them are required only during and post-event period.
(c) This sort of information should be collected during system study and development.
(d) The availability information is carried into cost calculation in next sheet to be studied and titled 'IaaS cost calculation'.

Third sheet to be studied is 'IaaS cost calculation':

1. This is the sheet where deployment servers are mapped on to IaaS ideal server sizes (see Table 4.1).
2. This sheet also gives the operating system or other infrastructures that are required for each server and hence, each corresponding instance in the IaaS. The cost of infrastructure software is also usually on pay-per-use model from IaaS providers.
3. There is a fixed one-time cost and there is a pay-per-use cost.
4. The cost indicated here is an estimated cost and not actual cost; actual cost will be pay-per-use plus the one-time cost.
5. Readers' attention is drawn to the details one needs to have as estimate before calculating the cost; these details are data storage requirement, bandwidth requirements, etc.

4.8 Summary

- The main objective of this chapter is to illustrate how to arrive at a deployment architecture suitable to map a public IaaS.
- In addition, this chapter provided details of mapping a deployment architecture to public IaaS.
- One can also learn how to move from requirements to ABBs and then to identify corresponding SBBs.
- A detailed calculation of cost of IaaS is provided.

Chapter 5

Characteristics of Cloud SaaS Software

5.1 Introduction

Software provided as service through cloud has certain special characteristics. This chapter describes a set of attributes that explain these special characteristics.

The attributes and their explanations are provided from the perspective of a service provider. Such a perspective helps understand the behaviour of cloud Software as a Service (SaaS) software. Understanding these attributes will help architect SaaS software for cloud environment.

Reference [24] indicates the following as essential characteristics for cloud computing and, in turn, cloud SaaS: on-demand-self-service, broad network access, resource pooling, rapid elasticity and measured service.

Reference [5] indicates multi-tenancy, scalability and customization by self-service as three important characteristics of cloud SaaS software. 'Resource pooling' as one more characteristic mentioned in Ref. [5] assumes significance in architecting or designing the software for cloud SaaS. Pay-per-use is the key model for cloud SaaS, and hence resources utilized by end-user should be 'measurable'.

This chapter will discuss most of these characteristics.

Generally, cloud SaaS solutions are designed for individual industry segments. This way, multiple enterprises in a particular industry segment can conveniently use a single instance of the cloud SaaS software. This optimizes the cost of producing the software.

Therefore, understanding the following industry characteristics becomes necessary in identifying requirements for cloud SaaS solutions:

(i) The nature of the enterprise
(ii) The industry segment for which the SaaS solution is provided
(iii) Provisioning enterprises model within the software (see Chapter 1 for a detailed discussion on this).

5.2 Multi-Tenancy

Multi-tenancy is the single most important attribute of SaaS in any cloud solution.

In a generic sense, multi-tenancy refers to many tenants residing in the same house simultaneously and paying rent in proportion to their period of stay, or to the extent of use of various facilities.

Multi-tenancy, in the context of SaaS in cloud software, refers to any software's ability to serve multiple enterprises simultaneously. 'Tenants' in this context refer to enterprises using the software (SaaS in cloud model). In essence, *multi-tenancy refers to many enterprises that simultaneously use the same running instance of a software.*

Here, each enterprise pays a fee as rent based on the duration of their usage of selected functionalities or facilities in the SaaS solutions or products.

As discussed in Chapter 1, in a hosted model, each enterprise will have its own dedicated instance of the software, which is contrast to the concept of multi-tenancy.

In the latter, although a single instance of the cloud SaaS software serves many enterprises simultaneously, it is expected to behave as if:

(i) it is a dedicated copy for each subscribing enterprises, unaware of other co-tenants using the same instance.
(ii) it will be available to each tenant (enterprises) at their own disposal for performing any tenant-specific actions such as customization of the software.
(iii) it has the ability to perform as an extended arm of the enterprise.

To make a single instance of software serve multiple tenants, various tiers and components of the software should have been architected differently (see Chapter 9 for detailed discussion on architecting cloud SaaS software). Each component needs to be designed suitably to achieve this characteristic. For example, the Web tier would require customization of user screens through metadata. Similarly, the data tier would require providing the right data model – either a dedicated DB for each tenant, or one DB for tenants (permitting customization).

But on the whole, to entertain multi-tenancy, the software needs to be architected much differently from the conventional way. (See Chapter 10 on CCRA and Chapter 9 on cloud product SaaS for a complete treatment. Chapters 4, 7 and 8 will provide different other flavours of architecture of cloud SaaS software.)

This chapter discusses how to architect various components or tiers of cloud SaaS software for multi-tenancy with a focus on describing various characteristics of cloud SaaS software. Section 5.8 (see also Section 9.10) is dedicated for improving and making the application more multi-tenant efficient. Chapter 6 discusses about what is cloud compatibility of a software solution or product and its relationship to characteristics of cloud SaaS application.

5.3 Customization

Customization is a provision available in software which allows customers to specifically modify the same to some extent to suit customers' specific needs. In addition, one customer's customization should not affect the behaviour of the software in any way to other customers of the cloud SaaS. Architecting and designing goal is 'to allow end-user customization' possibly for each feature (or components) of the software.

Some example components of the SaaS are as follows:

(i) User interface (their font, colour and logo for business promotion)
(ii) Business rules
(iii) Business processes
(iv) Database schemas or extensions for custom fields
(v) Reports

Typically, an enterprise performs customization of the software solution based on its organizational structure and how the cloud service provider would like to promote its business.

A software solution architect provides facilities to configure and customize the software. Conventionally, configuration and customization are done after installing the software, but before using it. Once customized, it remains so forever. If the organization wants to re-configure, the software needs to be re-configured and started again, or the solution needs to read the re-configured details from a file before loading the solution for subsequent use.

Configuration may refer to a simpler way of selecting from a set of prescribed values for every customizable aspect of the software solution. This method of customization is referred to as the parameterized method.

Customization may also involve a complex modification of a baseline solution by attaching an elaborate algorithm implemented in a code.

The following section examines how customization needs to be architected.

Customizable Needs of Enterprise and Customizable Components of Software

5.3.1 Web Tier: User Interface

Problem description

The enterprises would like to customize their user interface as per their internal quality. Corporate, at the upper level, will define some guidelines for the sub-units, such as permitted colour pallet to choose from, to further customize at sub-units level. The enterprise may be organized geographical region-wise such as Europe, India and rest of Asia, North America, etc. Each regional office should have the freedom to choose the colour and font that are right for their region. But, for example, the regions may not be allowed to use their own logo but only corporate logo.

At corporate level, they might have defined where on the screen the corporate logo can appear. At regional level, corporate rules would have prescribed what the permitted company logos are.

Thus, one can see a complete hierarchy of customizations possible, permitted and finalized for a user. The hierarchy goes as such corporate-level customization -> region level -> unit or department level -> individual end-users level personalization.

Solution hints

Changing code for customization is the technique of conventional hosted model where code change will be confined only to the version provided to the specific customer.

But in cloud SaaS, where multiple enterprises are using the same instance, any code change will affect all the enterprises, and hence that is not the technique.

In conventional software, configurations are stored in a configuration file, and the same is loaded into the software when it is restarted. This would not work for cloud SaaS, as the software is not started on the event of every customer joining to consume the service.

An appropriate user interface needs to be provided for taking all the customization that tenant/customer would like to specify. A 'skinnable' application architecture and use of style sheets help extensive customization needs of the user interface required for each customer.

The customized details have to be stored (as metadata) in a database (DB) against a composite key consisting of enterprise ID, department ID, user ID, etc., for each customer/tenant–user subscribed to SaaS in the cloud. (Metadata are data that describe other data). Customization details are stored as data; these stored data are not the exact description of customization, but may be the recording of only the changes made to benchmarked screen format.

Hence when one user logs into a running instance of the SaaS solution, the SaaS software needs to dynamically pick up all the customization permissible for the user and 'play' it 'on-the-fly'. The SaaS software needs to pick up the customization aspects while forming the server pages but before serving each page. The SaaS software needs to read the specific customization details recorded in the metadata file against the specific end-user using the 'composite key' and apply all the customization to the screen. All these happen at the Web tier just before rendering the screen to complete the request coming from client.

A metadata *service* available within the system provides access to the required metadata.

The techniques are:

(i) Providing necessary user interface screens to take customization details
(ii) Storing them in appropriate metadata DB (or file) with tenant–user ID as the (composite) key for the row
(iii) Retrieving on-the-fly through metadata service.

The above are more or less the ideal technique for storing, retrieving and playing all customization of various components of cloud SaaS software such as workflows, business processes and business rules.

5.3.2 Business Tier

Workflows and Business Processes

Reference [18] discusses the distinction between workflows from business processes. It also describes the best way of implementing workflows and business processes.

Problem description

Business processes are considered to be the asset of enterprises. They are also considered a differentiator from competing enterprises in the same segment[22]. Therefore, competitors using the same SaaS solution should be able to customize them and keep their version of customized processes secured.

In general, business processes are customized only at the enterprise level, and not at the individual level (see Chapter 9 for further discussions) (See 'Business Tier' under Section 9.7).

For example, one subscribing customer would like their sales personnel to get his/her sales managers approval before confirming an order, whereas another subscribing organization would like their sales personal to confirm by getting approval from stocks manager to ensure that the order can be fulfilled.

Solution hints

The only additional information that needs to be stored against each enterprise's ID in a metadata DB is the customization information for each of the default business processes provided.

Business Rules

You may know that business rules are handled in the business tier of software as best practices. It goes without saying that modern architecture of software encourages business rules not to be hard-coded into the system. This helps the enterprise add, delete or modify business rules as and when required without changing the code. It also allows business people themselves to make the changes, instead of relying on IT specialists.

Most of the time, business rules can be stored in an 'if-then–else' format and users do not have to worry about the formats to store. This naturally allows enterprises to have easier user interface to create custom business rules. Employing dedicated business rule engine is also in practice.

It should be noted that some business rules can be quite complex and may require custom coding. Such custom codes need to be kept in a DB and retrieved, 'played' and executed.

Using the same metadata DB, a SaaS solution can store all the customizations specified against each of the business rules for every enterprise ID. Even the code that needs to be executed for special rules for any specific customer of SaaS can also be stored in the same DB.

Custom Functionalities

Many users would like to add a bit of their own customized functionality that will be necessary for integrating or extending cloud SaaS solutions to be used by subscribing enterprises. These custom codes and logic or functionalities will also be stored with the metadata DB with (composite) key being customer ID or enterprise ID.

5.3.3 Data Tier

The number of concurrent online users is very large when compared to conventional solutions where one copy of the solution is dedicated to each customer enterprise.

This has two implications on the SaaS solution:

(i) Number of connections to DB that are required at any point of time is in proportion to the number of concurrent users accessing the data.
   (a) Therefore, the performance is directly proportion to available connects to DB for running queries on the DB. Efficient use of connections is an essential part of the architectural design.
   (b) Each connection requires some amount of main memory; hence, there are finite limitations to maximum number of connections in a DB server that is mostly determined by its memory. Each DB query will also require CPU time. Hence,

if more users come into the system, then the DB server should scale with additional servers in a cluster.

(ii) The storage space required to store data for each user is in direct proportion to the number of registered users of the system. Normally, it keeps growing.

(iii) In SaaS solutions, pricing the usage of storage by every user is common. The cost of storage is in proportion to usage of storage by each user, and hence the billing is as per total storage used by the enterprise.

5.3.3.1 Database Software

SaaS software product or solution should have a database (DBMS) software for managing the solution or product-specific data.

SaaS software should provide at least three options of DB for customers:

(i) Provide separate DB for each customer or tenant.
(ii) Provide one DB for all customers, with limited or fixed customization for all tenants.
(iii) Provide one DB for all customers, with flexible customization for each tenant.

Hence, the RDBMS software product should have basic capabilities for providing these kinds of models.

Most of the popular commercial off-the-shelf (COTS) RDBMS now have the required capabilities to serve cloud SaaS applications.

5.3.3.2 A Multi-Tenant Data Model

Each cloud SaaS software will have its own DB designed to meet its purposes. But the design should accommodate a reality of an expectation of each customer would like to have their extensions to the basic DB.

For example, a banking software (account opening software) in cloud SaaS would like to have their own DB and would not like their data to lie along with other bankers.

In a HR module used for collecting resumes from probable aspirants, subscribing customers did not mind sharing the same DB (since the applicant's resume has not yet crossed the enterprise boundaries to say it is their own data), but each customer would like to collect additional data along with resume.

A complex requirement is faced in a cloud ERP solution to be provided for small- and medium-sized enterprises (SMEs). Some aspects are discussed in Chapter 7.
This section briefly reviews three general approaches to solve this problem:

1. An independent tenant DB
2. A shared DB with a fixed extension set
3. A shared DB with custom extensions

Independent or Dedicated Tenant Database

Problem space

(i) Customers in certain verticals such as banking are worried about security of data in cloud.

(ii) Such customers are averse of idea of their data being in the same DB with other customers data.
(iii) Certain enterprises consider that their corporate data are their unique property such as their business processes.
(iv) In addition, some customers have not come out of earlier paradigm of having dedicated DB.

Solution

For such situations, providing dedicated DB for each customer is the solution.

Since it is dedicated DB, they can create their own relationships, queries, stored procedures, extensions to specific tables or define their own tables too, limited only by the user interface and program logic that the cloud SaaS software allows the subscriber.

A metadata created at the time of provisioning will point to this table against this customer.

Advantages of this approach are as follows:

(a) It is easy to provide one DB per customer.
(b) It allows maximum freedom to customers to customize the data model.
(c) It provides a high data secure feeling to customers who prefer that.

The disadvantages of this approach are as follows:

(a) As there is a finite limitation on the number of DBs that can be provided per RDBMS server, the cost of providing this solution will be high.
(b) The cost of providing services is high compared with other alternatives discussed here.

Database is Common (to all tenants but) with Fixed Extension Set

Figure 5.1 shows custom fields in a shared database.

Customer ID *Integer*	First Name *String*	Date of Birth *Date*	Custom1 *Integer*	Custom 2 *String*	Custom 3 *Untyped*
4531	Raj	1995-07-02	Paid	Null	Null
6532	Ram	1997-09-25	Null	Null	45
3451	Jyothi	2001-12-21	Null	Null	Null
4531	Murugan	1998-03-08	Null	Paid	Null
2457	Ganesh	2000-11-04	Null	Madras	Yes

Figure 5.1 Custom fields in a common database (shared by all tenants). Custom data is stored in separate custom fields

Same table is used for all tenants; therefore, records of all tenants will be intermixed in the same single table. Records are identified by composite key that will have customer ID and a few other identifiers to make it unique for any specific customer.

To facilitate customization, the table is provided with a set of pre-defined fixed number of columns; some of the tenants will use all the columns, but some of the tenants will use only a few of them.

There is no universal rule on how many of these columns to be provided. After the SaaS solution is launched the solution can suffer because of too many custom fields or too less; and this needs to be fixed after gaining experience.

Corresponding to these columns, user interface can be altered to permit data capture or data entry or block it or to validate data entry with custom logic. Tenants can decide what for to use these fields.

This table needs to be horizontally partitioned or 'shared database design' is appropriate for this since the architect needs to expect the table can grow enormously and then querying such a huge DB will consume more time and resources. The horizontal partitioning also should occur automatically as and when the DB grows and any one partition become too huge.

The main advantage is one single DB for all customers and easy for service provider to maintain. The cost is cheaper than the dedicated DB model discussed earlier.

The main disadvantage is that the fixed number of custom fields limits extensibility of the data model.

Data backup and restoration may affect other customers data access, and hence the overall design must be proper to avoid this issue through a mirrored DB.

Database is Common (to all tenants but) with Custom Extension Set

This third model overcomes the limitation of 'fixed extension' discussed in the previous sub-section. All other facts remain the same.

It is a single DB shared among all the subscribing customers. To allow arbitrary extension, the extended data are stored as a name–value pair in a different data table. The row index is kept in the main table. Each subscriber will be assigned a unique record ID, and the same is stored in record ID column of main table. This record ID is used to locate the data in the extended table.

Since it is name–value pair, each customer can have nil or any number of name–value pairs. Hence, name–value pair acts like extending the main table with column name as 'name' and value in name–value pair in the extended table.

Since the type can be anything, it is advised to provide one more column where the type can be stored along with name–value in the extended table.

While retrieving a customer record, the application performs a lookup of the extended table, selects all rows matching record ID and casts the custom data as per the type and returns them to be treated like any other field data.

Customer ID *Integer*	First Name *String*	Date of Birth *Date*	Record ID *Integer*
4531	Raj	1995-07-02	329
6532	Ram	1997-09-25	275
3451	Jyothi	2001-12-21	Null
4531	Murugan	1998-03-08	824
2457	Ganesh	2000-11-04	501

Record ID	Name	Value
329	Student	Yes
275	Enrolled	Science
Null	Finishing year	2014-07-29
824	Student	No

The main advantage of this approach is to offer flexibility to customers in extending arbitrarily the custom data while retaining the cost-benefits of shared DB. Solution architects can consider this approach when they anticipate that the customers will require a large flexibility in extending default data model as illustrated in case study of Chapter 7. Also recommended when reports requirements are diversified as used-to-be in solutions for SMEs or 'long tail' segments.

The main disadvantage is additional processing complexity while retrieving data or searching data or while querying or updating or indexing data.

Therefore, customer should be provided with facility to customize user interface to collect the custom data; at the same time, presentation logic should provide customization to display them too. In addition, customization should provide to add additional business logic to process these custom data.

Scaling and Performance of Database

As discussed earlier (under the sub-section 'Database is common (to all tenants) but with Fixed Extension Set'), the size of data will grow enormously in SaaS solutions.

Therefore, putting in place a partitioning strategy such as horizontal partitioning of the table needs to be considered.

Even re-partioning already partioned segment is also a must since data will continue to grow. Even this need to be automated – meaning that re-partioning algorithm needs be automatically started sooner a partition exceeds a pre-determined size limit.

Depending on the clues from data (such as geographical data) may be good only in very specific applications; the strategy cannot be blindly applied in all situations.

Efficient data organization is also possible by wisely using the knowledge on the data. For example, data can be partitioned based on geographical regions; the geo reference should be part of data. But such strategies are not universally applicable, and one cannot find such help from the nature of the data in all situations while architecting itself.

5.3.4 Reports

There is a lot of need for customizing reports for every tenant (enterprise). Most software provides many principle reports; many times, there is a need for even customizing specific reports. Customization may be very simple – like adding their own respective company logos, or very complex – like manipulating highly customized table data to get a specific report.

In a community cloud, a SaaS solution serving many SMEs, the requirements for customizing reports conflict with one another. This poses many challenges in providing satisfactory customizing features.

One can even choose a separate COTS reports software that has extensive features to get custom reports. But if such software is multi-tenanted, it is more desirable.

Even how data are organized in DB tables and schema affects how the system facilitates customization of reports. Refer to the sub-section titled 'Shared Database with Custom Extension Set'. Custom reports may be required involving data stored in custom extension of tables.

To keep up the performance, a master–slave DB structure can be created. While one main DB will be used for transactions, another will act as a mirror to produce reports. Unfortunately, if report generation is also done on the same operation DB, serving transactions will slow down the response dramatically. But such techniques are not specific to cloud SaaS alone.

5.3.5 Abilities to Choose Functions at Fine Granular Level

Choosing Functionalities of SaaS Solution

Every customer would like to pick and choose the functionalities in a SaaS solution unlike a dedicated copy per customer in the hosted model of 1990s.

Customers in SMEs segment and in 'long tail' would like to minimize their spending by using only those functionalities that their business needs. Hence, customers from this segment demand to split aggregated functions/services to finer ones and also request proportionate lower cost.

If cloud SaaS software is architected as SOA, naturally the above is achievable. Finer functions wrapped in services can be orchestrated to get aggregated larger services. Exposing the finer service as such is a business decision of SaaS providers.

While subscribing, enterprises themselves will choose functionalities and they will further allow role-based user access to functionalities among the chosen ones. (This is controlled by the role-based access in identity and the access management sub-system of SaaS solution.)

Hence, SaaS software products or solutions should have facilities to keep track of functionalities chosen by each enterprise and permitted for each end-user.

The same data structure discussed in the previous sub-sections can be modified and used for keeping track of this customization also. Permission to use any service needs to be checked every time before connecting the service to service requestor (or end-user).

5.4 Scaling (Auto-Scaling and Auto-Provisioning)

SaaS usage can go up or down during any part of time; also, the number of users may increase unexpectedly. Therefore, the important implications of this situation are as follows:

(i) The SaaS solution should accommodate any number of growing customers and users.

(ii) In the true spirit of cloud, best solution should scale up when the demand for use goes up and scales down automatically when the demand comes down too to conserve resource utilization. The demand here refers to the number of online and concurrent users of SaaS solution.

This is true for SaaS solutions that have seasonal peak and tough demands. The 'season' can be within a day or in a week or month ends (as payroll processing services) or in a year during holidays or festival seasons.

(iii) Unlike conventional architecture, the SaaS solution cannot be designed to accommodate the peak demand of it; such architecture will necessarily employ infrastructure that is suitable for peak load. That implies a huge cost investment up front making the cost of solution to go up and in turn the subscription fees will be higher for customers, and also the risk of going wrong along with the prediction of 'peak load' by deploying either too large or too small number of hardware.

In cloud, practically SaaS solution will be architected for minimum number of concurrent users.

On SaaS solution being deployed in Infrastructure as a Service (IaaS) platform, hardware will automatically scale up to accommodate the additional performance required. Also when the users come down, it will also automatically scale down the hardware in line. That is how the SaaS solution will be architected. Thus, the SaaS solution will scale up or scale down on demand. (See Chapters 4 and 9 for how to architect such a SaaS to achieve this.)

(iv) **Web Tier:** When the number of online users increases or number of logged-in users increases the demand on Web tier will be increasing. Hence, more processing power has to be brought in to support the additional on-demand workload at Web tier. Additional hardware means increased cost. But the cost is proportional to the number of increased users. Therefore, in SaaS billing certain fee is charged as a minimum monthly fee per month for every signing up end-user, and hence it becomes a welcome situation to service provider.

(v) **Business Tier:** This is the tier that directly produces values to customers. Business functionalities in SaaS solution fulfils customer's requirements. The processing power and memory requirements will be in direct proportion to the number of concurrent users of SaaS solution.

(vi) **Data Tier:** As the number of online users increases, there is a likely increase in data access. Cloud SaaS such as enterprise resource planning for enterprise analytics are examples to this. When the data access increases, the number of connections to DB needs to be increased and that will demand more memory (see Chapter 9 for details). Number of data access objects that will be active also will demand more processing power.

More instances of RDBMS may be required to accommodate additional users. (How do RDBMS scale is discussed in Chapter 7).

(vii) **Data Storage:** In SaaS solution's billing model, the customers are charged an amount proportional to the data storage used. Therefore, if there are more users and more storage space on demand, then the cost of storage is directly proportional to the billing amount for storage per user. Hence, it is a welcome situation. For the service providers, the expenditure is in proportion to the revenue.

(viii) **Customization:** Additional processing power and memory is essential to handle the customizations discussed in the previous section. (This additional processing power is in comparison with the software not developed for multiple tenants; hence simple customization; no on-the-fly retrieval of customized information through metadata services, etc.) This is directly proportional to the number of concurrent users. In a conventional hosted model, this additional processing power and memory is not required.

Higher demand for business tier, customization, data tier and RDBMS will require more CPU and memory. This aspect has to be rolled into the cost of providing solutions, and hence it will reflect in the pricing model of SaaS services.

In all the above situations, on implementing the solution on IaaS, IaaS platform provides mechanism for 'auto-scaling' and 'auto-provisioning'. Hence as explained in Chapter 4, additional processing power or memory will be added on-demand or removed or scaled down when the demand comes down. Hence, the additional cost of resources utilized due to increased user traffic is in proportion to billing, and it is less burden to operate the SaaS services. This is also one reason why IaaS is recommended for running cloud SaaS.

5.5 Operational and Billing Support Services

SaaS solution software will have a provision for metering the usage of each functionality of the software at various granular levels.

This is a special characteristic and feature of any SaaS software. This feature will not be there in conventional software.

By this ability, SaaS solutions track and report usage of software features, and other resources for every end-user for billing purposes.

Fine granular-level usage tracking can be rolled up as per the pricing policy prevailing then. Change in pricing policy or pricing strategy will change different ways of rolling the fine granular usage metre.

Refer to Chapter 10 for its implementation suggestion in the cloud computing reference architecture (CCRA). This functionality is a cross-cutting aspect across all the functions of the software. Therefore, it is summarized and provided in common cloud management platform (CCMP) layer of the CCRA.

All these functionalities are unique built-in functionality that one needs to provide as part of any SaaS solution or product.

Main constituents of CCMP are operation support services (OSS) and business support services (BSS). These terms are same as that used in telephone industry.

OSS provides support to operations of running the SaaS services. Some simple examples are account activation, provisioning, service assurance and data backup.

BSS refers to the functionalities that are supporting the business of providing cloud SaaS services to customers. See Chapter 10 for a little more detailed discussion on BSS functionalities. BSS comprises services to raise invoices for every customer for the consumption of services and resources. In a multi-tenanted environment, automating this is essential.

5.6 Software Upgrades and Maintenance

A single instance serving multiple tenants needs to be architected properly even for maintenance and upgrades. The single instance cannot be shut down for the sake of maintenance or software upgrade.

Since it is a single instance, upgrades or bug fix releases are done monthly without disturbing the users. Users get the latest version automatically without paying any additional fee or buying a new version.

A traditional technique is to have an alternative site where the upgraded or maintained software is deployed, and it is switched to point that new site, which has the least down time. This is done by swapping virtualized servers' addresses of new site to the existing one (see Section 5.2 also).

'Spring' kind of middleware gives a mechanism for 'hot swapping' of modules without bringing the system down to replace a defective module with a bug-fixed one. This technique is to use the inversion of control and inject module dependencies into Spring™; before jumping into the next module, Spring™ will look up the virtual server where the module is available. At that level, server pointing to the new server having the maintained module name can be re-directed for smooth swap.

Hot swap also inherently assumes high modularization of the software.

Architect needs to think and come out with an elaborate strategy for maintaining and upgrading the software when the instance is still serving many tenants.

5.7 Maintenance of Database

In the 'independent database for every tenant' model, taking regular backup is easier, and it is maintained for each subscribing company. Hence, restoring is also easy and can be done on tenants' request too.

But in shared data models restoring a company's specific DB is difficult. (A special sequel should be run with the company ID as a key to retrieve data from back up and populate live tables.) But taking backup of the entire DB is easy.

5.8 Efficient Multi-Tenancy

In this chapter, readers can see multi-tenancy is a characteristic that impacts many components of the cloud SaaS software – be it user interface or data model or business rules or business processes, maintainability, etc.

The efficiency refers how many tenants are packed into one single instance of software. Since cloud SaaS software is pretty complex and has many modules and tiers, each component is likely to accommodate varying number of users (see change from tenants to users). Depending on the nature of application, certain modules will become critical modules where all the traffic (most of the user's request) will go through (see Section 3.7 and refer Figure 3.2). Architects need to envisage the same and guide its design to maximize the number of tenant – users processed by this module.

5.9 SaaS Architecture is Unique

From the above discussions, readers can easily infer that the architecture of cloud SaaS software is going to be pretty different and unique compared to conventional software applications architecture.

The difference is so vast, and one can easily conclude that the architecture being unique also characterizes the cloud SaaS software.

Further details of architectures of cloud SaaS software are discussed in Chapters 7 through 10.

This uniqueness is also used as one of the measures for cloud compatibility (along with other characteristics mentioned here) of a given software. Chapter 6 deals with cloud compatibility measure.

5.10 Summary

- This chapter summarizes characteristics of cloud SaaS software.
- Multi-tenancy, customization and scalability are all intermixed in rendering the special characteristics for cloud SaaS software.

- For achieving the characteristics required for cloud SaaS software, enough hints are provided in problem–solution style for architecting each sub-components.
- Three types of data model that are mostly suitable for various types of cloud SaaS solutions are discussed.
- Efficiency in multi-tenancy and special architecture of cloud SaaS software are also briefly discussed.
- This chapter will serve as a pre-requisite to understand Chapter 6.

Chapter 6

Cloud Compatibility Measure

6.1 Introduction

For architecting a software solution, we need a lot of solution building blocks (SBBs) that make up the solution. Each of the SBBs may be mapped onto one or many software products. Chapter 18 in Ref. [21] indicates how to architect solutions using off-the-shelf components or software products. For cloud Software as a Service (SaaS) solutions, it is preferred that each of this software products also be a cloud compatible SaaS product. (This chapter gives the answer to the question 'Why is it preferred?'.)

Expected ideal characteristics of a SaaS software – be it a product or solution – is discussed in detail in Chapter 5. In reality, many of the software products do not meet this long list of ideally expected characteristics of SaaS.

This chapter proposes and discusses an empirical method to measure how much of these characteristics are met by any given product. Such a measure is here referred to as cloud compatibility measure.

6.2 Motivation to Come Up with Cloud Compatibility Measure

This measure is a kind of yardstick that is used to measure against and compare products to know how much they are cloud compatible.

Such a comparison will help in selecting better suitable products to meet SBBs for building cloud SaaS software solution. While other factors such as functionalities or performance, etc., being equal in meeting the requirements, the one having better cloud compatible index will be selected.

In addition, this book discusses that SaaS solutions are possible with three kinds of cloud compatible indexed products: (qualitatively speaking) (1) fully cloud compatible (100%) products, (2) fully non-compatible (0%) products and (3) semi-cloud compatible (anywhere in between 0 and 100%) products.

Making a software product fully cloud compatible requires re-architecting and building it ground up[23] as discussed in Chapter 9. Such an effort is huge and justifying with a business case or providing a convincing ROI may even elude. Therefore, the market will continue to have semi- or non-cloud compatible products that architects have; no other choice but, to use them to build cloud SaaS solutions.

Also business requirements or business models may dictate whether it is essential to go for absolutely cloud compatible SBBs to build cloud SaaS solution. The use case given in Chapter 7 demands low-cost solution (security is not a major issue), and hence there is no need to use (may be costly) SBBs that are perfectly cloud compatible to build a cloud SaaS solution.

Hence, architects may have to use less (or non-) cloud compatible SaaS products as SBBs to build cloud SaaS solutions.

Thus, there exists a necessity to have techniques to architect solutions with products having any degree of cloud compatibility; that has resulted in such techniques described in this book – Chapters 7 and 8. This chapter provides a preliminary step for those techniques: measuring 'cloud compatibility'.

By following techniques described in this chapter, if product vendors also mark on their product brochure as to what extent their products are cloud compatible, that information will reduce a lot of effort for solution architects.

Just like specifying 'minimum hardware required' or suitable 'operating system' on the pack of software products, vendors can specify 'cloud compatibility index' also.

Cloud compatibility measure as applied to any existing products has other uses such as to improve them to make them absolutely cloud compatible, if that is an objective.

While that gives enough motivation to come up with a common yardstick for cloud compatibility measure, let us see how a scale can be set up as well as how the scale can be used.

6.3 Definition of 'Cloud Compatibility'

How to define 'cloud compatibility'? A software is said to have complete cloud compatibility if it has all the necessary characteristics (mentioned in Chapter 5) to the desired level. If it does not have even a single characteristic, then it is said to have absolutely no cloud compatibility. This is more of operational explanation rather than a theoretical definition.

Cloud compatibility is referred with respect to its ability to satisfy all characteristics necessary to become very efficient cloud SaaS software.

Literature Refs. [5, 24, 37] cloud compatibility in various different ways – one of them[24] is whether a cloud SaaS software service is compatible to in-house software. We do not enter into any such meanings.

There were similar thinking to measure cloud compatibility, and a need was felt by many in the past; here, we will review one prominent and the most comprehensively discussed in literature[5] before embarking into the main idea of cloud compatibility that this book prefers to explain and use in the remaining chapters.

6.4 SaaS (Solutions) Maturity Model

Reference [5] uses a terminology 'SaaS maturity model' as a way of measuring cloud compatibility. A fully matured SaaS product is the ultimate cloud compatible product. Thus cloud compatibility measure is also a way to measure SaaS maturity of the software.

The term 'maturity' also indicates that softwares need to progress (mature) in this direction of having absolute cloud compatibility.

Although Ref. [5] identifies four levels of maturity, it has acknowledged that SaaS maturity is on a continuous scale. That means cloud SaaS maturity is in a continuous scale of 0 per cent through 100 per cent as this book points out the cloud compatibility measure.

As per Ref. [5], the basis for SaaS maturity is based on three characteristics of a SaaS software: scalability, multi-tenant efficiency and configurability.

Based on the three characteristics, the Ref. [5] defines four distinct levels of maturity:

(i) At zeroth (or technically the first level) level, all the three characteristics are absent.
(ii) At the fourth level, all the three characteristics are fully present to desired degree.
(iii) Each level is distinguished from the previous or other levels by addition or absence of one of the three attributes.

Refer to Figure 6.1 below[5]:

Level 1: Ad hoc/custom

(a) Each customer has its own customized instance.
(b) Has customer-specific hardware for each instances.
(c) This was popular in 1990's and referred to as 'hosted model' (see Chapter 1).

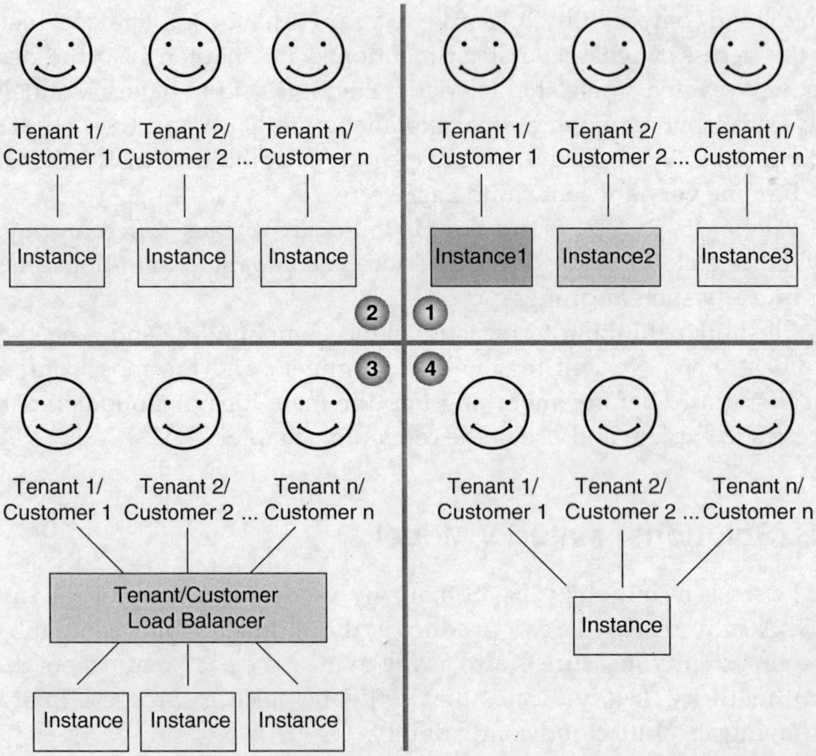

Figure 6.1 Four levels of cloud SaaS maturity model[5]

Level 2: Configurable

(a) Same as Level 1 but with one difference that the software is configurable. Hence, each customer will have their own same code base since their configuration customization would have changed the initial common code base.
(b) Upgradation of software is possible across customers.

Level 3: Configurable, multi-tenant efficient

(a) Single instance serves many customers.
(b) Use of metadata for keeping the configuration parameters set to each customer.
(c) From end-users' perspective, they are unaware of the existence of other customers using the same instance.

Advantages:

(a) Same hardware is efficiently shared across customers and cost saved.

Disadvantages:

(a) It cannot scale efficiently; scaling (scaling up) by moving to more powerful hardware is the only possible solution.

Level 4: Scalable, configurable, multi-tenant efficient

(a) SaaS providers can host multiple customers.
(b) A load balanced form of identical hardware instances help scaling up or down on-demand.
(c) Rolling out updates to the software is easy, since it is single instance at single point.
(d) Customer data can be kept separately.
(e) Configurable metadata provides a mechanism for both recording preferred user experience and as well as highly flexible and rich user experience provisions[5].

Thus level 4 provides all the advantages.

(a) The above model is good to understand the subject 'cloud compatibility measure'.
(b) This model is proposed from the perspective of revamping (re-architecting or re-developing) or maturing any existing software product to make it a cloud compatible SaaS software. Therefore, how to make a product more 'mature' as a cloud SaaS software is the key perspective here.
(c) Such a measure sets a goal or target state to be aimed at; as well as it defines a path to travel to reach the target state. The 'goal' or 'target state' is reaching level 4. 'The path' to travel is improving from level 1 through level 4.
(d) But from the perspective of architecting a SaaS solution for cloud, this measure is not adequate.

1. Solutions architects face, most of the time, a situation to select a product from a set of available ones in the market. Among the choices of products available, solution architects need a measure to compare otherwise equal products to choose a much more matured SaaS software. From that perspective, defining a measure is attempted in this chapter.

(e) SaaS maturity model discussed so far, makes use of only three characteristics of software for measuring SaaS maturity; the one discussed in this chapter takes into account all the characteristics of cloud SaaS software as solution architects need many intermediary levels between the first and fourth.

6.5 SaaS Maturity Continuum Scale

The same Ref. [5] also brings in an interesting observation that SaaS maturity (Figure 6.2) is not 'all or nothing' proposition.

It is better to visualize SaaS maturity as a continuum between *isolated data and code* on the one end and *shared data and code* on the other end[5].

Per-tenant SLA, code and data isolation are at the one end, and economy of scale and simpler management are at the other 'sharing' end.

On declaring a software – be it product or solution – being fully matured (as SaaS for cloud), the code of the software's single instance is sharable across multiple companies for simultaneous use, whereas the data are preferably isolated from one enterprise to another. That is at the highest end of fully matured desirable SaaS solutions or products.

Contrast this to lowest level where the data and code are isolated from other enterprises.

The continuum only supports a reality between these two extreme ends where there are numerous possibilities.

The numerous possibilities are due to variation in the levels of each of the characteristics of SaaS software.

This principle of 'maturity continuum' is applicable to cloud compatibility also. 'Cloud compatibility' is also not 'all-or-nothing'. Its value ranges from 0 to 100 per cent, and there can be many intermediate values. (Even at 0% still one can possibly build a cloud SaaS solution using the same, but the cost of it may be higher.)

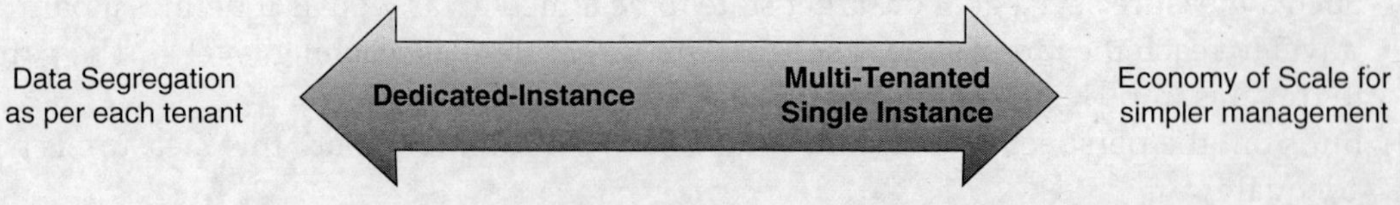

Figure 6.2 SaaS maturity as a continuum scale[5]

6.6 Cloud Compatibility Measure

This section describes how to measure cloud compatibility of a product. This is an empirical method. This section also shows an example of how to put in use to select products that are more cloud compatible while architecting cloud SaaS solutions.
There are three sub-sections within this section:

(i) Section 6.1 discusses a method to set up cloud compatibility measure (for the purpose of solutions architecting or evaluating a product).
(ii) Section 6.2 indicates ideal values for each of the characteristics of the ultimately cloud compatible SaaS solutions or products. It also discusses or reveals further details of measure.
(iii) Section 6.3 discusses on applying this measure to products through a case situation.

6.6.1 Procedure to Set Up the 'Cloud Compatibility Measuring Scale'

This section describes a procedure to arrive at cloud compatibility measure for products in an architecting project. The procedure consists of setting up or defining a scale and then use it to measure 'cloud compatibility' for each components or products that need to be evaluated for providing cloud-based SaaS solution.

In this method, architects use an ideal 'value' for each characteristic of fully matured SaaS software – Solutions or products. Ideal values are described in Section 6.2 for most of the characteristics and are listed in Table 6.1.

For example, against a characteristic of 'business rules', an ideal value suggested in the table is 'alteration of business rules can be allowed to alter workflows/business processes'. The value indicates the solution that allows customers to define or modify default business rules that come along with the software; and at the same time when such an alteration is done, the system automatically points out all the other areas that also need to be modified. For example, sometimes a change in a particular business rule, such as approval amount being increased from a default of 5000–10,000 rupees, may prompt for altering workflow, such as to get additional approval from the senior manager of the bank; otherwise, the manager him/herself can approve.

Complete absence of the ideal state, for any characteristic, is assigned a value 0. In the above example of business rules, the pre-defined business rules cannot be altered by any subscriber to cloud SaaS.

A software product or component is said to be cloud compatible fully if it meets the ideal state for all the characteristics.

Complete absence of the ideal state for all the characteristics is assigned 0 per cent compatibility.

Between these two extreme values, architects are encouraged to use or define either 5 or 10 levels. (See Table 6.2 along with the case study discussed in Section 6.3 for an illustration of this point.) Weighted average method is used for commercial off-the-shelf (COTS) product described in the case study in Section 6.3 and Table 6.2 will show the values.

Table 6.1 Cloud-compatibility calculation

	<-------100% compatibility values (for each attribute) 0% compatibility------>								
Customization									
Customizable needs of the enterprise and customizable parts of the software			Customization of one component can highlight customization required in other components; e.g. change in business rule should indicate the workflow need to be changed.	Customization is possible as per organization hierarchy (for each subscribing enterprise) down to individual end-user level; personalization possible for Web tier, business tier, and data tier as explained in the following.	All parts of software starting from Web tier to data tier are customizable.	Simple customization at all levels by each enterprise. (Such arrangement is good enough for small- or medium-sized enterprises.			
Web tier									
Web tier – user interfaces	At personalization too	Examine the architecture for skinnable, or use of style sheets, etc.	Customization at various hierarchy levels of enterprise from federated organization down to unit level.						
Business tier									
Workflows, business processes	Workflow can get modified by the values in business rule parameters.	Each enterprise can set extreme boundaries for their business units to define their own business processes.	Each customer can define or alter the default process to suit their business not at user level.						

	<-------100% compatibility values (for each attribute)				0% compatibility------>				
Business rules	Alteration of business rules can be allowed to alter workflows/ business processes.	Business or users can also add, delete and modify rules.	Only IT professionals can modify rules.	Custom code can be added for any new rule definition.					
Custom functionalities		Ability to add custom code as additional functionalities by each enterprise.	Give a summary credit points for custom database table, custom stored procedures						
Data tier									
Database software	Multi-tenanted RDBMS package that as services exposed to hook to BSS and OSS.		Need to write custom code to hook to BSS and OSS in the platform. (Do not do double entry both here and or BSS and OSS row too).						
A multi-tenant data model	Independent or dedicated tenant database	Easy or tenant-based backup and recovery – ease of maintenance.	Shared database with fixed extension set	Shared database with custom extension set					

(*continued*)

Table 6.1 Cloud-compatibility calculation (Continued)

	<-------100% compatibility values (for each attribute) 0% compatibility------>								
Reports	Custom reports with independent database or dedicated tenant database.	Complete customization of reports – having used multi-tenanted reporting tool.				Ability to change only logos formats of custom reports.			
Multi-tenancy	The six sub-parameters below this can be simply 'yes' or 'no', or a percentage mark can be given based on the knowledge against each of the components.								
Scaling									
Web tier									
Business tier									
Data tier									
Data bases									
Data storage									
Abilities to choose functions at fine-granular level	Having implemented service component architecture and exposed most of the component services at xx level layer.	At least component services are accessible for 'service creators' to select and configure.							

	<-------100% compatibility values (for each attribute) 0% compatibility------>								
Scaling (auto-scaling, auto-provisioning)	Architecture supports module-wise scaling.	Deployment architecture is on IaaS.	Scaling algorithm (such as exact number of users) for each module is available.	Highly scalable RDBMS and also data tier	Separate data storage for each user	Highly scalable business tier architecture	Web tier can auto-scale on scaling of online users.		
Operational and billing support services	Has enough provision to use CCMP common for both IaaS, BPaaS and this SaaS software too.	Software should have enough 'hooks' to allow cloud environments BSS and OSS to get metrics from various sub-parts of software and its implementable deployment infrastructure too.	Has provision to hook BSS and OSS, but it requires custom code to hook them.	Provides a neat feature to measure usage of any fine-granular level of system functionality usage and independently measured the infrastructure usage including for infrastructure usage at user level. Ability to allow flexibility to roll up or combine various usage metering as per SaaS solution providers pricing strategy.	Modify as per changing pricing policy, cost affecting prices, government policy regulations, etc.				

(*continued*)

Table 6.1 Cloud-compatibility calculation (Continued)

	<-------100% compatibility values (for each attribute) 0% compatibility------>								
Software upgrades and maintenance	Architected to replace modules at run time.	Needs a backup deployment infrastructure (mirror site) to switch to maintained or enhanced software							
Maintenance of database	Easiest to maintain: individual databases for each enterprise/ tenant and hence secured and faster backup and recovery.	Independent schema	Very tough to maintain: same common schema with custom extension of columns.						
Efficient multi-tenancy	How many concurrent users and how many login users can be allowed on the whole for the entire SaaS software.	Get the same measures (number of concurrent users) for each of the modules or tiers	Calculate the cost of deployment unit architecture per each user for each module or tier (see Chapter 7 for further details).						

	<-------100% compatibility values (for each attribute) 0% compatibility------>								
SaaS architecture is unique.	Architecture is completely based on CCRA and within that SOA RA.	Possible to implement security as an aspect; also able to set security policies	Highly modularized structure; highly layered structure; detailed deployment architecture is possible.	Securable at thread level; securable at every service level.	Examine the architecture for each of the points mentioned in Chapter 9. If all are present, then it is 100% scored on this attribute.	Possible to have individual databases for each enterprise	Inter-tier interfaces are loosely coupled through service APIs.	Only service APIs are provided for each of the exposed function-alities.	Monolithic architecture. Inter-tier interactions are not visible or tightly coupled. Not amenable for any external provision of security or analysis.
Number of users it can accommodate within one instance	On comparing between two products, the one that can accommodate more users per unit cost of hardware is better software.	(This aspect is discussed in more detail in Chapter 7.)	The least number among the various modules or tiers of SaaS software being the measure for comparison between two products or solutions.						

(*continued*)

Table 6.2 Cloud-compatibility measure for two products

	<------100% compatibility values (for each attribute) 0% compatibility----->									
	For open-source product					For COTS		Score out of max 10	Relative weightage	Weighted score
Customization										
Customizable needs of the enterprise and customizable parts of the software		Customization is possible as per organization hierarchy (for each subscribing enterprise) down to individual end-user level-personalization possible for Web tier, business tier and data tier as explained in the following	User interface at individual level, work flow and data folders are customizable.			Simple customization at all levels by each enterprise. (Such arrangement is good enough for small- or medium-sized enterprises.)		4 out of 10	6	4 * 7 = 28
Web tier										
Web tier – user interface	At personalization too		Customization at various hierarchy levels of enterprise from federated organization down to unit level.			Simple customization at enterprise level for user interface is available.		4 out of 10	8	4 * 8 = 32

	<------100% compatibility values (for each attribute) 0% compatibility----->									
Business tier										
Workflows, business processes			Each customer can define or alter the default process to suit their business not at user level.			Cloud SaaS can create or customize processes but not at tenant level (zero value for tenants).		3 out of 10	3	3 * 3 = 9
Business rules			Only IT professionals can modify rules.			Cloud SaaS can create or customize business rules but not at tenant level (zero value for tenants).		0 out of 10	4	0 * 4 = 0
Custom functionalities			Give a summary credit points for custom database table, custom stored procedures			Not possible		5 out of 10	6	0 * 6 = 0
Data tier										
Database software	Multi-tenanted RDBMS package that has services exposed to hook to BSS and OSS.		Need to write custom code to hook to BSS and OSS in the platform. (DO not do double entry both here and or BSS and OSS row too).			Integrated database software		0 out of 10	4	0 * 4 = 0

(continued)

Table 6.2 Cloud-compatibility measure for two products (Continued)

	<------100% compatibility values (for each attribute) 0% compatibility----->									
A multi-tenant data model	Independent or dedicated tenant database	Easy or tenant-based backup and recovery – ease of maintenance				Single tenant model extended for cloud SaaS purpose		0 out of 10	8	0 * 8 = 0
Reports	Custom reports with independent database or dedicated tenant database		Ability to change only logos formats of custom reports			Ability to change only logos formats of custom reports		0 out of 10	7	0 * 7 = 0
Abilities to choose functions at fine-granular level								0 out of 10	5	0 * 5 = 0
Scaling (auto-scaling, auto-provisioning).	Architecture supports module-wise scaling.	Deployment architecture is on IaaS.		Highly scalable RDBMS and also data tier.	Separate data storage for each user.	Highly scalable business tier architecture.	Web tier can auto-scale on scaling of on-line users.	4 out of 10	8	4 * 8 = 32
Operational and billing support services	Has enough provision to use CCMP common for both IaaS, BPaaS and this SaaS software too							0 out of 10	3	0 * 3 = 0

	<------100% compatibility values (for each attribute) 0% compatibility----->									
Software upgrades and maintenance	Architected to replace modules at run time.							0 out of 10	6	0 * 6 = 0
Maintenance of database	Easiest to maintain: individual databases for each enterprise/tenant and hence secured and faster backup and recovery							1 out of 10	7	1 * 7 = 7
Efficient multi-tenancy								0 out of 10	8	0 * 8 = 0
Cloud SaaS architecture			Highly modularized structure; highly layered structure; detailed deployment architecture is possible.	Securable at thread level; securable at every service level		Possible to have individual databases for each enterprise.	Inter-tier interfaces are loosely coupled through services APIs.	0 out of 10	9	0 * 9 = 0

(*continued*)

Table 6.2 Cloud-compatibility measure for two products (Continued)

	<------100% compatibility values (for each attribute) 0% compatibility----->									
Number of users it can accommodate within one instance				These data were not available and also not calculated during architecting or product selection phase.				9 out of 10	8	9 * 8 = 0
								Weighted average score = sum of (score * weight)/ sum of (weight)	100	1.08

For example, for the characteristic cloud SaaS architecture, there are about nine possible values that are indicated in Table 6.1. In addition, Table 6.1 gives a lot of possibilities for value for each characteristic (whether those characteristics do matter or not and hence what are the values that need to be chosen can be project specific).

Solution architects should have the flexibility to define each level and criteria to determine and assign a value to each level.

Criteria for determining levels may be unique for each characteristic (attribute); it can vary from solution to solution as the solution architect decides.

The variation from solution to solution may be due to project requirements or criticality of that parameter for that product. Defining intermediary values also depends on the business requirements and the criticality of the characteristics of SaaS to the project.

This will look like a laborious process for the first time, but its continuous use will accumulate the values and criteria defined for each project. The accumulation will serve as a project asset for subsequent projects too.

Constant use of this method will provide a ready reckoner for many software products being used in various project situations.

Evaluating and accumulating such values for infrastructure software products – such as operating systems, app servers, portals, e-commerce products and content management systems – will be used repeatedly for most of the subsequent projects.

This work is less for solution architects, if the product vendors provide more generic and absolute measure of cloud compatibility value for each of their product.

Also use of weightage for the characteristics is sometimes appropriate and recommended.

Such pre-determination to assign weightages clearly brings out the priority of the characteristic that the architect is looking for in that solution.

Sometimes, it is not possible to find 5 or 10 different intermediary levels for some of the characteristics. In that case, architects can settle for only three distinct intermediary levels too. Assigning lower weightages to those characteristics is normal practice.

Instead of finding 5 or 10 distinct levels, it will be advisable to use a grading system. In this case, a score between 0 and 10 is assigned, based on architects' judgement about the characteristic for a given product, for each characteristic of the product. And collective grade is determined based on total score obtained.

If weightage is used for each characteristic, weighted average score is calculated for each competing product and the results are compared.

Alternative to find 3 or 5 or 10 different intermediary levels, a simple 'yes' (100% compatible) or 'no' (0% compatible) scheme will also suffice.

6.6.2 Ideal Values for Characteristics

Chapter 5 discusses highly desirable characteristics of SaaS solutions and products.

This section summarizes the essentials, from there, required for the purpose of cloud compatibility measure.

Refer to Table 6.1 and the explanation for the table is as follows:

(i) Against each attribute, the table lists as much as possible idealistic expectation.
(ii) In a way, this is a different collated tabular summary of what is discussed in detail in Chapter 5. Therefore, comprehending Chapter 5 is more important.
(iii) Each of the values against any attribute is explained in Chapter 5; some understanding of importance of these values can also come from Chapter 9.
(iv) The list is not exhaustive.
(v) Certain attributes such as 'multi-tenancy' or 'scaling' depend on many other (sub-) attributes; those attributes are highlighted bold and against them no values are provided.
(vi) It is very difficult to indicate which one should be given a higher importance weightage or priority.
   (a) But the presentation is such that: for any attribute, the highest idealistic figure is given in the left-most column (column 2), and the least important values are given in the columns as far to the right as possible.
   (b) For some of the attributes, all possible 10 values are given; for most of them, all the 10 values are not possible to list because it may not make sense.
   (c) Depending on project requirements and situation, priority of values for any attribute need to be re-assigned; also priority among the attributes may need to be re-arranged; the list does not suggest any importance or priority among attributes; in some projects, certain attributes is not at all important.
   (d) Also based on the same – project requirements and situations – may be many more 'values' that are not listed in the table can be considered.
(vii) Although listed last, examining and giving high importance to SaaS software's architecture is most recommended.
(viii) Multi-tenant efficient is mostly described in the table as a comparative measure between two and more products or solutions. The data that need to be collected are indicated there in the table column; but the comparison can be done in the following way:
   (a) First collect for each module or tier or component how many number of users it can accommodate for one instance on one deployment infrastructures set.
   (b) The <total cost of deployment infrastructure> divided by <the maximum number of users it can accommodate> gives one measure called 'module cost per user'. But that is not enough.
      1. Some of the 'modules cost per user' may be low or high; it does not indicate any.
      2. Comparison of 'cost per user' for the entire deployment infrastructure can be used between two different competing products or solutions.

3. But sometimes, the above may be deceiving; all the users may not go through all the modules (or tiers); therefore, it may be appropriate to select a set of most frequently used modules and calculate their cost per user and compare them.

6.6.3 Case Study – Measures for Two Products of Similar Functionalities

6.6.3.1 Introduction to this Illustration Through a Specific Case Study

(i) The actual product names are purposely avoided.
(ii) The application for which these products are compared is to develop a cloud-based enterprise document storage solution.
(iii) Enterprises (subscribing customers') main criteria were of the following
   (a) More of low-cost solution (pay-per-use)
   (b) Ability to interface with many in-house systems
   (c) Ability to interface with other cloud services such as Salesforce.com™ or Google™ maps, etc.
(iv) The content management system needs to work with Salesforce.com™ (another commercial cloud SaaS service) to exchange stored multi-media content.
(v) The cloud enterprise content management (ECM) SaaS solution also needs to interface with other enterprise systems across enterprise boundary from its own cloud (outside enterprise boundary).
(vi) The objective of this exercise is to select one good cloud compatible software product so that a better cloud SaaS solution can be built to meet customers expectations.
(vii) Two ECM software products, which are used for required solution, are compared here: one is open source and the other is a COTS product.

6.6.3.2 Open-Source ECM Products Basic Information

(i) The product basically has multi-tenant architecture.
(ii) JBPM™ is used as its Business Process Management (BPM)/workflow engine; this can accommodate multiple tenants so that any subscribing customer can customize workflows within the product.
(iii) Has a multi-tenanted database to accommodate most of cloud ECM SaaS solution.
(iv) It has an open RDBMS software that is also multi-tenanted.
(v) Most of its functions are exposed as service APIs; it is not clear whether its inter-tier communications are service oriented; but being open source, the source code is available for any modification required.
(vi) It is built on J2EE platform.
(vii) Being open source, it can be made amenable for many things:
   (a) Run time hot swap of upgraded software.
   (b) Security can be implemented as 'aspect' using spring™ or any such platform.

6.6.3.3 COTS ECM Products Basic Information

(i) This COTS is an established product in the market.
(ii) This is also a Java-based system.
(iii) The product is in existence even before cloud computing becomes popular.
(iv) On license basis, this software can be procured and integrated with rest of modules for any solution, or it can be in used standalone in enterprises for content management needs.
(v) It is a multi-tier architected product; implying scaling can be supported through additional hardware for the required bottlenecked modules or tiers.
(vi) Functionalities are exposed as services for consumptions.
(vii) Inter-tier communication within the product is not service oriented.
(viii) Obviously, source code is proprietary and not available for solution architects to modify them to suit solutioning requirements.
(ix) The concept of multi-tenant has to be simulated outside this product for subscribing enterprises.
(x) Individual subscribing enterprises content need to be stored in a labeled file folder. Customizing subscriber-specific user interface or storage is not possible.
(xi) Workflow or BPM is an external module whose license needs to be purchased separately. BPM module is also not architected for multi-tenants.
(xii) Storage use for every user needs to be calculated by an external module based on file size both during storing and deleting. This is a round-about means; laborious custom algorithm needs to be developed and implemented separately for this functionality; it will consume additional time during file creation and deletion.

6.6.3.4 Selection of Product Based on Cloud Compatibility Measure

The following discussion is based on Table 6.2 where the above discussed two products cloud.

(i) Although all the attributes' values are listed for both the products, the architecture of the products immediately reveal which one is more cloud compatible.
  (a) Architecture indicates the open-source software is more cloud compatible and also being open-source amenable for implementing needed aspects.
(ii) (This example chosen here is two extreme end-products for comparison; and hence the difference between them or which is more cloud compatible than others is pretty clear, hence the resultant choice. But the way to go about is what is more important).
(iii) The open-source product (OSP) is declared by the software publisher as multi-tenanted.
(iv) OSP has a dedicated workflow/business process engine that is also multi-tenanted; hence, each customer can customize workflows/BPM to meet their requirements.
(v) Since the solution is on content management, it is expected that each user and hence each subscribing tenant enterprise will have different storage needs. Ability to finely measure the secondary storage use and also ability to allocate additional storage

space on-demand are important characteristics expected. This is directly possible with least development effort for OSP-based solution compared with the COTS-based solution.

(vi) The COTS product does not have service APIs to integrate with other cloud services or other enterprise systems, whereas as the open source had a reasonable interoperable services, it is expected to have easy connections to other cloud services such as Salesforce.com™ or Google's™ cloud services (including maps).

(vii) For the project, comparing these characteristics adequate to select the final ECM product.

The above discussions and the comparison chart (Table 6.2) clearly indicate what can be the product of choice for the solution. Obviously, the cloud compatibility of the 'open-source product' is more than the COTS. Here, an absolute measure on the maturity or ideal perfect cloud compatibility measure is not attempted. Relative comparison is adequate for selecting products as SBBs suitable for cloud SaaS solutions.

6.7 Combined Discussion about All the Three 'Cloud Compatibility Measures'

This chapter discussed the following three models of cloud compatibility measure:

(i) The 'SaaS maturity model' referred in Ref. [5] and discussed in Section 6.4.

(ii) The cloud compatibility measure that is discussed in sub-section 6.6.1.

(iii) A variation of 'cloud compatibility measure' where in to use many intermediary values between 0 and 100 per cent compatibility with weighted average among the attributes discussed in sub-section 6.6.1.

Some observations about these (cloud compatibility measuring) methods are as follows:

(i) The first level or the lower extreme end of all the three methods discussed here coincides – it is not at all cloud compatible in the scale.

(ii) Similarly, the fourth level of matured product coincides with the absolute cloud compatibility of the scale.

(iii) The major differences between the two models of measure suggested in this chapter and that of the one in Ref. [5] are as follows:

  (a) The fine difference between two extreme ends is essential to compare many maturing products coming up in the market. Maturity model[5] gives only four levels, whereas 'the cloud compatibility measure scale' gives flexibility to set a large range value from 0 to 100.

  (b) Assuming only two stages between 'nothing and all' as mentioned in SaaS maturity model is good if one plans a road map for a product to mature to the fullest level; even in that situation, this book suggests it is better to have many more finer milestones on the road map of maturity (to reach the target architecture) rather than confining only to two major milestones.

(iv) In 'cloud compatibility measure scale', the intermediary levels can be fixed to serve many purposes: for example, for measuring maturity with calculated ROI for every additional compatibility the product gains.

(v) 'Cloud compatibility measure' method is more of practical use also in the solution architecting space, especially to select a product or component objectively from a qualifying list of them. There the solution architects have least influence on the product architecture or its current status. This is a little pragmatic empirical way to convince the stakeholders for the choice made. In addition, it has a good engineering analysis basis.

In conclusion, the 'cloud compatibility measure' introduced in this chapter can be used both for selecting most suitable product as SBBs while architecting solutions and for re-architecting a given product and draw a road map for making it completely cloud compatible.

6.8 Summary

- This chapter discusses motivation for devising a cloud compatibility measure.
- It describes an empirical method that is handy to use both for:
  - (a) Selecting most suitable one from competing products while architecting a cloud SaaS solution.
  - (b) Finely defining a road map to make any given product to be absolutely cloud compatible.
- The cloud compatibility measure is compared and discussed with a SaaS maturity model of Ref. [5].
- It showed a few variation of using the cloud compatibility measure scale and that will be handy to tweak it depending on the practicality of any project situation.
- It also illustrated the scale's use through a case study.

Chapter 7

Architecting SaaS Solutions for Cloud Using Semi-Cloud Compatible SBBs

7.1 Introduction

This chapter gives a method of architecting cloud Software as a Service (SaaS) solutions using semi-cloud compatible products.

Hence, this chapter also tries to integrate all the knowledge a reader would have gained thus far from previous chapters.

Chapter 2 describes a couple of architecture development methods; one of the methods is for developing cloud SaaS solution for a special case of group enterprises namely for small- and medium-sized enterprises (SMEs).

The case study presented here is for developing cloud SaaS solution for SMEs, and hence the method discussed in Chapter 2 is applicable here.

Chapter 3 is a pre-requisite to grasp how Infrastructure as a Service (IaaS) works, what is auto-scaling, etc., for architecting any cloud SaaS solution, and hence the case study presented here also.

Chapter 4's knowledge of how to architect a solution for cloud IaaS is assumed here for this case study, and it is very much applicable to all cloud SaaS solutions.

Chapter 5's knowledge of being familiar with all the characteristics of cloud SaaS solution is a pre-requisite for architecting a solution of this nature described in this chapter.

Chapter 6's knowledge of how to measure cloud compatibility of a given software product is essential for the solution discussed here for choosing from a bunch of possible solution building blocks (SBBs), suitable ones for the solution.

This chapter provides additional details on the following:

(i) How to use cloud compatibility measures to arrive at a final choice of software products for the solution as SBBs.
(ii) How to come out with auto-scaling algorithm for a cloud SaaS solution based on the individual component software products (SBBs).

Software products used (SBBs), in the case study discussed in this chapter, are semi-cloud compatible; hence, they provide required but limited multi-tenancy. Since they are software products (from various vendors), solution architects have no control over their cloud compatibility nature including how many concurrent users each product in the solution can handle (for a given minimum hardware recommended configuration by product vendors).

Reference [19] contains many information discussed here.

7.2 Case Study

7.2.1 Introduction to Case Study

This case study is about architecting a SaaS solution for a group of small- or medium-segment manufacturing industry; we can refer them as a community or a consortium of enterprises. The characteristics of SMEs are a lot different, and these are discussed in Chapter 2.

7.2.2 Description of Customer

(i) Customer is a consortium (community) of SMEs.
(ii) There may be totally about 8,000 users from about 600 enterprises.
(iii) It is not guaranteed that all the 8,000 users may opt to use the solution; but this number gives an idea of the maximum size of the 'market' for which this solution is aimed at. This number will give some business economics too.
(iv) If the number of users for the solution exceeds 3,000, then the consortium will take over the solution and run its operations. (This will limit the operating profit of the solution.)
(v) Usage volume is not committed by the consortium at any point of time in the life cycle of the solution.
(vi) Some enterprises will subscribe for a large number of users, and some enterprises may subscribe only for one or two users for the solution.
(vii) The consortium will not invest any money.
(viii) Maintaining the system is the service provider's responsibility.
(ix) Average literacy level of prospective users is low.
(x) Solution provider can charge strictly on pay-per-use per functionality or the services consumed:
    (a) Should not charge for any fees for the entire month based on logged-in users.
    (b) But charging should be strictly on the basis of duration of usage of any (opted) functionality.
    (c) Consequently, there cannot be any charge for enrolling in any new user such as one-time registration fees.
    (d) Also, there cannot be any penalty for withdrawing or dropping any particular user.
    (e) (These sub-clauses along with others imply that it is the service provider's responsibility to maintain the users).
(xi) Consortium expects a proven solution and not custom developed. (This implies that solution should be an integration of proven software products rather than developed from scratch as custom modules of software).
(xii) Industries in the consortium are involved in textile manufacturing.
(xiii) Each enterprise may produce one or more product or service for textile manufacturing.
(xiv) They also compete with each other very fiercely in the same market place for their share of business.
(xv) Since their customers are international, each enterprise need to provide a world-class service, and some of them need to show transparency of production progress by integrating their enterprise resource planning (ERP) systems (which is nothing but the intended cloud SaaS solution) to their customer systems. (Implying each enterprise in the consortium may have their own customers and each enterprise's

data are confidential, and hence the connection to customers system also should be highly secured.)

(xvi) Each member need to interface their systems with customers' system for exchanging information that are relevant to customers.

7.2.3 Customers' Requirements

(i) Customer is looking for an ERP solution for textile industry.

(ii) Human resources management and accounting modules are also need to be included.

(iii) Sales, inventory and stores management features are a must.

(iv) Some of the enterprises or companies in the consortium may use end-to-end ERP functionalities; most of them may not use end-to-end but a few sub-modules or functions.

(v) Hence, enterprises are looking for fine granular functionalities of the solution be made available as service from the intended cloud SaaS solution. That will help each enterprise can pick and choose only those functionalities what they require and pay only for them.

(vi) Many of the enterprises provide a specific product or service within textile industry.

(vii) Customers look for heavy customization of user interface, databases (DBs), mainly reports and also workflows.

(viii) Most member enterprises will also interface their own in-house other (information technology) systems with the cloud SaaS solution that the vendor will provide.

7.2.4 Solutions Implications and Constraints

(i) The customer is not willing to invest either in hardware or software; that means the solution provider needs to invest in these and offer as a service. It is natural for SMEs to defer or avoid upfront investments.

(ii) There is no minimum usage guarantee or stickiness to consume the solution. This meant that neither market size was predictable nor success of solution being consumed is guaranteed. The ROI of this service eludes calculation. Therefore, even a solution provider had to be conservative in investments to provide the solution; hence, deploy the cloud SaaS solution for minimum users, but the solution should scale on demand.

(iii) There is a need for appropriateness (as finer as possible) in granularity of functions in the solution. That would allow member enterprises to pick and use only functionalities what each one of them requires to conserve cost.

(iv) It is essential to allow subscribers to perceive that the cost is in proportion to usage of functionalities.

Customer is highly sensitive to cost of using solution: Both in pay-per-use cost per unit time as well as total duration of use.

Each enterprise would like to customize their reports, processes or screens to meet their specific requirements. Hence, multi-tenants co-existing in the same solution instance is inevitable, which is nothing but a typical cloud SaaS solution.

(v) The solution is for a group of enterprises rather than for a single enterprise (please recollect similar discussions in Chapter 2); even among those enterprises in the community providing same products or services, they differ vastly in business processes or rules. The enterprise model would not be homogeneous even to model them. In addition, many will not have any documented enterprise architecture to attempt any study and then derive some commonality among them in the enterprise models.

Solution needs to address the following usage pattern as it is evident from the requirements:

- Each company will use some or a few functionalities of the solutions implying fine granularity in offering solutions functionalities.
- Need for integrating cloud SaaS solution both with each subscribing enterprise systems.
- There could be a possibility of interfacing this cloud SaaS solution to a large number disparate systems of customer-to-customer systems.
- The peak demand or load on any of the modules will be highly fluctuating between high and low of estimated demand.

7.2.5 Case Model

Table 7.1 summarizes unique problem this case faces[19]:

Table 7.1 Summary of the problem in this case

Problem characteristics ⇨ / Solution Characteristics ⇩	Build business capabilities for a group of enterprises rather than for a single entity	All are either small or medium enterprises	Usage is not a predictable model
Using TOGAF's ideal ADM	?	?	?
Using less 'cloud-ready' COTS to provide a cloud based solution	?	?	?
Architecture a cloud based (rather than hosted) SaaS solution	?	?	?

7.2.5.1 Explanation for the Table

Table 7.1 summarizes the characteristics of problem and possible solutions' space. The cross junction of these two 'spaces' – problem and solution – is where the solution lies.

Both *problem* and *solution* space has three major 'dimensions':

First in problem space:

(i) The solution is for a group of enterprises and not for a single company.
(ii) Within that, it is for SMEs where cost is a constraint, and not for very large enterprise.
(iii) Usage of the solution is not predictable; hence, the cost cannot be determined in easy steps. Profitability eludes, since the consortium may take over and run the services when the number of paid users exceeds 3000.

Note: *Chapter 2 completely discusses the above situation and provides how a methodology can be evolved around the central architectural development method (ADM) of the open group architecture framework (TOGAF) for these kinds of project situations.*

It also has three significant dimensions in solution space:

Row 1: Using TOGAF's ADM

(a) TOGAF's ADM for solution architecting need to be used for a group of enterprises, which is not obvious.
(b) Within that 'group of enterprises', another special case comes in – 'SMEs'.
(c) The methodology should be taking into account the uncertainty in the usage model and hence pricing model.

(A solution for this – a methodology for architecting cloud SaaS solutions for SMEs – is completely discussed in Chapter 2).

Row 2: Using semi-cloud compatible products to provide cloud SaaS solution

1. Using semi-cloud ready commercial off-the-shelf (COTS) as SBBs for the solution for group of enterprises.
2. Cost will dictate selection and optimal use of COTS products for the solution; hence, less cloud compatible products may be forced into the solution.
3. But the final solution should behave as if it has absolute cloud compatibility.

Row 3: Architecting a cloud-based SaaS solution (rather than conventional hosted model).

7.3 Architecting Solution

7.3.1 Building Business Capabilities for a Group of Enterprises

Identifying architectural building blocks (ABBs) by appropriately grouping the requirements is one of the first significant first steps in architecting solution. Chapter 2 has discussed this step in detail. Chapter 4 has illustrated this step though a solution that is non-cloud SaaS solution, the illustration is useful for novice professionals.

(Next major step is to locate suitable SBBs to meet the ABBs. But before that step)

From the functional requirements and the ABBs determined, architects can come up with a preliminary functional architecture. Key modules required for this solution is ERP module. One can further detail various sub-modules that are required for the solution. HR module is also required but assumed to be part of the ERP module for referring here.

An RDBMS package is essential but that cannot be counted as functional module.

Other software required (including infrastructure software such as operating system, app servers, Web servers, anti-virus software, etc.) are based on technological requirements. These are also not functional modules.

There may be more than one possible SBB option that could have been identified matching each ABB. Then, each SBB need to be further analysed for cost effectiveness by analysing their license fee, implementation and maintenance cost.

That will give a set of short-listed options of SBBs against each ABB. In this set, we need to run the cloud compatibility measure on each of the SBBs, as discussed in Chapter 6. Subsequently, one that scores more cloud compatible can be finalized.

Sub-section 7.3.2 gives an overview of cloud compatibility discussions done for this ERP module.

7.3.2 Calibrating COTS against Cloud Compatibility Criteria

Within the cloud compatibility criteria discussed in Chapter 6 and in Table 7.2, the discussions narrow the characteristics expected out of SBBs. Therefore, evaluation of each software product, that got qualified as SBB, need to be carried out keeping these additional narrowing down criteria. The final selection depends on the closeness of expectations mentioned in Column 3.

Table 7.2 Calibrating COTS against cloud compatibility criteria[19]

Cloud compatibility criteria (major ones; others do not get weights in this solution)	Calibrating criteria for shortlisted SBBs (COTS) in simpler descriptions	
Multi-tenant efficient	'Number of users per instance' ratio influences cost per user.	Products that offer maximum number of users per a specific hardware will be selected.
Configurable *Customization of screens, reports, work flows/ business processes or rules*	Without customization, system adoption becomes difficult. Therefore, these expectation need to be met by SBBs.	SBB that gives maximum configuration and customization options will be selected.
Extension to data models *Each enterprise would like to have its own DB*	It is compromise to use DB extensions either to allow each tenant to customize, or solution provider uses this feature (consume it) for implementing certain common functionalities across similar group of enterprises.	The data model that will give extensive customization of reports more closer to almost independent database allowing as much DB extensions and customization.

(*continued*)

Table 7.2 (Continued)

Cloud compatibility criteria (major ones; others do not get weights in this solution)	Calibrating criteria for shortlisted SBBs (COTS) in simpler descriptions	
ACL	Ideal expectation is ACL need to be maintained out side any package including ERP. Most of the COTS software assume single tenant and hence even if we maintain ACLs outside the software every time ACL need to be loaded into it for proper functioning; and this is quite challenging in cloud SaaS usage circumstances under 24 × 7 ops.	ACL will be maintained outside any package and role-based access will be used for allowing users the requested services.

7.3.3 Key Challenges and Solutions in Finalizing SBBs

Table 7.3 below indicates how the solutions have been finalized against odd or challenging reality. The column to the right indicates the final decision taken in this solution against those cloud compatibility criteria.

Table 7.3 Key challenges and solutions in finalizing SBBs[19]

Cloud compatibility criteria	Solutions to challenges
Multi-tenant efficient	Many COTS do not have this feature. So we need to filter those that are at least multi-tenant architected though not efficient. We need to device scaling algorithm as discussed in Section 7.5.
Configurable	Most of the COTS do not handle configuration through 'metadata', and hence not suitable for multi-tenants to use the same instance.
Extension to data models	In this solution, the architect chose to use DB extensions to provide functionalities common to similar enterprises in the group. There was still some scope for tenants to customize.
ACL	The solution benchmarked the roles and access rights. Still left certain roles for custom creation within that group, which means, if a new role is created, it will be available for all the tenants in the group. User access control was done outside the package; allowed the tenants to manage their users. The roles defined have to be, somehow, taken into or injected into the COTS product to make it work.

7.3.4 Security Requirements and Solutions to the Final Solution

Customer's security requirements were very simple. Enterprises expected a basic data protection for privacy and the entire cloud is private and visible only to subscribers. (This is typically a community cloud meant only for a set of known possible customer enterprises.)

7.4 Summary of Cloud-Based SaaS Solution

Having selected and finalized the required SBBs, the solution architecture can be drafted. In this case, it will be as follows:

7.4.1 Deployment Architecture for Minimum Usage

(i) Terminal server (software from Microsoft™) (Figure 7.1) will act like Web tier software to handle all incoming HTTP requests or page requests; each instance of the terminal software can entertain comfortably 50* simultaneous users.

(ii) MS Navision™ can be assumed to be the ERP software; this is multi-tenanted, but each software instance cannot handle more than 200* simultaneous logged-in users.

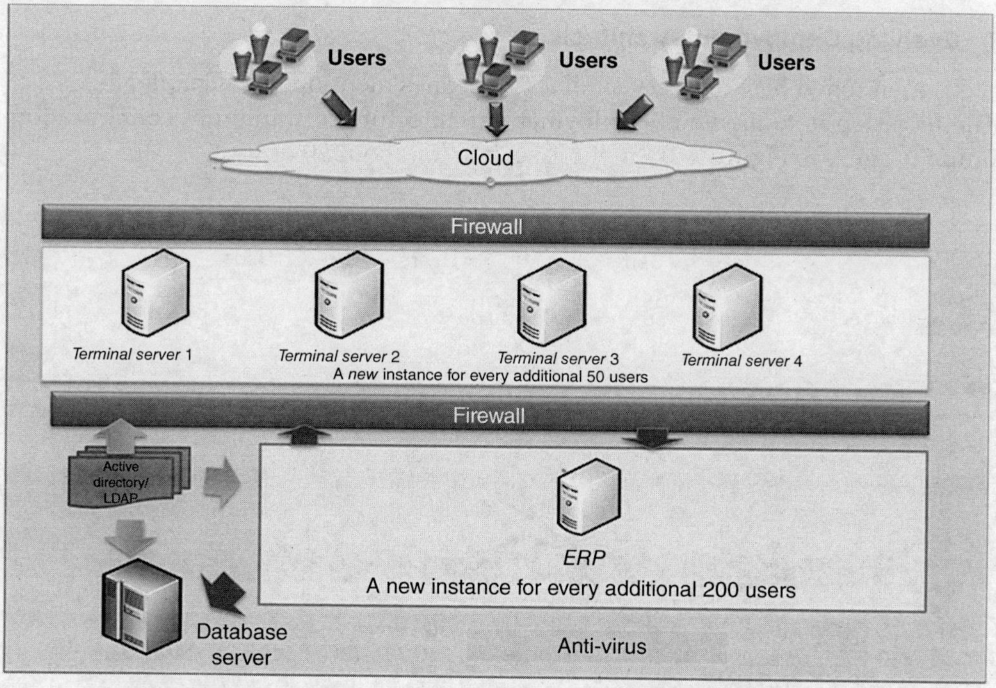

Figure 7.1 Terminal server, auto scale to accommodate 200 users

*The number of users that is mentioned above as these software can simultaneously be handled is based on specific usage pattern and is arrived after initial POC; and this should not be assumed as manufacturer's specification.

(iii) MS SQL server is the chosen DB.

(iv) Other supporting software are Active Directory™/Lightweight Directory Access Protocol™ (LDAP).

(a) One instance is enough for all 8,000 users or even more.

(b) Of course antivirus software.

(v) Users will be validated and authenticated through Active Directory™/LDAP™.

(vi) Authorized users will be allowed to use the signed up (or permitted) features in ERP software.

(vii) ERP software will use the RDBMS.

(viii) For each customer, same RDBMS is used but different schemas. This also will help them have their custom reports and information collection for the same purpose.

(ix) A SAN is used for data storage.

(x) All the hardware are under a hypervisor and h/w infrastructure is virtualized using techniques similar to the one described in Chapter 4. Additional instances of the hardware can be requested on-demand, thanks to the hypervisor's ability.

7.4.2 Evolving Deployment Architecture

The steps mentioned here are very similar to the ones mentioned in Chapter 4.

The first step is to arrive at deployment architecture of minimum configuration for minimum usage (see Figure 7.2). In our case, it is for about 50 users.

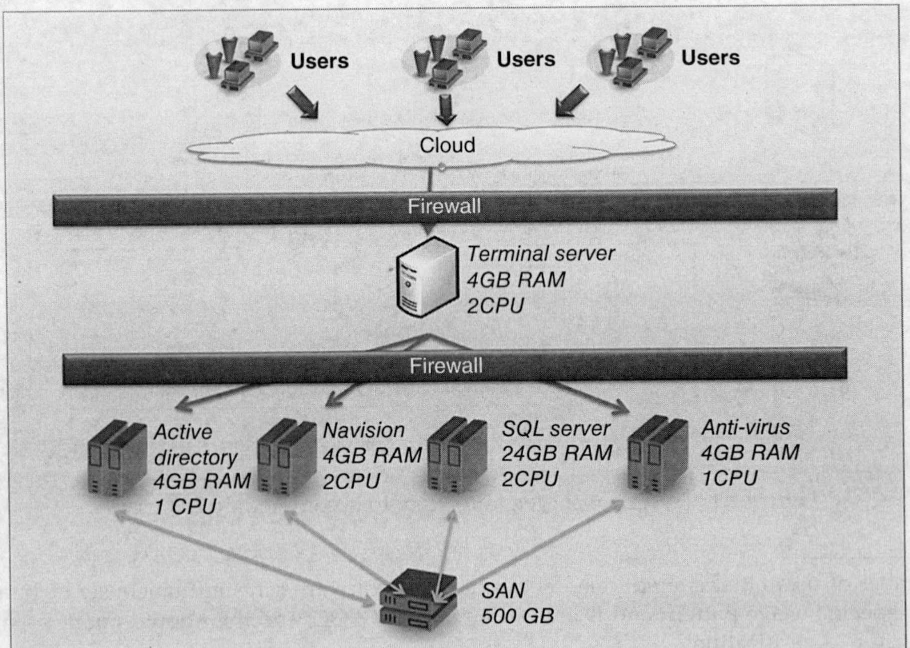

Figure 7.2 Deployment architecture for minimum usage – 50 logged in users

7.4.3 Size Software for Scalability

The second step is to identify the scalability factors for each of the software.

For terminal server, the maximum number of users per box* can be only 50. Therefore, for every additional login user beyond 50 users, we need one more set of hardware box* and an instance of the software to entertain additional incoming users to maintain the same response time.

For the ERP software, one instance can handle up to 200 users. For every user beyond 200 till the next limit of (additional 200) 400, we need one more set of hardware box* and corresponding software instance. This includes the operating system and the associated micro-ERP software.

To coordinate these two ERP servers, a load balancer is essential; this can be even software as in this case.

However, RDBMS software normally does not scale based on the number of users. The ideal parameter is the central processing unit (CPU) utilization and memory utilization. If CPU utilization crosses 40 per cent or maximum of 60 per cent and memory utilization crosses 60 per cent, it is better to kick off its next instance. There are many ways of calculating the scaling trigger point for RDBMS package. The above is not true always, but useful common way.

7.4.4 Determining Scaling Algorithms

The auto-scaling algorithm will be more like the one listed below:

(i) For the first 50 users, the minimum hardware/deployment configuration will work.
(ii) The moment 51st user logs in till 100th user, the next instance** of terminal server will start, and this process repeats for every additional 50 users.
(iii) When the total number of users crosses the first 200, the next instance** of ERP server will also start; this will repeat for every 200 users. Bring a load balancer to coordinate these two servers.
(iv) RDBMS software will start next instance** based on the composite parameter of CPU utilization and memory utilization.

7.4.4.1 Scalability and Performance Illustration

(i) Figure 7.3 explains how the scaling will occur as and when new users log in. This is in tune with the scaling algorithm explained in Section 7.4.4.
(ii) For first 50 login users there will be only one terminal server and one ERP server will be deployed.
(iii) On 51st new login user, the second terminal server will be kicked-in to work, that the first scaling occurs.
(iv) On 101st and 151st, new simultaneous users, third- and fourth-terminal servers will be brought to live.

---

*In cloud paralance, the "hardware box" is one instance of H/W with the corresponding specification.

**An instance here refers to the H/W instance for the specific S/W SBB + one copy of S/W instance. Bringing this instance and earlier ones under load balancer is also automated under this step.

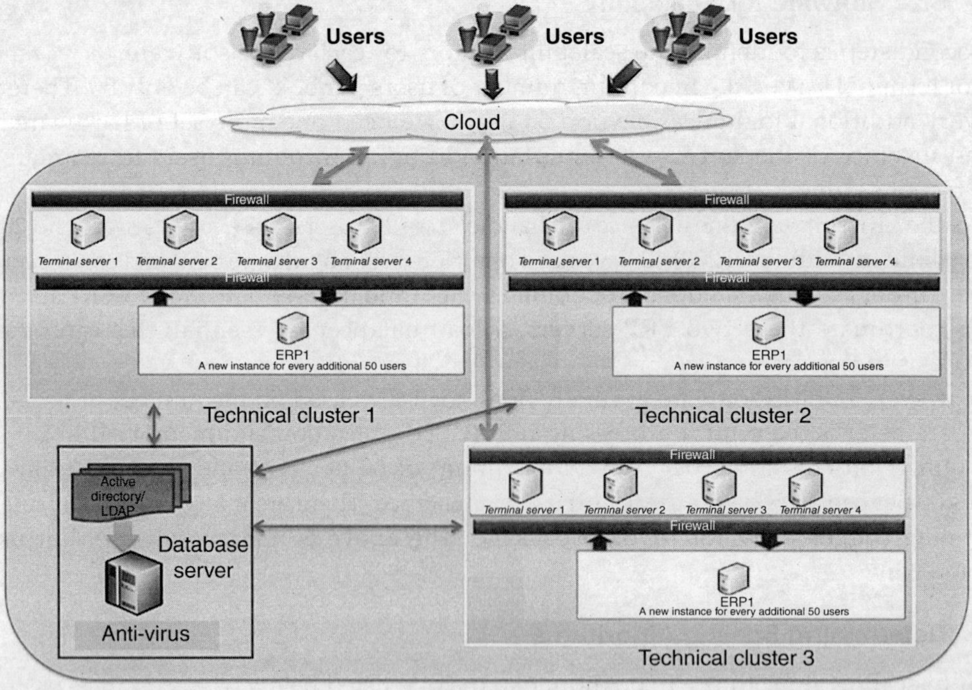

Figure 7.3 A snap shot of actual auto scaled-up architecture that is serving when the users are above 600

(v) On 201th new login user, second cluster will start with one terminal server and one ERP server. This second cluster will keep scaling by adding additional terminal server until its 200th but over all 400 users log in… and so on.

(vi) In all the above situations, the hardware housing RDBMS, anti-virus, active directory server will be only one. (RDBMS server scaling is not dependent on number of login users; it depends on how intensive the computational work is invoked by users; even if less than 50 users invoke a large CPU time or memory intensive work at data tier (assuming RDBMS will be directly taxed), it will begin to scale as per its scaling algorithm mentioned in Sections 7.4.3 and 7.4.4).

7.5 Other Routine Steps for Implementing the Solution

(i) The steps mentioned in Chapter 4 for choosing IaaS is applicable here.
(ii) Choose the appropriate hardware instances in the targeted virtualized IaaS environment.
(iii) And install each of the SBBs/products in the appropriate instances.
(iv) Install also the scaling algorithms using the provisions in the virtualized environment – this will be mostly using a cloud watch patterns.

7.6 Less Cloud-Ready Software Costs More for Per-User/Time

The cost to end-user is directly dictated by the maximum number of users that can be accommodated in one unit of deployment hardware configuration. Here for 200 users, the solution needs four terminal servers and one ERP server. Therefore, the cost of these 4 + 1 servers is divided by 200 users. If, say, 30 more users logs in, then they cannot be accommodated in the running 4 + 1 servers. Additional one each of terminal and ERP servers are required as explained in the scaling algorithm. Therefore, the cost does not always go down with increased users. Further, the cost of the solution is dictated by maximum number of users that can be accommodated in single instance of software.

If the software is highly scalable, it can accommodate more users per instance, and hence cost of hardware required per user will be less.

Therefore, configuring minimum deployment architecture, and providing scaling algorithm almost brings the solution architecture phase to conclusion.

7.7 Summary

The key takeaway from this case study are as follows:

This use case:

- Summarizes experiences in architecting a solution as follows:
  - For a group of enterprises rather than for a single entity.
  - For using semi-cloud-ready software to provide cloud-based SaaS solution.
- Summarizes key challenges and solutions.
- Contributes the following to architect cloud-based SaaS solution for a group of companies.
- Uses the measure for cloud-readiness to select the needed SBB for building cloud based SaaS solution.
- Provides detailed steps to build a cloud solution.

Recommendation for further work

(i) Although ADM's steps are technology independent, the open group can give some guidelines on optimal set of steps for architecting cloud-based solution.

(ii) We need to examine our reference models and enterprise continuum to include cloud extension of corporate assets to represent in EA repository.

(iii) Architecture forum such as TOGAF can examine more formally the use of ADM for applying or using the same in situations such as providing solutions to group of enterprises as the need for the same is going to increase.

(iv) Coming up with a systematic set of criteria to calibrate any given software for 'cloud-readiness' seems to be a must. I tend to recommend a software product – neutral body can bring a regulation even to stamp them for its cloud readiness using the commonly agreed criteria.

(v) Also, the software products can contain scaling guidelines rather than relying on experience from other projects. Right now, mostly we find a suitable hardware configuration for deploying them.

Chapter 8

Architecting Cloud SaaS Solutions with Cloud Non-Compatible Products

8.1 Introduction

Chapter 7 describes how to architect cloud Software as a Serive (SaaS) solutions using semi-cloud compatible software products. Chapter 9 provides a complete discussion on how to architect cloud SaaS products that are aimed to be absolutely cloud compatible. The information found in these two chapters will definitely also be useful to architect solutions using non-cloud compatible software products. As discussed in Chapters 1, 5 and 6, very often solution architects are forced to provide a good cloud compatible SaaS solutions using cloud non-compatible (cnc) software products.
To recap quickly, the main reasons are the following:

(i) Many of existing software products are *not* cloud compatible.
(ii) It may take long time (and cost) for software product vendors to re-architect their software products.

Therefore, architects have to live with the reality of providing cloud SaaS software solutions using utterly non-compatible cloud software products. This chapter shares experience of such situations. Solution architects can benefit of the discussions in this chapter. The technical architecting method shown and adapted in this chapter cannot be generalized and applied to all solutions that use absolutely non-cloud compatible software products.

8.2 Classification of Solutions Using Not-at-All Cloud Compatible Products

A typical industry grade software solution may typically require more than 5–20 different software products: big or small. A few of them may provide main functionality for the solution. If some of the remaining software products are not main and happen to be non-cloud compatible, then architecting a solution is relatively easier and not discussed in this book.

If the main software products required for a solution are not fully cloud compatible, some of the techniques discussed in this chapter can be used.

Figure 8.1 summarizes the possibilities of using completely non-compatible cloud products in solutioning situation.

Note: *Readers have to know the important caution that is in the form of limitations of the method discussed in this chapter.*

(i) Unlike Chapter 7 or 9, the method discussed is not a generic one that can be applied to all cloud SaaS solutions that require the use of perfectly non-cloud compatible software products.
(ii) The above point is true even if some or all the main products are not absolutely cloud compatible.

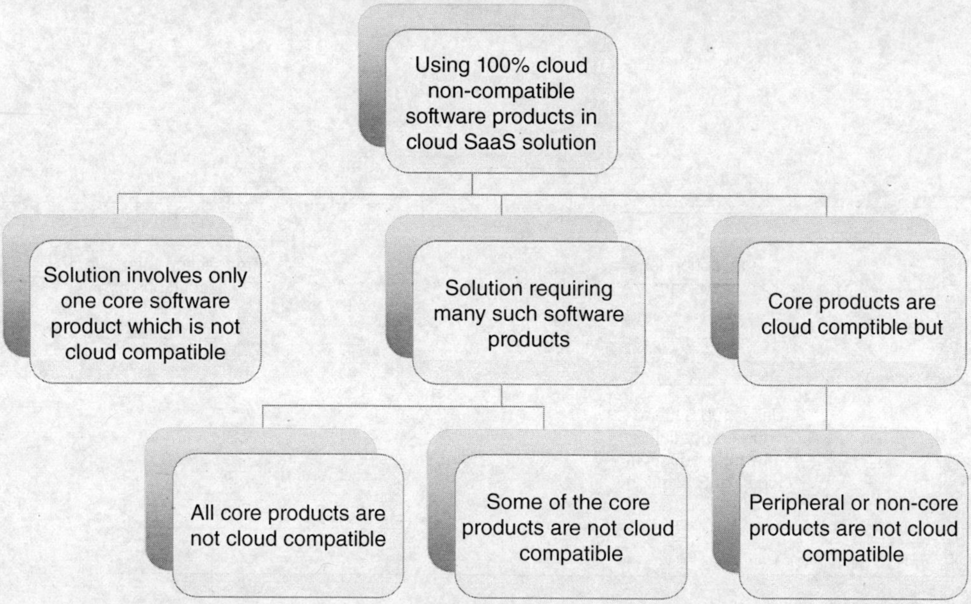

Figure 8.1 Summary of classes of cases possible in cloud SaaS solution situations using completely non-compatible cloud software products

(iii) This chapter illustrates a method using a case study.
(iv) In this case study, only one main product is involved and that is not cloud compatible.
(v) The techniques used in this case study and also the tips and tricks adopted in this case study can be used in many similar projects.
(vi) After sufficient experience, any solution architect will be in a position to provide solutions that he or she encounters. The contents of this book will be of great help to any person to start the journey and also produce simple to medium complex cloud SaaS solutions. Probably, very complex solutions may not be possible directly with the knowledge gained only from this book.
(vii) Another important aspect that a reader should bear in mind while reading this example is as follows:
   (a) The cloud SaaS solution that needs to be architected can be classified into two broad and main categories as follows:
      1. Those that are transactions intensive (see Chapter 9 for brief explanations on additional complexities that these classes of solutions bring in for architecting them).
      2. Those that are transaction-less solutions.

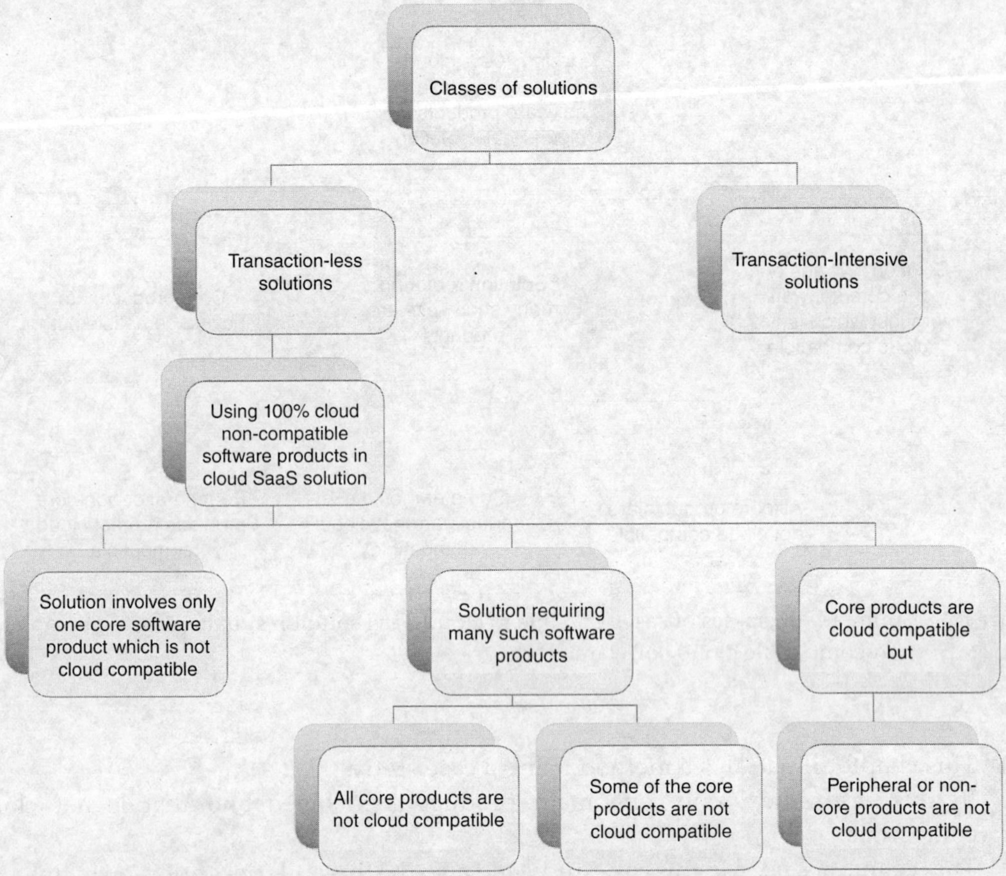

Figure 8.2 Summarizes various classes of solutions possible including transaction-less and transaction-intensive solutions

Figure 8.2 is a modification of Figure 8.1 by incorporating the above two classes, namely transaction-less' and 'transaction-intensive' solutions. Most of the techniques discussed in this chapter will be useful for *transaction-less* solutions and not for *transaction-intensive* solutions.

8.3 Some General Strategies

While architecting a solution using completely non-compatible cloud products, some of the following general principles or tricks or tips can be used by architects. Some of these can even become guiding principles for specific projects too:

(i) Gather all cloud characteristics and requirements of target cloud SaaS solution. To meet the above requirements, provide separate SBB that is cloud compatible (modules or products), but outside cnc core product(s):

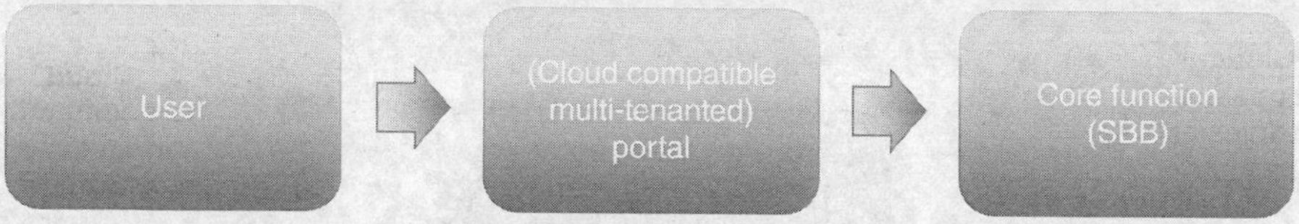

Figure 8.3 User accessing core function only through multi-tenanted customizable portal

(a) For example, consider a situation where cloud SaaS solution has a requirement of a good and highly customizable user interface (UI), but its core product is completely non-cloud compatible, then think of a multi-tenanted highly customizable portal facing users. Figure 8.3 illustrates the solution.

(ii) Therefore, in architecting procedure (see Chapters 2, 7 and 9), after identifying SBBs, solution architects need to segregate those SBBs that meet the core functionality for which absolutely non-compatible cloud products are mapped and those for which cloud compatible modules are identified. (See Chapter 6 for 'measuring' cloud compatibility characteristics of products that become SBBs of the target solution. The same measuring technique can be used to measure cloud compatibility characteristics of target solution too.)

(iii) For the non-cloud compatible modules or products, identify all the cloud compatible characteristics that are required in the target solution.

(iv) Create modules that will meet the above (point (ii)) requirements and supplement the cloud compatibility for all those non-compatible SBBs.

(v) Probably, architects may need to optimize such supplementing modules by consolidating similar requirements coming from various cnc SBBs into a few common cloud compatibility providing modules.

Therefore, the solution consists of two major identifiable components: (1) Those modules that can handle cloud compatible features, and the same make the overall solution as much as possible nearer to completely cloud compatible. (2) Those core modules that provide core functionalities but are absolutely non-cloud compatible.

Figure 8.4 provides one high-level view of a typical solution architecture, thereby reflecting the above points.

Those non-core functional modules that are make the overall solution more cloud compatible may be mostly custom developed in all the projects. As these common modules that make the solution cloud compatible are very often required for each cloud SaaS solution, it is quite natural for solution architects to look for software products to fulfil these requirements. At the time of writing this book, the author was unaware of such software products. In future, if products do come up, then those will not only decrease the effort of custom developing these modules but also can be a well-tested, defect-free SBBs of the target solution.

Consequently, availability of such software in future and use of the same in solutions will ensure extension of (non-cloud compatible) products' life without re-architecting to make it absolutely cloud compatible products too!

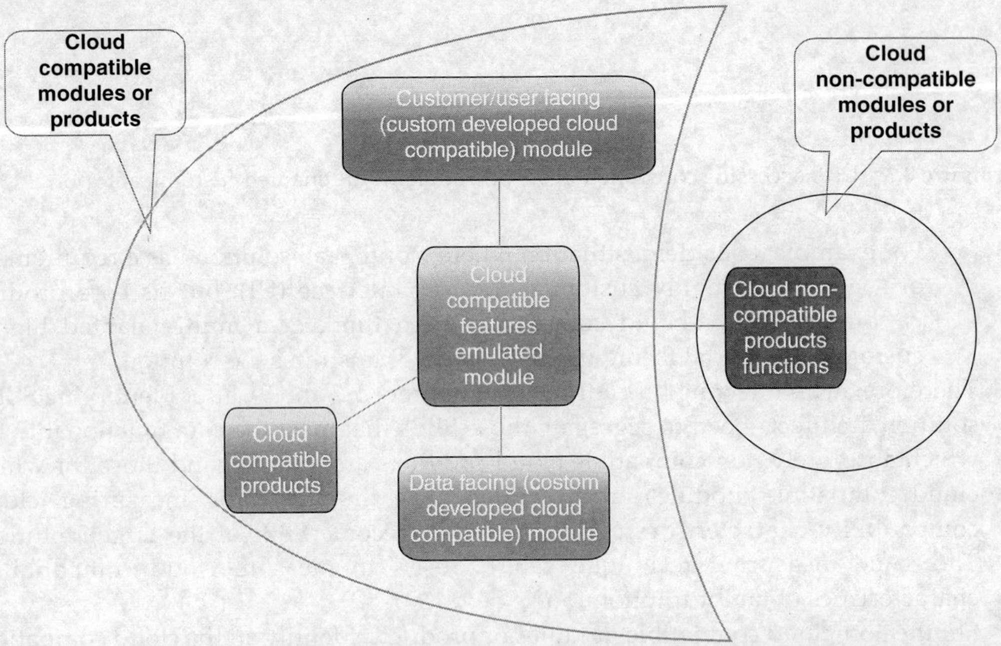

Figure 8.4 Conceptual view of solution architecture with absolutely cloud non-compatible product

Examining what kind of software products could be non-cloud compatible but still required (urgently – not waiting until it is re-architected to be cloud compatible) is a good proactive exercise for solution architecting team in any typical solution architecting companies that put in use thousands of software products. Typically, they have functionalities that are highly specialized, domain specific and highly custom developed ones.

Therefore, solution architects can even develop a specific architecture for using these cnc software products. Such regularized architecture would have identified solutions for all required cloud compatible features.

Identity and access management could be one component in a cloud SaaS solution, data access modules including multi-tenanted relational DB software could be another, and a portal could be a third one, and these are some examples of modules that will be required for most of cloud SaaS solutions with high cloud compatible characteristics. If workflow is available in the platform itself rather than from a separate product such as in .Net, achieving or providing cloud compatibility characteristics for workflow module may be easy or difficult depending on the provisions available in the platform; it may trivially become easy if the platform itself provides multi-tenancy. (The author is not implying anything on the current capability of .Net; for specific information on .Net capability, please check the respective product manual.) It becomes difficult if the workflow is a separate product within the overall solution. This should be treated like any other product and subjected to analysis of cloud compatibility measures. If it turned out to be a completely non-cloud compatible product, then the treatment is very similar to what has been discussed in this chapter. Similar argument holds good for other components such as business rules engine too.

All the above-discussed SBBs need to be cloud compatible and absorb many of the cloud compatibility requirements of the solution. Even the cloud compatibility characteristics requirement that comes from cnc products need to be absorbed and included in these products. These SBBs can surround the cnc products and apparently even 'hide' them from getting exposed to users (or other interfacing systems) directly. Figure 8.4 gives a pictorial view of a typical solution architecture that implements the above discussions.

This will become more clear as the reader goes through the case study presented in this chapter. The common practice at this stage of solution architecting is to expose all the required functionalities from the core software product as service. Sometimes, this is also referred to as 'service API'. Most of the readers may know API as an abbreviation for application programming interface. Traditionally, product vendors used to provide only APIs that are programming language dependent; and if the API is not available for any particular programming language of choice for the developer, then that will hinder the use of product functionalities in the solution. Service APIs are language independent and provide a loose coupling for integration. Nowadays, product vendors themselves provide these service APIs, which will decrease the workload for solution developers.

These services need to be exposed in the functional layer of a ideal service-oriented architecture (SOA) (or cloud computing reference architecture). See Chapters 9 and 10 for a detailed discussion on this.

The exposed services should be visible only to 'cloud services creators' and not to 'cloud services consumers (or customers)'. (see Chapter 10 for proper definition of service creators and service consumers from cloud computing reference architecture (CCRA) vocabulary.)

Other cloud compatible modules and software products (in the total solution) will consume these services and produce results to users.

With this background, we will understand the case study that uses only one core functional product that is perfectly cnc.

8.4 Case Study

8.4.1 Use Case 1

Set of small and medium banks decided to have a cloud-based solution to facilitate their prospective new customers to open new bank accounts with them.

While signing up for a new bank account, the potential customer may need to supply a lot of supporting documents such as a copy of his or her telephone bill as proof of their mail address, proof of identification such as driver's license copy, a proof of being in the sate – mostly ration card or voter's id. Like that, the list of documents to be provided is large and each scanned copy can occupy more than over 5 MB of storage space. (5 MB was the limit in popular cloud SaaS customer relationship management (CRM)).

Until they become customers, it is the banks' responsibility to hold the proofs and keep them safe. It should be tamperproof for hacking or stealing such information about individuals. Once their application is approved by the bank, then these papers will be once and for all moved to folders within the boundary of the bank. Leaving them on the cloud is not advised as part of banks' requirements.

In this use case, each bank is a customer for the cloud SaaS solution. Within a bank, there may be many users. Some of them will be internal users or bank employees, and there may be many external users who are potential customers who try to open new bank accounts.

8.4.2 Use Case 2

A catalogue-based product selling company would like to keep a copy of multimedia-based catalogue of the product that every customer selects and orders. This ensures the complete description of the product a customer ordered. It also captures the customization details of the selected product. Even if the company drops that particular product or product line, the details remain in the DB forever. In case of later dispute on the part of customer such as if there is a difference between the ordered product and that delivered to the customer, then this will act as a reference.

The mash up (or multimedia) description of any typical product in the catalogue exceeds 5 MB.

Order entry, tracking sales to delivery is done by a cloud-based popular SaaS CRM system. Due to size limitations of the mash up that can be stored in the CRM, the product descriptions as found in the catalogue cannot be stored along with the purchase order.

Entire product catalogue is stored in a content management system (CMS). The product catalogue itself is a multimedia catalogue and will occupy a lot of storage space.

Individual product descriptions from the catalogue is taken, copied and stored in a separate place in CMS against the purchase order number and a unique identification number to the purchase order.

The URL of the storage location in CMS is embedded back into the purchase order, and the purchase order is saved in CRM as per CRM's workflow.

Therefore, when the purchase order is retrieved from the CRM for any clarification, using their impeded URL in the purchase order, then one can retrieve the exact catalogue description of the product from CMS.

8.4.3 Some Common Observations

In both the use cases, the end-user or the users of the cloud SaaS solution do not interact with CMS directly.

CMS provides a functionality of storing (and retrieving) a large amount of unstructured data whose size is not a restriction. The data can be in any format such as MP3, MP4, etc. The data are very often referred to as unstructured data in contrast to those that can be stored in relational DB and retrieved through SQLs. The data will be typically comprise voice, video or images or a combination of text too.

In this case study, the CMS is a non-cloud compatible product. This is the one that provides main and core functionality to the solution as discussed in Section 8.4.4.

Refer Chapter 6 for a description of the product and analysis of the non-cloud compatibility of the same product.

8.4.4 Solution Description

(i) As indicated earlier in this chapter, all the required functionalities of the CMS need to be exposed as service in the functional layer of the CCRA (or SOA). These services will be visible only to service creators and not visible to service users for both the solutions.

(ii) Multiple tenants need to be maintained outside the CMS.

(iii) User management and the privileges of their access rights to various functionalities of the system have to be maintained outside the CMS.

(iv) While accessing the CMS functionalities, the appropriate access rights that the user may have need to be checked by the other modules before accessing CMS.

CMS is at the backend, and it will not face users or customers.

(v) CMS need to be connected in a trusted mode through the *accessing module* to rest of the solution. This implies that no users will directly access CMS. In addition, it implies that CMS is aware that only one system will access it, and such an accessing system is trustworthy to transact. Normally, in such situations CMS will be behind a firewall, blocking any other possibility of directly accessing CMS.

(vi) Any CMS, and especially this one, requires a relational DB as well as a file system. CMS will store multimedia contents in the file system and keep a pointer of the storage in the relational DB. This DB is different from the DB that the solution itself will be having and maintaining one.

(vii) This pointer along with the row of information maintained in the DB of CMS is passed back to the *accessing module*. This information is in turn stored in the solutions DB against <customer id>, <user id> and <purchase order number> combination as a key for later retrieval. This information is also passed on to the CRM for it to store it along with the purchase order, and that is the requirement of the system.

(viii) The solutions DB can be a multi-tenanted model as desired and designed by the solution architect. It can follow any one of the three possible designs indicated in Chapter 5, or it can be any other model suiting to the requirements of the solution.

(ix) Although the overall solution is cloud-based and multi-tenanted and can concurrently entertain many users, the *accessing module* will access CMS functionality only one at a time either to store or retrieve the contents (a conceptual view of this is same as that in Figure 8.4).

(x) For the use case 2, the CRM itself can provide all the user interfaces. Hence, the required cloud compatible characteristics required at user interface level are left to be provided by the CRM itself. CRM being cloud SaaS, it has the required capabilities naturally.

(xi) CRM will face and interact with the users directly. Hence, the target solution itself is at the backend and not exposed to users.

(xii) In use case 2, most of the workflow will be handled by the CRM itself. Similarly, the business rules too. Therefore, the business tier of the cloud SaaS solution that is being architected will be thin and basic, and it need not have separate modules either for workflow or for business rules. CRMs modules for these itself can be extended for this part too. Thus, using the same for both CRM and target solution fits within the general principle of cloud computing to optimize resources and pass on the gain of scale of economy.

(xiii) For use case 2 from the description of requirements and solutions, it looks like that the solution that is being worked out tries to extend the capability of the CRM; CRM has the basic limitation of not able to store over 5 MB of content.

(xiv) In addition, as mentioned earlier, CRM is a cloud SaaS. Salesforce.com™ is one such example of a CRM existing on the cloud. The target solution is also conceived as cloud SaaS.

(a) Solution also can reside on the same Infrastructure as a Service (IaaS) and Platform as a Service (PaaS) platform as that of CRM (see Figure 8.5). For example, Salesforce.com™ provides one such platform having IaaS and PaaS for both developing as well as launching the solution. Incidentally, Salesforce.com™ is a cloud SaaS CRM in the cloud.

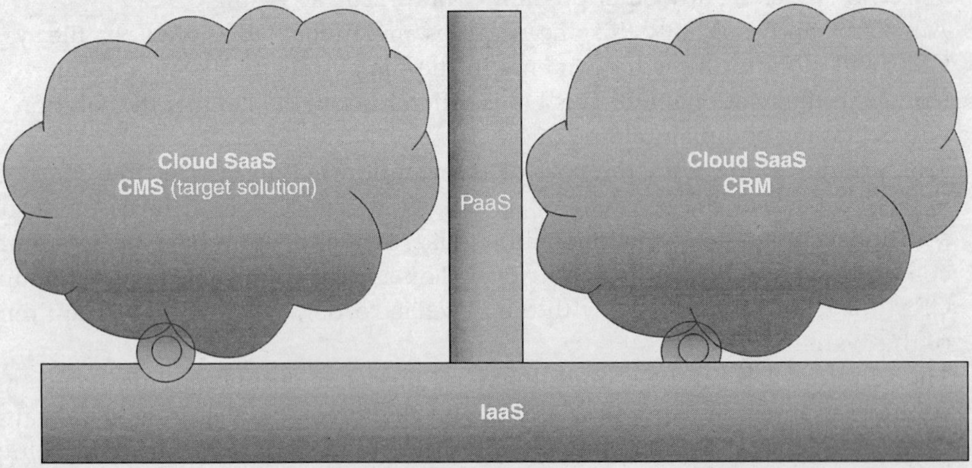

Figure 8.5 Both CMS solution and CRM reside and share the same IaaS and PaaS platform

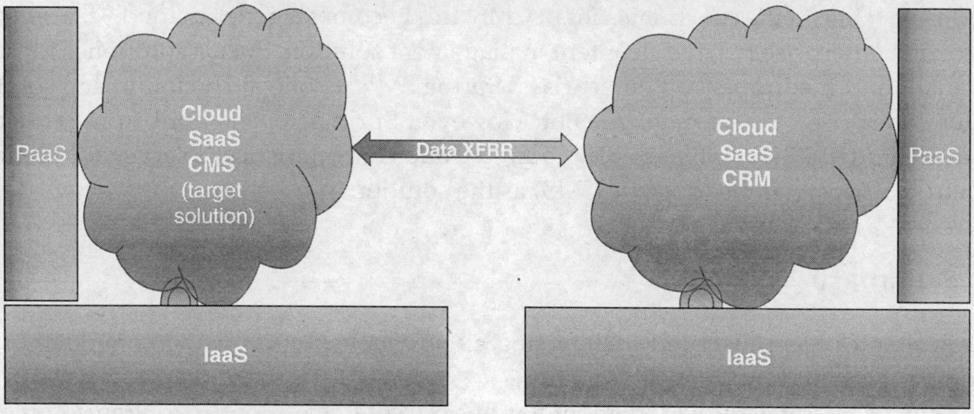

Figure 8.6 CMS solution is offered from a public IaaS cloud, which is different and away from CRM cloud

(b) Such an approach of both CRM and CMS solutions being in the same IaaS + PaaS platform offers a lot of benefits: One such benefit is that the data transfer between them is secure, faster, and the size (of content data to be passed to CMS solution) does not matter. Since IaaS and PaaS platform is shared between them, the cost will be lower.

(c) Alternatively, the CMS solution can reside in a separate public IaaS cloud. Since the CRM is also in its own cloud, one can clearly see that the two clouds – CMS solutions cloud and the CRM cloud – will exchange data between them (see Figure 8.6).

1. In that situation, high security has to be provided for the connection between the two clouds to securely exchange data.
2. The data also need to be protected during the user (flight) transmission on this connection.
3. Service interfaces are not really a suitable mechanism for exchanging high-volume data, such as multi-media content, through them[10–12].

Use case 1

(i) For the use case 1, the solution needs to provide an exclusive Web tier, and all multi-tenanted user interface facility.

(ii) The business tier needs to have separate business rules engine and business process systems in order to meet the requirements.

(iii) Data tier will be very similar to the one described earlier for use case 2.

(iv) In reality, the entire solution needs to be architected as cloud SaaS with all cloud compatible features, except for the core functions coming from complete cnc product. But the functions from complete cnc product will be made available to end-users from the rest of the modules of the solution in a true cloud SaaS solution characteristics.

(v) On exposing all the functionalities of CMS, this becomes a generic cloud SaaS solution for any enterprise to have a content management solution. Such a solution is ideal for small- and medium-sized enterprises. SpringCM™ is one such cloud SaaS solution for enterprise content management. However, SpringCM™ is built from scratch as true cloud SaaS with all possible required cloud characteristics to serve multi-tenants and (*not having* embedded cnc CMS) as the solution.

8.5 Summary

- This chapter has illustrated architecting cloud SaaS solution using completely non-compatible cloud product.
- A brief discussion is provided about various classes of solutions involving completely non-compatible cloud products.
- The general points that may be useful for most of similar projects is summarized and discussed in the beginning of this chapter.
- One particular solution is illustrated using two use cases; but, both the use cases need to use a CMS that is not cloud compatible at all. (Although there are cloud compatible products in this class, project situation forced to choose the cnc product.)

Chapter 9
Architecting Cloud Compatible SaaS Software Products

9.1 Introduction

In order for a software product to be deployed as cloud compatible software as a service (SaaS), it has to meet the characteristics mentioned in Chapter 5.

Whether an existing software product is cloud compatible or not can be assessed through the cloud compatibility measures described in Chapter 6.

Many of the current versions of software products in the market are not cloud compatible. Reference [24] confirms the same. Reference [5] also indicates the same although it was chronological earlier.

Therefore, the question of 'how to make the existing products as near as ultimately cloud compatible' is the main topic of this chapter. The body of knowledge is too enormous. This chapter touches upon many areas at top level. It also skips a few, thinking it is not critical for a quick overview.

Although any existing software can be deployed as such without any modification to it, in infrastructure as a service (IaaS), such a deployed software cannot be considered as 'cloud SaaS'. It will not have automatically on its own all (or at least required) the characteristics, pointed out in Chapter 5, for cloud SaaS software.

Continuing to answer the main question raised, there are two options to make an existing product completely cloud compatible:

(i) Option 1 is to develop the software product again ground up by completely having an ideal cloud compatible architecture.
(ii) Option 2 is to retrofit the existing current version of the product to make it more cloud compatible. Reference [5] also indicates the same.

Option 1 is highly time consuming and also a costly approach. Business economics may not permit such an approach.

However, on examining the characteristics of cloud SaaS software, one can easily conclude that cloud characteristics stem from architecture (of software products) rather than from a functionality of the products. Therefore, for 'cloudifying' (meaning making closer to absolutely cloud compatible) an existing product altering its architecture is more appropriate. Thus, retrofitting an existing product to meet this objective is difficult. Option 1 of re-architecting seems inevitable.

As it is a costly and time-consuming exercise to re-architect, many of the software product vendors have not taken their products for making it cloud compatible.

As a domino effect, the same reason leaves a less number of cloud compatible products in the market. This in turn has resulted to invent mechanisms such as those described in Chapter 7 or 8 to provide cloud SaaS solutions with no or partially cloud compatible products.

However, service consumers need some solutions until the market gets cloud compatible SaaS products. Therefore, the customers need solutioning techniques such as those described in Chapter 7 or 8.

Such an action will help software vendors to provide a cloud SaaS solution using existing products. Hence that can give additional revenue from new emerging markets such as small- and medium-sized enterprises (SMEs) or 'long tail', which are possible to reach only because of cloud-based software services. That in turn will give both money and a good data point to know the potential market size of 'SME' or 'long tail'. Hence, product vendors can evaluate their product position on whether to invest for making their products fully cloud compatible or not.

Also during this time, gray-scale solutions may emerge between nothing or only re-architecting and redeveloping as an option. If some such option emerges, it may reduce the cost of re-architecting their products.

Some examples of gray-scale intermediary approaches are re-pack a non-compatible existing version of the software into cloud compatible product using techniques described in Chapter 7 or 8.

This chapter explains a Greenfield approach of starting from scratch, a ground-up approach to build a cloud compatible SaaS software product. Although it is little idealistic, the content of this chapter will provide an ideal architecture that any cloud compatible software must have. Engineering knowledge discussed in this chapter is useful even for architecting cloud SaaS solutions; also architects can use this knowledge to evaluate architectures of any software product for its suitability to provide cloud SaaS or include architecture as one of the criteria for cloud compatibility assessment of software products.

There are no major big differences between architecting solutions or products. But in architecting solutions, the differences are as follows:

(a) The major concentration is on integrating functional modules.
(b) Wherein the functional modules (SBBs) may be mostly be filled by products.
(c) Thus, product (SBB) selection is important aspect.
(d) There are very little custom code being developed (since most of the functionality is met by the products and their customization).
(e) Solution architects will have least control over the inside code of the constituent products; custom code being developed specifically for the solution will
   1. Either fill in those additional functionality not covered by any of the products – this is very rare situation, or
   2. Integrate various modules and products that constitute the solution.
(f) The major role for the solution architect is to find solution building blocks (SBBs) meeting architectural building blocks (ABBs) – meaning identifying appropriate products (SBBs) that will meet the functional requirements (ABBs).
(g) The focus on functional realization will be at broad top level unlike the fine granular-level focus on functional realization for product architects.
(h) Evolving solution architecture is much simpler in this sense.
(i) If the constituent products are more cloud compatible, architecting, subsequent realization and operations becomes much easier, less costly and hence can be competitively priced lower.

But on the other hand, product architecting involves a lot of critical decisions that may affect product architecture. Product team needs to pay a lot of attention to detail during product realization from its architecture. This chapter will explain these in detail, as much as it could.

9.2 Cloud SaaS Product Architecture Development Methodology

Architecture development methodology (ADM) is to put a process governing architecture development projects to get intended desired work products – the architecture of cloud SaaS product in this case.

TOGAF Version 9.1 ADM provides the umbrella process.

Adopting it and customizing it to suit product vendors' organizations must have been preceded at the beginning of this specific project.

Adopting it further to specific project is left to product stakeholders.

Chapter 2 discusses additional points and methods. Chapter 2 provides two types of special situations encountered in architecture development project:

(i) Where the probable customers are a large number of SMEs.
(ii) Agile architecting process is another situation where architecture needs to be developed while functional requirements are evolving; that demands architects to be more agile (rather than waiting for functional requirements to be fully collected and frozen before start of architecture development project).

Adopting the open group architecture framework (TOGAF) will give a set of architectural principles.

Adopting service-oriented architecture (SOA) RA and cloud computing reference architecture (CCRA) will give a few more architectural principles that will be useful for this class of projects also.

All relevant phases of TOGAF will be applicable to this class of architectural development projects also.

9.3 Drivers Influencing Architecture of Cloud SaaS Products

There are many factors that influence arriving at an appropriate architecture for a product:

(i) Most of them come from business decisions.
(ii) Some of them come from the target market segment to which the product is aimed at.
(iii) Key drivers come from the business model of providing cloud SaaS (which is briefly discussed in Chapter 1 but that is not adequate to know the intricacies of cloud business models).
(iv) Also, the functionalities of the software product aimed to offer.
(v) (For the purpose of this section, we highlight those that come from other sides.)
(vi) Cloud SaaS itself will bring a set of architecture-influencing drivers:

    (a) Scalable, multi-tenant efficient and customizable (explained elaborately in Chapter 5) are important parameters that differentiate between well-architected to poorly architected SaaS product.

        1. Multi-tenancy is a challenge to architect as it demands a paradigm shift in architecting. Chapter 6 explains this characteristic in detail.
        2. Customizing is a self-service for customers, and hence it should be easy to do without any programming effort for customers.

Notes: *As discussed in Chapter 5 and illustrated in Chapter 7, 'scalable' in cloud SaaS architecture refers to on-demand scaling design provision (especially by horizontal scaling) to accommodate more number of simultaneous users for a given implementation architecture. This is discussed in detail in Chapter 6 and some finer details are provided.*

(b) 'Long tail' – one possible market segment is a large number of small enterprises and also they may be small IT consumers. Their requirements are different and briefly covered in Chapter 1.

(c) A special class of 'long tail' is SMEs whose characteristics and the factors emanating from them for considering before architecture is discussed in Chapters 1, 2 and 7.

(d) Building a business model into a product is somewhat new for product development! And most of the hooks need to be provided in the architecture, and balance is nicely taken care if the architects chose to align with any of the CCRA. CCRA prescribes and will help architects in giving a list of aspects to be covered apart from giving a templatized architecture itself.

(e) Cloud compatibility is not zero-or-nothing proposition. Using a correct judgement of on what are all that parameters it should be more cloud compatible and what are all not important is project-/product-specific decision for architects.

(vii) Adapting the natural choice of SOA and CCRA will bring another set of influencers, which can be had from their respective Refs. [24, 26, 28]

(viii) Providing a robust 'operational model' that will provide SLAs both legally and financially viable is another influencing factor.

(ix) This book including the contents of this chapter focuses on providing information to architect cloud SaaS software. In enterprises, architects need to be more pragmatic such as consult infrastructure team on using either in-house private cloud or sometimes even utilizing public cloud.

All these factors influence the final architecture; these will also set various architectural principles that will guide subsequent realization steps of the architecture.

9.4 Characteristics Required for Cloud-SaaS-Products' Architecture

Characteristics required for a cloud SaaS product is described in Chapter 5. Chapter 5 also discusses the characteristics as 'requirement–solutions pair' and that provided realization of these characteristics as well. Here, we give architectural implications.

(i) Highly scalable: Highly modularized multi-tier architecture gives a natural room for auto-scaling as explained in Chapter 3.

(ii) Multi-tier architecture: Multi-tiered architecture that is a variation of three-tier architecture is preferred and

(a) This helps in achieving highly modularizing the functionalities that are provided to users.

(b) Such a model will help many of the SaaS users to select their needed functionality and
(c) Provider can track usage and bill only for the selected functionalities.
(d) Highly bundled function is difficult to split into fine granular level if customers demand to save their spend as explained in case study in Chapter 7.

(iii) N-tier or multi-tier architecture is also referred to as distributed architecture (since each tier and also constituent modules can be deployed on independent hardware servers on a distributed computing environment such as LAN or WAN).

(iv) All functionalities need to be exposed as a service in the functional layer of the SOA of the CCRA:

(a) Some of the functionalities may be consumed by the service providers or by service creators themselves.
(b) But those functionalities that the ultimate end-service consumer will use and pay for it is the purpose for which the product is being built. These set of functionalities can be collectively referred to as 'payload' (the 'load' that ultimately pays, and all other loads are dead loads and helps in making this one pay. The term 'pay load' is adopted from aeronautical industry – the passengers or cargo that brings revenue to the airline operators).
(c) (Currently, in the market some of the software vendors provide service APIs for the functionalities over the existing version of the product. Thus, it will give a look to consumers that the software is 'service oriented'. But that is not adequate for using this software to provide SaaS through cloud. One simple and obvious reason may be that a given software may not have inherent multi-tenancy).

(v) The functional layer is part of CCRA.

(vi) Customizable: As discussed in Chapter 5, writing a custom code is not the appropriate solution for cloud SaaS software as it is *single-instance multi-user* software. Instead, each customer's customization should be recorded as metadata to configure the way the software appear and behave for themselves.

Cloud SaaS product should have provision for end-user customization of each possible functionality of the solution.

(vii) Deployable on IaaS: the software product is recommended to be architected for deploying on IaaS.

(viii) With a strong emergence of mobile devices – such as mobile, smart phones or tablets, it is essential to consider architecting to address use of even mobile clients also. Designing data model as a service to enable mobile devices to access them is one of the examples; another one is the UI that needs to be amenable for mobile devices also. (See Refs. [31–33] for a little more details on functional requirements that come from mobile device use alone).

9.5 Selection of Basic Architecture for Cloud Compatible SaaS Product

Selection of Architecture Style

(i) Conventional two-tier architecture definitely would not meet the above epectations.

(ii) Its extension of Web-enabled a two-tier architecture also would not fit in for this purpose: The main reason is we are looking for 'single-instance serving multiple enterprises'. Hence, either option 1 mentioned above or any existing desktop-based or traditional client–server(two-tier) 'Web-enabled' application can never be made to run in a single logical instance (that too with metadata centric approach)[5].

(iii) Basic architecture will be a three-tier architecture; but that needs an appropriate modification to be adopted for cloud SaaS purposes as will be explained next.

(iv) As scalability and performance will be a major guiding factor, a multi-tiered architecture is ideally recommended.

(v) This will have an SOA approach as we are talking basically about providing SaaS where SOA is a natural choice.

(vi) The CCRA[24] discusses SOA-based approach in depth (see Chapter 10), and it is built over SOA reference architecture. Therefore, by adopting CCRA makes the product automatically SOA based.

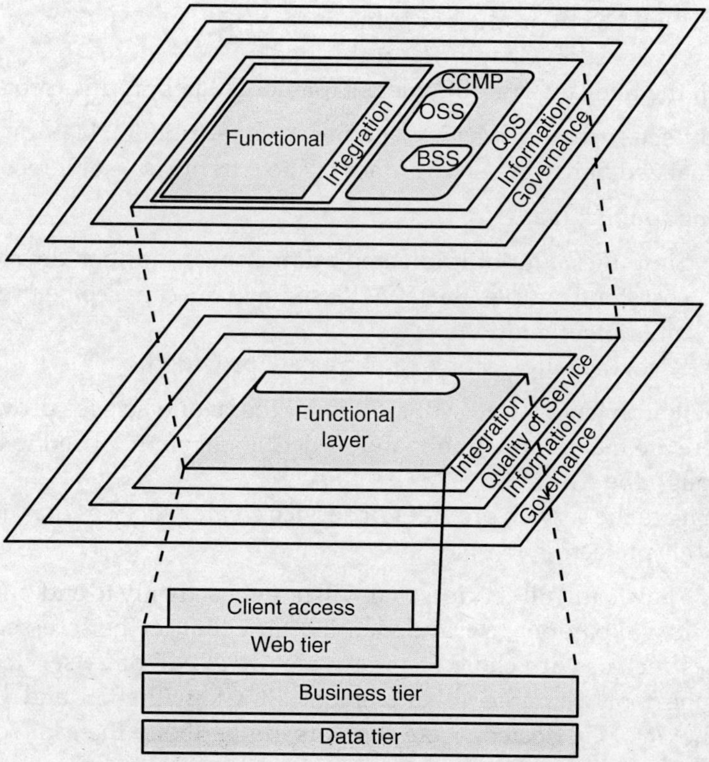

Figure 9.1 A multi-tiered service oriented (distributed) architecture-schematic

(vii) Therefore, the selected architectural style is service oriented at the top level; and at anatomy level, the software's architecture is multi-tiered distributed computing system. Figure 9.1 indicates the various relations here.

9.6 Starting Points for Architecting Projects

Development of architecture for cloud SaaS products requires knowledge from two important areas:

1. ADM (already covered in Section 9.2 of this chapter)
2. Technical engineering aspects

There are two starting points for technically starting the architecture development project:

1. CCRA
2. Functional requirements of cloud SaaS product that need to be developed

9.6.1 Starting from CCRA for SaaS

(i) CCRA provides a templatized SOA-based architecture that is complete in all respect to offer a cloud SaaS product or solution.

(ii) CCRA is reviewed in Chapter 10 of this book.

(iii) Select all the relevant building blocks for cloud SaaS product project. For example:

   (a) Architects need to decide whether to use (public) IaaS or an in-house un-virtualized hardware environment (The latter is not at all recommended.):

   Using (public) IaaS

   - Simplifies a lot of implementation issues, shortens development time and cost; for example, the CCMP used by IaaS can also be used for the product on implementation.
   - Also, the auto-scaling can be easily provided.

   (b) Whether to have PaaS or BPaaS from other cloud service providers or not

   (c) There are many more fine granular decisions too that need to be taken on going through the ABBs.

   (d) What are the service provider or service creator services that need to be retained for this project?

(iv) Identify ('pay load') all services that will be exposed only to end-customers for which customers will pay-per-use; and identify those that can be accessed only for internal purposes such as with cloud SaaS provider or CCMP or by service creators.

(v) Determine tools required to implement CCMP with BSS and OSS functionality; if (public) IaaS is selected, these will already be there; the same can be used while

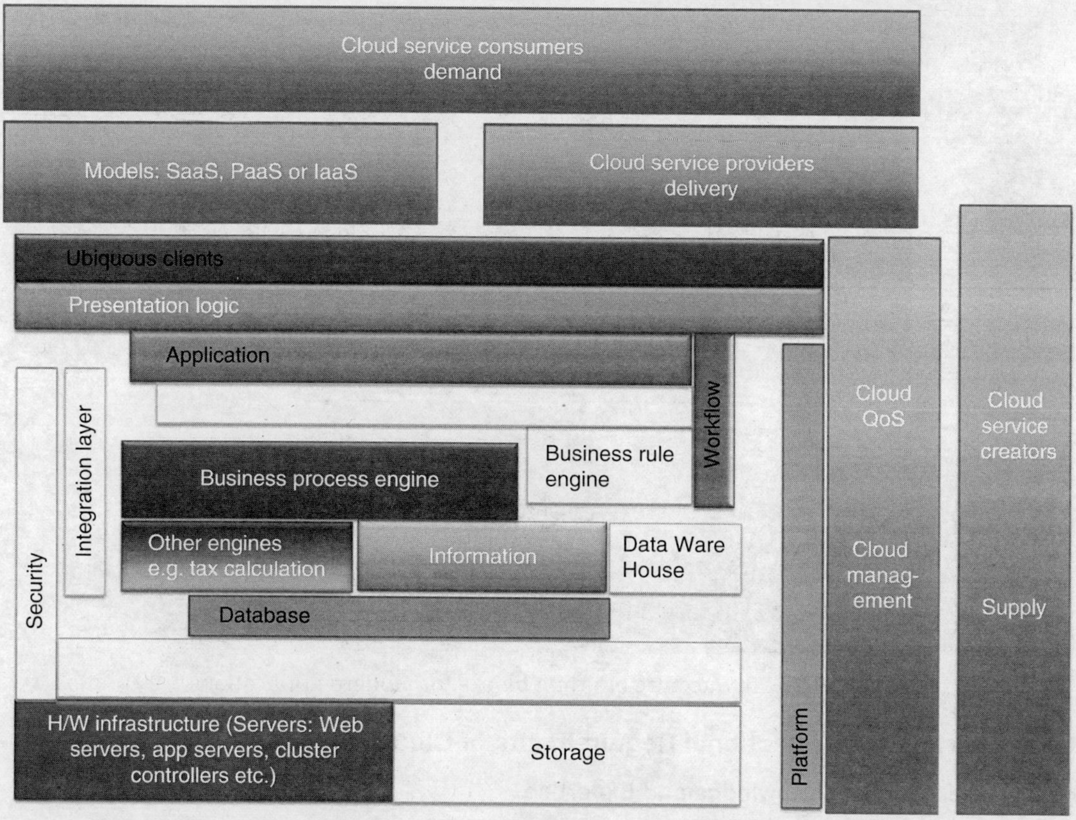

Source: Reproduced from Ref. [25]

Figure 9.2 Common building blocks of CCRA (a high leve abstraction)

providing this specific cloud SaaS too. This is also a recommendation of CCRA, and that lessens the burden on the architectural development project.

(vi) The common building blocks that are necessary to complete and launch a software product as a full-fledged SaaS in cloud can be obtained from CCRA: Figure 9.2[25] summarizes common building blocks at a very high level of abstraction from the published BIG three's (HP™, IBM™ and Microsoft™) CCRA.

Figure 9.3 gives a basic idea of major inevitable ABBs that are present in modern days software. Also the same figure shows the security layer as crosscutting 'concern' layer, which includes logging, authentication configuration, caching, etc.

(vii) Now architects need to locate SBBs meeting the selected ABBs of the finalized lists. Having now removed the worries about the paraphernalia that are required to launch a software product as cloud SaaS, let us dive into details of the main internal architecture of the product.

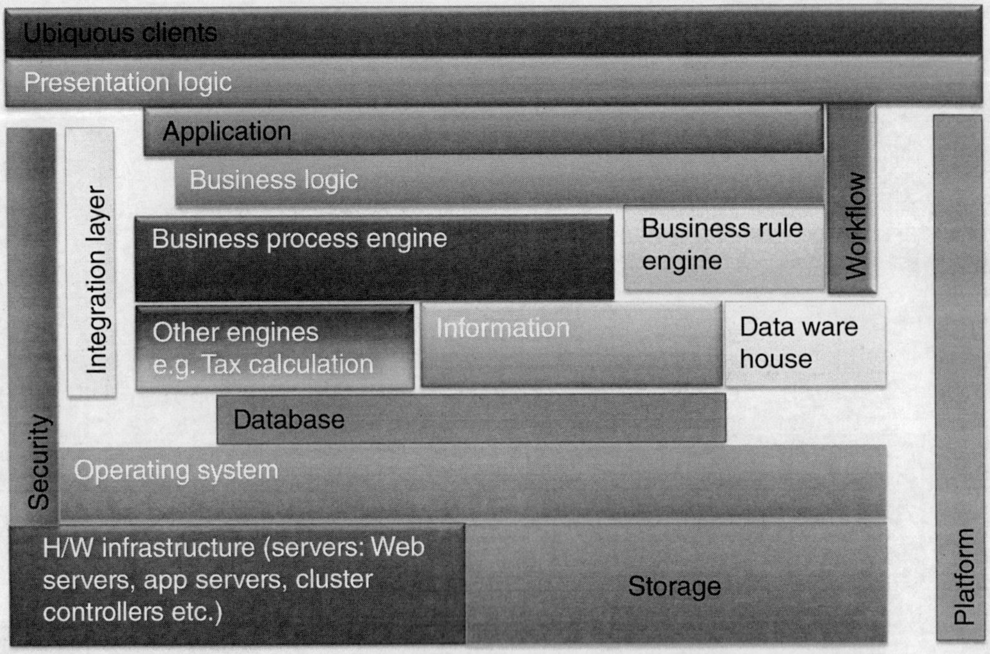

Figure 9.3 Architecture building blocks for modern applications

9.6.2 Starting from Functional Requirements of Cloud SaaS Product

9.6.2.1 Pre-Requisite Knowledge and Expertise

Architects will benefit from reviewing SOA reference architecture Ref. [TOGAF's SOA RA]. That knowledge and experience is essential for architecting cloud computing solutions including architecting cloud SaaS products.

CCRA document in Ref. [24] gives a complete list of TOGAF'S SOA RA documents that an architect can consult: also Ref. [14] will be of some good use to practical architects to gain insight into how to architect products using SOA and SOA RA. Reference [16] gives a good account of taking care of security inside the product. Some brief points are touched upon on security in Chapter 11.

Understanding how to make a software as 'server' is another essential knowledge, since most of the times cloud SaaS will function as a server either in a solution where this plays a part as component or even in standalone services.

Understanding to develop 'skinnable' applications is another subject area that needs to be mastered before getting into Web tier or user interface.

A thorough evaluation and in agreement with business stakeholders to finalize the business model of providing SaaS cloud services is a key step before starting this project.

The functionalities will be grouped in ABBs.

These will be provided as a service APIs for service consumers (both internal and external consumers). It will be prepared for getting listed in the service directory.

Decide on how crosscutting functionalities/services (such as security aspect) will interact with every payload services. Guidelines are already given in CCRA, and this is the time to nail them down. For example, identify all the hook points from where a payload service will start engaging a billing service to track the functionality use. This will be later used by billing services to charge the customer as per billing policy for the customer for this specific functionality/service.

Realizing ABBs

(i) The functionalities grouped into ABBs;
(ii) Map each ABB to SBB;
    (a) Identify actual SBBs that will be either any software product or 'engine' or
    (b) May be a custom module to be developed
    (c) Sometimes, one single ABB may map to more than one SBB or vice versa too.

Deciding on inter-tier communication

In a multi-tiered SOA, it is better to keep the inter-tier or even inter-module communication as services. These services need not be registered in service registry of the product that will typically be in CCMP layer. These are just service APIs.

That provides a loose coupling between modules and any module become easily replaceable.

Replacing a faulty software module with bug fixed one is a very common requirement in cloud SaaS providing situation. Hence, avoiding hard coding of interfaces between the tiers or even critical modules is desirable. Retrieve the interface address between layers from a lookup table. There are many more techniques but recognizing the problem situation is important.

Service API can not be decided unilaterally and blindly in all cases; for example huge volume of data can not be sent through service API.

Asynchronous or completely loose-coupled interface through message exchanging can be a last option: The size of data and the speed at which it needs to be exchanged through the interface will limit the use of this mechanism. References [10–12] will give some idea about this point.

Other options available are push or pull, synchronous communication, asynchronous communication and file drop.

9.7 Distributed Applications Architecture

9.7.1 Tier-Wise Specific Points Relevant to Architecture of Cloud SaaS

This section gives further finer points about 'hows (how it has to be) and whys (why it has to be)' of the internal architecture of the product.

(i) Functionality of SaaS product:

(a) It is better to identify as much fine-granular functions as possible; being identified as fine grained, later these can be combined to provide coarse-granular services or functions. As discussed in Chapter 7, customers will look for high flexibility to choose fine-granular functions to minimize cost.
(b) If it is a service-oriented approach, coarse-granular services can be formulated from fine-granular ones. Reference [13] will provide guidelines to formulate well-formed services from constituent fine-granular services.
(c) Collecting functionality for the entire domain is not new for product vendors; but collecting functional requirements for 'long tail' or SMEs – as discussed in Chapter 7 – provides new challenges.
(d) Designing every function, as much as possible, as end-user configurable is desirable.

(ii) Well-defined application layers: presentation, business, data access layers:

(a) Naturally develop application components in multiple tiers/layers.
(b) Presentation layer: this is conventional Web tier; but it can have a separate module to handle all possible clients; if there are any screen flow logic, then that must be separated out from tight coupling to screens presentation themselves. Appropriate workflow services can be employed even for navigating screen flows. Later, this can be easily extended by configurable plug-in for customizing screen navigation.
(c) For ubiquitous presentation – to ensure present the screens on any client – one needs a strategy to adapt 'universal' any (past or present or even future) clients. For some guidelines for handling conventional desktop clients with mobile devices, readers are referred to Refs. [31–33].
(d) User interface

1. All brand-specific information should be kept separate. They should be retrieved from metadata files that are in the path similar to organization/lang id/file type/filename.
2. On the landing page if multiple portlets are there, facility should be provided to enable/disable the portlets and rearrange the same.
3. Facility should be provided to have two or three themes of interface with respect to menu. It should be possible to have either a ribbon menu or a menu as a left-hand pane. This should be set at a customer level.
4. The entire user interface properties should be set through style sheets. No property should be hard coded. The style sheets can be selected specific to an organization/customer. The use of style sheet can facilitate customization of 'look and feel' of fonts, colour, adding customer logo, etc. These are also referred to as 'skin' of an application and software should be architected for 'skinnable'.

5. It should be possible for 'literals' to be modified for different customers. Ensure that the literals are available as a separate pack that can be modified for different customers/organizations.
6. Have information for controlling the control visibility outside the page. The information on the visibility and other visual attributes of all controls in a page can be kept in a database (DB) or property file specific to an organization/customer. The page rendering will use this info for displaying the right set of controls with the right attributes.
7. Have some additional controls available which is hidden. Based on the customer needs, this can be enabled to support for capturing/showing additional information. The enabling info is available in the DB/property file specific to a customer.
8. UI services also need to be developed to support mobile devices such as smart phone's or tablets; this means all needed UI functionalities also need to be provided as 'services' to facilitate these devices could consume them.

(iii) Business layer: high modularization is advised.

(a) Internal workflow within the software has to be segregated from customer workflows; business processes need to be separated out from the remaining workflows.

(b) Screen flow logic also needs to be segregated from screen logic; it is worth considering implement the screen flow through platform-based workflow module (such as in .Net).

(c) Reference [10] explains design principles on how to segregate workflows from business processes; this segregation will allow some customization of business processes to individual customers' need.

Certain work flows such as approval workflows can be customized without affecting main business process; even if the workflow needs to be modified for customization of business rules (as discussed below), this approach, of taking platform-based workflow (as in .Net) or workflows within software products, will be useful. Every product such as e-commerce or enterprise content management (ECM) software come with internal workflow module to design and carryout work flows specific to them that need to run internal to their products such as shopping cart to cash point exit in ecom. Such workflows can be left to those internal to those products rather than being brought to main business processes.

(d) Business rules need to be separated from the application business logic to facilitate each customer to customize as many business rules as permitted. Thinking of employing a business rules engine is advisable. (But it is desirable that the rules-engine is also a cloud compatible product.) Customization of business rules left as self-help by customers can also be facilitated through this approach.

(e) Program flow control logic should be separated from program or business logic. Consider implementing the program flow control also through platform-based workflow modules (such as in .Net).

(f) Also, separate validation logic from main business logic.

(g) Business process engine: (employing commercially available multi-tenanted BPM product is more advisable). As per CCRA's recommendation, these need to have been exposed as service in process layer of functional layer of the CCRA. Process services can be consumed both by the internal of the product software and also by the customer (cloud SaaS service consumer). But there is no need for employing two different products – one for workflow and the other for BPM.

- Customers will heavily customize the business processes while initially setting up use of cloud SaaS and also later. For example, one subscribing customer would like their sales personnel to get his/her sales managers approval before confirming an order, whereas another subscribing organization would like their sales personal to confirm an order without such procedure but get approval from stocks manager to ensure that the order can be full filled.

(h) Integration server: the role of integration server is to integrate all the components in this layer and also those including the third-party tools that may be used. This component is not common in earlier architectures.

(i) Communication server: it has become common to provide many communication provisions with customers – email is one obvious example; fax has not yet died; also business processes are communication enabled with audio–video-text kind of software and SMS think these functional blocks as a part of architecture is advisable. An extreme example is illustrated in Figure 9.4 where a complete *unified communication* module is presented.

(j) Business logic: Extension requirements to solutions need not be cosmetic alone. There will be various situations where certain additional validations need to be added to the business logic or other requirements such as doing additional postings on successful completion of a particular transaction. Hence, have callouts on different transactions to support these types of specific changes, have specific callouts at end of transaction for terminal actions of each page such as 'save document', etc.

(k) Wherever business functionality is required to be configurable, go for engines. For example, have a tax engine to handle tax or pricing engine for pricing purposes.

(l) Business tier should be designed as a 'server'.

(iv) Data tier: There can be three different modules or sub-tiers or better called as components under data tier.

(a) Data access objects (DAOs)

(b) Relational database management system: DB

(c) Data storage

1. Encapsulate access to DB, and this is a general technique.
2. Cash data on server and/or client for improved performance.

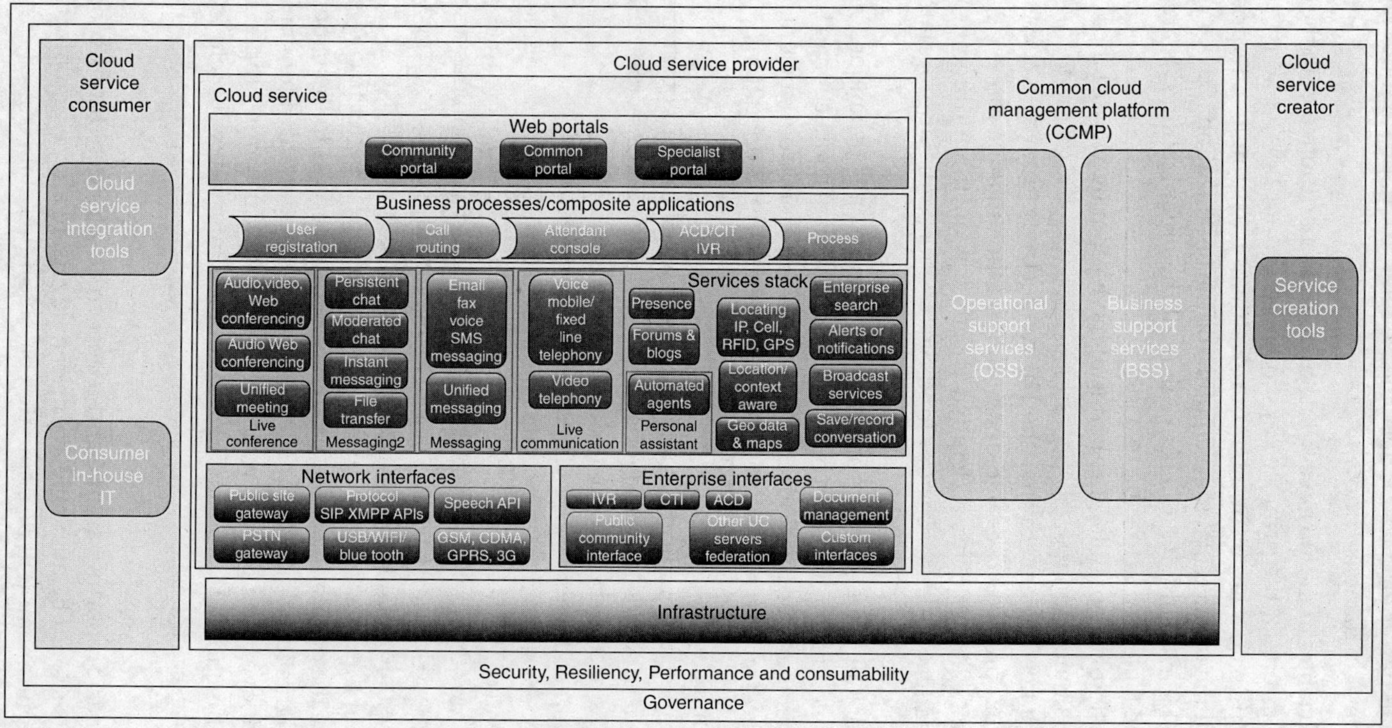

Figure 9.4 Unified communication

3. For DB design or data models, please refer to Chapter 5 for details.
4. DB design: database implementation
    - All tables in the DB have to be horizontally partitioned with the organization id as one of the primary keys. (One reason for horizontal partitioning is to anticipate a larger number of rows than usual single-enterprise solutions.) All the tables will have a column for the organization ID.
    - All joins will have to ensure that all the organization IDs are same for all the tables participating in a join.
    - Wherever possible, it is better to have separate DB instances for different customers groups.
    - We need to ensure that the DB connectivity from app server is obtained from property files/DB depending on the organization.
    - See Chapter 5 for a detailed discussion on three different data models that can be choosen for cloud SaaS. Choose the appropriate one for the product.
    - For all data access operations, employ all techniques to maximize concurrency – This can be optimal utilization of connection to DB (as pooling them and 'acquire or release' connections from pool), or unless absolutely necessary do not lock record in DBs such as read operations.

(v) Closed architecture
'Closed architecture' indicates that modules in a tier can call other modules in the same tiers or modules in one layer above or below; but cress-cross calling jumping across layers need to be completely avoided.

(vi) Loosely coupled layers
The inter-layer calls and inter-module calls should be highly loose coupled or precisely service oriented. This helps in on-the-fly replacement of defective modules with corrected ones (there are other methods available to replace defective module as discussed later in this chapter and also see Chapter 5), also to implement security as 'aspect'.

(vii) Incorporate failover and redundancy for disaster recovery (DR).

(viii) Wrapping of third-party products and components: It is better to choose third-party tools where the development team can have a direct access to their source codes and can have rights to modify them. Tucking them as proper SBB and wrapping it in the designated layer with custom wrapper is advised. Custom wrapper and accessing products' functionalities through loose-coupled interface will help in replacing or maintenance situations.

(ix) Reports

(a) Use a basic reporting engine and report creator for generating reports.
(b) Reports should be available at different levels, to all the organizations.
(c) The report menu will be populated based on this mapping.

(d) Considering specialized products for report generation is also good, if the customer expectation is high. Expecting a multi-tenanted product will limit the choice of available reporting product to choose from since not many are multi-tenanted. Most of SMEs customers or customers from 'long tail' may also demand two extreme expectation on customization of reports, which has a lot of practical limitation to architect or implement. DB also should permit enough customization (as discussed in Chapter 5) to support certain type of reports requested.

(e) Architects need to identify through evaluation process cloud compatible scalable reporting engine.

9.7.2 Architecting to Scale the Application

Scaling is possible in two ways: one is known as 'scaling vertically' and another is known as 'scaling horizontally' (see Chapters 3 and 4 for some detailed discussions on scaling).

Scaling vertically refers to have more processing power such as higher speed processor (CPUs) or adding more processors to the same server; in addition or alone adding more main memory. Essentially, this means going for higher performing hardware. This is also referred in literatures[5] as 'scaling up'.

Scaling horizontally is adding more servers of same processor speed and memory; these hardware work in a cluster under a load balancer; and in these additional servers, additional components of software will function in parallel. This is also referred to as 'scaling out'. Scaling out can be achieved through on-demand provisioning of additional servers as explained in Chapter 3.

In cloud SaaS software, scaling horizontally (scaling out) is what is mostly preferred as discussed in Chapter 4. Cloud SaaS software should scale out (horizontally) with a priori (arbitrary) number of servers; each of the servers have one or more instance of the application or its components to accommodate any arbitrary number of users.

Apart from architecting the SaaS application as highly modularized and tiered to allow scaling of each of these independently, as discussed in Chapter 4, the internals of the application need to be specifically designed and implemented with some more of the following points, in addition to other points discussed earlier in this chapter. A detailed discussion of these topics need a separate book.

The following provides some finer details that can be used in the software design:

i. In a horizontal scaling (or scale out) means, many instances of the same software are luckily to run in the operations. To take advantage of this, the product should be in a position to move around transactions to any available instance. This can occur many a times even during a single transaction. Transactions should be totally unaware of the fact that it is being moved around to various instances. A software behaving in this fashion is said to be 'statelessness.'

ii. To achieve a software to function in a 'stateless' fashion, many more aspect has to be taken care of. One of them is to store user data on client side so that any instance can access it and use it rather than storing it on server side (in Web tier).

iii. In case 'state' is stored in the Web layer, it is better to go for affinity-based access. Do not store session info in the app server.

iv. Technique of 'pool'ing has to be adopted both for optimizing computing resources and also collect metrics on their usage for resources such as DB connections, threads or even network connections.

v. A common age-old technique of handling I/O asynchronously will help in freeing resources for useful work till the slow I/O operation is complete.

vi. It should be possible to add new access elements specific to customer for supporting access authorization specific to an organization or customer. Details are discussed in a separate section below named 'identity and access management (IAM)'.

vii. For horizontal scaling, the tier/component model expressed in earlier chapters is a key consideration.

(x) Architecting for maintenance

Maintainability is one of the key attributes for this architecture:

(a) Most of the cloud SaaS offering is 24 × 7 in use.
(b) Single instance is used by multiple customers.
(c) Many things including customization are left to self-service of users/customers.
(d) Any one customer may bring down the system, or any one of the components such as DB may bring down the whole system due to 'illegal operations'.

Hence, the system is highly vulnerable for going down.

(e) System cannot be stopped for maintenance or upgrades or for applying patches, but they are inevitable operations.

1. Normally, a redundant site is used for upgrading and regular maintenance; at one time when the upgrades are ready, the Web server will point out the new server in a blink of moment.
2. High modularization and multi-tiered approach will give flexibility to upgrade at individual component level.
3. There are specific discussion about DB design and recovery in multi-tenant situation elsewhere in this book.

(f) Designing DB for roll-back or recovery, especially when a single customer has crashed the DB, is an important aspect. Some of them are touched upon in Section 5.7.

(g) Fault isolation is another important aspect in the architecture design: fault of one customer should not bring down or crash the entire cloud SaaS software.

If a fault occurs because of one customer, then that customer should be isolated and can terminate the specific customer.

(h) An enterprise-scale architecture needs to include DR plan as well as business continuity plan in the overall design. As the concepts for these are simple extrapolation of what is being currently practised for non-cloud solutions. However, these are specialized area, and it is not covered here.

9.7.3 Service Orientation of Entire Product Architecture

The entire cloud SaaS product architecture is SOA. Chapter 10 discusses this point a little more elaborately using cloud reference architecture.

Providing only service APIs for non-SOA products cannot be counted as 'service-oriented architecture' as discussed in Chapter 6.

Figure 9.1 is a unique contribution of this book, which clearly explains the integration of service-oriented + multilayered + distributed architecture that is essential for cloud SaaS software.

Having said the same, this book will not introduce SOA or attempt to go into any detail of SOA. References [14–16] will help a lot.

Important points on service orientations that are essential for cloud SaaS software are highlighted below:

Inter-module or inter-tier communication will be strictly service oriented and not conventional tight coupled. If a very loose coupling is desired, then message oriented-service interface can be thought of as design option. Queuing techniques need to be incorporated to architecture as queuing is inevitable for handling messages.

A large volume of data cannot be sent through service interfaces. This is one of the restrictions of service interfaces. Therefore, other methods need to be exploited.

Use of appropriate service protocols either SOAP or REST depends on the nature of the interface whether the communication across the interface be asynchronous or synchronous, respectively.

Obviously, all these services are not relevant for end–users, and hence these will not be exposed to end-users.

Service orientation has another weakness of security. Reference [16] gives a detailed method to secure service interfaces and access even at module level.

9.8 Identity and Access Management

Most of the products in the market give two options for system integrators who will make a solution using the product:

(i) Access enterprise IAM and provide a role-based authentication.

(ii) Inside the product have features to set role-based authorization; it can sync up with enterprise IAM for user management.

Such an approach is not suitable in a multi-tenanted environment; many of the popular ECM products, in the market, have these kinds of facilities, which is a huge limitation while architecting cloud solutions using these products.

Ideally, a product dynamically, on-the-fly should be in a position to get authorization and authentication for every logged-in user before entering into every function or service of the product.

Therefore, IAM can be a separate module; it can be made to work with customer's enterprise IAM too.

One is user identity and the other is role-based authorization for feature access. In many cloud SaaS service consumption, customers also desire to define their own roles and assign access rights to various SaaS features – which makes implementation more complex. Sometimes, business rules also may control access to features.

For a further discussion on this topic, readers should refer to Refs. [5, 16]

IAM is the main entry point for any user to get in to consume the services offered. Thus, IAM, being the main entry gateway in, can be connected to rest of the solution through a 'trusted mode'.

A connection between two servers are said to be trusted on fulfilling conditions such as the following (see Figure 9.5):

(iii) The product assumes that any call that comes from IAM can always be trusted.

(iv) Both IAM server and the product servers are under a fire wall, and hence no intrusion is possible.

(v) IAM can provide a token on authorization and a separate one for authentication. This token is carried into the product, and the product uses this for verification before entertaining the requested service at any level and every time. (Token based is one of the many possible approaches).

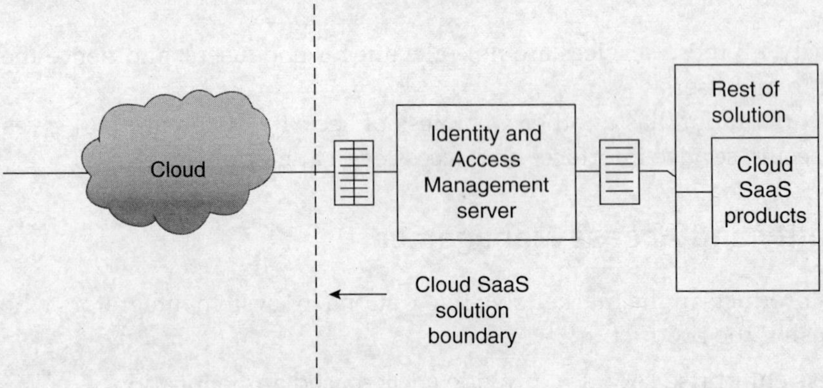

Figure 9.5 IAM and cloud SaaS product are connectedly 'trusted mode'

9.9 Transaction-less vs Transaction-intensive Products

The subject product for which architecture needs to be developed grossly influences the intricacies and difficulties of developing an architecture for it. These difficulties are at gross levels of the nature of the product.
This book classifies products, for this purpose, into two categories:

1. Transaction-less software product
2. Transaction-intensive software product

ECM software such as Alfresco is considered transaction-less software. The term 'transaction-less' need to be understood as 'transaction nil'. An ECM software stores or retrieves a file for the user.

(Contrast this with a banking software that allows a user to transfer the money from one account to another. Such a transaction needs double commits, and there is a *unit of action* and a facility for roll back. A relational DB software is another extreme example for transaction-intensive software).

The experience gained thus far indicates architecting a multi-tenanted product of transaction-less product is several orders easier than the other one.

9.10 Efficient Multi-tenancy

There is no universally accepted measure for 'efficiency' of multi-tenancy. The simplest guiding factor is how many of users can be served by the cloud SaaS in a unit hardware infrastructure.

This is a relative measure rather than an absolute one. This means comparing two situations for same hardware configuration:

1. One cloud SaaS solution can serve 50 users.
2. Another cloud SaaS solution can serve 100 users.

The second one is more efficient compared with the first. Such a measure is not practical because there can be no two solutions having the same deployment (unit) architecture.

Therefore, the basic question of efficiency is how many more users can be packed into a given set of deployment architecture and infrastructure software.

As discussed in Chapters 4 and 7, each module will require different hardware configuration; also, each module will inherently differ in packing maximum number of users per unit hardware instance. Hence, continuously finding ways to improve the number of users at module level is inevitable point in cloud SaaS architecting exercise.

9.11 Infrastructure Softwares' Architectures for SaaS Solutions

A cloud SaaS product relies on several infrastructure software during runtime. Some obvious ones are operating system, application servers, middlewares and DB software.

If these are also multi-tenanted, then it is an ideal situation. As of now, not many in the stack are available in the multi-tenanted form. The most critical of these is relational DB; thank God, we now have both COTS and open-source cloud-ready RDBMS, and these are in use for a year or more now.

If the subject of software product, say an app server or RDBMS, needs to be made cloud compatible, then the problem is much more complex. All the knowledge mentioned here are required and much more too; nevertheless, that will be a delightful project to be in.

The main reason for these need to be multi-tenanted are economy of scaling, efficient resource utilization by sharing and hence metering for pay-per-use for every user. Right now, such platforms are emerging.

Review of some of even publically available product architectures will be of high use to architects who take on cloud SaaS product architecture assignment:

(i) High availability architecture of Oracle WebLogic
(ii) The open-source and ECM software Alfresco
(iii) Multi-tenanted RDBMS architecture
(iv) Discussions on architecture of multi-tenanted middleware

9.12 Deployment Architecture Basics for Cloud SaaS Products

Multi-tiered distributed service-oriented cloud compatible CCRA-based cloud SaaS product provides a natural deployment architecture. It is highly scalable architecture. (Compare discussions in Chapters 4 and 7)

(i) Each tier can be on a single hardware server.
(ii) Major components or modules also can be on individual servers.
(iii) CCMP in CCRA provides a lot other components each of which also can go on individual servers.
(iv) The configuration of each server would have been calculated as per packing efficiency of multiple tenants in a minimum given configuration for each module/tier/product/engines. For further details on this aspect, refer to Chapters 4 and 7.
(v) The remaining steps will be exactly like the one mentioned in Chapter 7 for auto-scaling and auto-provisioning.
(vi) It is recommended to choose IaaS as the deployment environment.
(vii) Public IaaS provides a lot of OSS and BSS facilities that are required for providing cloud SaaS.

9.13 Future Direction

On software product vendors coming up with cloud compatible software products, it opens a lot of market opportunities for them: Unfortunately on the other hand, if the vendors could get completely cloud compatible software products, they will tend to offer more the product as cloud SaaS services or solutions rather than offering them as software product.

The interesting new possibility is to offer them as cloud SaaS or its functionalities as cloud services. (This can be in addition to selling them as a product itself in a conventional way in conventional or any market). This may open out a set of new market and revenue for the product vendors.

In this new possibility, system integrators, architecting cloud SaaS solutions, will face new challenges. The bunch of functionalities (provided by the product) is then available as cloud services or cloud SaaS and not as a product. Integrating these into an overall (cloud SaaS) solution is the key technical concern and the challenge is securing. Also, integration is taking cloud services and not necessarily taking products. Architecting solutions all involving cloud services is different in nature and not covered in this book in this edition.

9.14 Summary

- This chapter gives a lot of technical points for architecting absolutely cloud compatible software products.
- The starting point is CCRA.
- It recommends the product need to have SOA.
- The product will have highly scalable multi-tiered distributed architecture.
- For each of the tiers – Web tier, business tier and data tier, this chapter gives a lot of points that need to be taken into consideration while designing those tiers.
- It gives reasonable explanations how cloud SaaS characteristics such as customizing and multi-tenancy, scaling, etc., need to be implemented while architecting the product.
- Certain clues on architecting for maintainability are provided.
- It also provides some connecting explanations on infrastructure architecture, connecting IAM while solutioning are touched upon.

Chapter 10

Cloud Computing Reference Architecture

10.1 Introduction

Cloud computing reference architecture (CCRA) gives a templated architecture to architect any cloud computing solutions. This chapter will bring its relevance for architecting for cloud software as a service (SaaS) products or solutions.

The knowledge of CCRA can be essential for architecting for cloud SaaS products or solutions, and the same is discussed in Chapters 7 through 9. In addition, the CCRA discussed in this chapter can be the basis for solution architectures discussed in Chapters 7 and 8. Chapter 9 elaborately points out how RA becomes the starting point for architecting a cloud SaaS product.

Chapter 2 also discusses architecting method using CCRA.

In general, reference architecture (RA) brings 'best practices' of architecting from various architecting projects experience. In other words, RA is matured architecture in that domain or area. Since it is born out of experience, it is also error free and tested in practical projects. Therefore, instead starting an architecture project from scratch, it is better to start from RA, if one such is available.

In cloud computing, the industry has not yet come out with single regularized RA. A few are floating around; the CCRA taken here for discussion is the one proposed by IBM™ to The Open Group Architecture Forum (TOGAF). Neither TOGAF has expressed that this proposal is not accepted nor TOGAF has confirmed that this draft is under consideration at the time of writing this book.

This CCRA is very generic trying to address architectural needs of various types of cloud computing services such as PaaS, BPaaS, infrastructure as a service (IaaS) and also SaaS. We will focus only those relevant to cloud SaaS. Readers are encouraged to read Ref. [44] for complete treatment of it.

10.1.1 Review Bias

Reference [24] is reviewed with certain limitations or bias while reviewing the CCRA information given in the document that is available in the public domain. The review has kept some narrow objective, and it is biased towards the same. The aspects are explained as a caution to the readers not to expect a full review of Ref. [24].

Readers should bear the following points in mind, whereas reading the remaining part of this chapter that is attempting a quick short review of the CCRA:

(i) Reference [24] is the reference material used for the review; Ref. [24] itself is based on an overview of the CCRA, and it is not a complete elaborate specification.

(ii) This also indicates that there are a few more such industry-proposed RAs for cloud computing, which is not covered here; readers are encouraged to read and benefit from them too.

(iii) The review here is to comprehend at the top level necessary for the purpose of the book rather than going into details on what are all relevant or not for any CCRA.

(iv) The purpose of the book is to show 'how to architect cloud SaaS software'; hence, details that are necessary for other cloud services (such as those that are not highlighted or reviewed here).

(v) Even within the original proposed CCRA taken for review in this chapter, only those concepts and points that are pertinent and relevant for cloud SaaS is selectively reviewed, and others related to IaaS or PaaS or BPaaS are omitted.

(vi) Only those major components of CCRA and those relevant to cloud SaaS are relatively discussed in detail, and all others are omitted.

(vii) The objective is to help architects use the relevant architectural building blocks (ABBs) and layers from this CCRA into architecting solutions and products. The objective is to give architects a quick, minimum, but essential needed for cloud SaaS solution architecting.

(viii) Although this material can be studied on a standalone mode, the book has kept its relevance to the discussions in Chapter 9, and a few other chapters.

Hence, it will look like distorted for readers who are expecting any generic treatment. Readers are encouraged to refer to Ref. [24] for as-is presentation.

At the end of this chapter, readers can also find a review of comparison of three RAs from IBM™, Microsoft™ and HP™[25].

For an understanding on of what RA is and how to create one from scratch or a domain and what are similar such RAs that exist in other areas, readers can refer to Ref. [23]. Although this reference book is more on master data management, a novice architect can learn a lot about fundamental terms in architecture such as what is software architecture 'blueprint' and how does it differ from a 'reference architecture'.

This book does not intend to recommend any particular CCRA as a de facto benchmark. For each project, the respective architecting team needs to evaluate and select one suitable for their purpose.

For those who are hearing for the first time the phrase 'reference architecture (RA)', the description in the following paragraph will help in understanding the same.

No architect needs to start his or her work from scratch. As TOGAF's enterprise continuum points out any solution architecture does not exist in isolation; it is part of the continuum of architectures[30]. This philosophy reinforces that one does not need to develop an architecture from scratch; this is very much applicable to architecture development of any cloud SaaS architecture development projects including those explained in Chapters 7 through 9.

For any architecting project, the technical starting point is an RA. The architect takes, modifies, and customizes the RA and realizes a solution as per requirements of a specific project on his or her hand.

10.1.2 What Does CCRA Bring to Table for Solution Architects?

As it is true for any RA, CCRA also

(i) It brings a set of best practices from practical experience of implementing many cloud solutions.

(ii) It provides how a set of pre-meditated architectural decisions common to cloud computing are realized in the best optimal way.

(iii) Using CCRA gives a common and consistent architecture for all SaaS-related projects within an enterprise.

(iv) Such a consistency helps better quality and lowers the cost of realization.

(v) CCRA is independent of any implementation technologies.

(vi) It is also independent of deployment or delivery models such as private or public or community or hybrid clouds[24]. (Also see Ref. [24] for the explanations of 'private' or 'public' or 'community' or 'hybrid' clouds). Thus, its applicability and use cover a vast area of requirements.

(vii) CCRA better be used as a starting point for architecting for a class of all cloud computing projects including SaaS solutions and products.

(viii) It is intended to be used as a guide or blueprint for cloud SaaS implementation that may be driven by specific functional and non-functional requirements applicable to specific project.

(ix) However, CCRA by itself is not a fine granular deployment ready architecture for any single-cloud implementation.

(x) Architecture overview diagram (AOD) of CCRA gives fundamental ABBs that are making up the CCRA.

(xi) It also provides a set of fundamental architectural principles that are fundamental to deliver and manage cloud SaaS services.

(xii) It provides basic relationships among ABBs that constitute CCRA.

(xiii) It provides principles to integrate with other enterprises systems as well to enterprise architecture.

(xiv) Architectural principles that are defined as a part of CCRA need to be followed on all implementation stages such as architecture, design and deployment.

(xv) CCRA describes functional capabilities of constituent ABBs, user role and their corresponding interactions among themselves.

(xvi) CCRA provides a complete list of all ABBs that are required for any cloud computing projects including SaaS solutions and products; for example, cloud computing management platform (CCMP) identifies all business support systems (BSS) and operation support systems (OSS) that are required to run a cloud SaaS.

As this book follows TOGAF, this chapter will review the draft CCRA that IBM™ submitted to TOGAF and under consideration by TOGAF.

10.2 Cloud Computing Architectures Are Service-Oriented Architectures

10.2.1 Important Aspects of Cloud (SaaS) Services

(i) In cloud SaaS, one tries to provide SaaS; and this service is consumed by customers.

Many software vendors have exposed their functionalities as service. Providing software functionalities as a service is not new to industry, and it has been happening even before the cloud 'arrived'.

When providing and consuming of software (functionalities) is in the form of service, it is better the cloud SaaS software architecture reflect this – say the architecture style should be service oriented.

So service is the fundamental nature there and that implies and indicates to look into its relationship with service-oriented architecture (SOA).

Cloud SaaS architectures are basically service oriented.

There exists a fundamental relationship between SOA and cloud at architectural level, solution and service levels[24].

(ii) Next important aspect in cloud SaaS solutions is that any cloud SaaS service model includes cloud IaaS. The cloud SaaS software is deployed over IaaS rather than conventional deployment architectures (see Chapters 3 and 4 for the difference between conventional and IaaS-based deployment architecture).

A typical cloud SaaS solution provider may not offer IaaS as an independent service; for example, Salesforce.com™ offers only SaaS; but their underlying IaaS is not yet offered as a service to the customer. But their SaaS is inferred to be definitely deployed over IaaS.

(iii) Next important aspect of cloud SaaS solution is that they could be deployed in any one of the following four models:

1. *Public*: when the cloud (SaaS) solution exists across organizational boundaries
2. *Private*: when the cloud (SaaS) solution exists strictly within the organizational boundaries

or

3. *Hybrid*: a combination of the above two
4. *Community*: is like public but only to a set of authorized organizations

These deployment models define (or dictate) specific scope of cloud architecture and solution.

For example, in hybrid model, there is a need for integrating systems across enterprise boundaries to the cloud service.

For example, if an enterprise has deployed a solution on the cloud that will mull the data that are available in public domain, such as social media, and sends the resultant analysis (analytics) to enterprise, now the results have to cut in the conventional enterprise firewalls and deliver to the needed enterprise system. The data in public domain could be some opinion about the product or services offered by the enterprise; in addition, since the data are already in public domain, getting them inside enterprise is waste of enterprises information technology (IT) resources (storage, compute, people to manage, etc.). Also there is no secret about the data since it is already in public domain; but the processed results such as how many people have liked a particular product is definitely confidential to the enterprise.

This is something like business-to-business (B2B) integration requirement model. SOA has the ability of interfacing disparate systems across enterprise boundaries. SOA solutions for integrating systems across enterprise boundaries have been available even before the cloud 'arrived'.

Similarly, SOA solutions have been in existence for most of the aforementioned models even before the cloud.

But in cloud computing, these functionalities and requirements (coming out of the four models) take prominence, and they are no longer optional. Hence, the existing SOA solutions get exemplar across these models requirements and become specific ABBs in RA of cloud computing.

(iv) A few essential characteristics of cloud computing are as follows:
  (a) On-demand self-service
  (b) Rapid elasticity
  (c) Measured services
  (d) Resource pooling
  (e) Broad network access

(See Chapter 1 for discussions on some of these).

Again, as found in the four deployment models, these characteristics are also optional for SOA in many enterprise solutions, but they become essential and mandatory for every cloud (SaaS) solutions.

In cloud computing, industry is trying to regularize these requirements. Hence, cloud architecture requires a special set of capabilities to meet these requirements; and also cloud architecture specifies corresponding ABBs to meet these essential requirements that are otherwise optional in SOA.

(v) In addition to the above, some more functions that were optional in SOA solutions become essential for every cloud (SaaS) solution.

Some examples are:

  (a) Security across enterprises boundaries and
  (b) Service management automation

Security across business boundaries is related to access to the cloud (SaaS) services from enterprises systems cutting across the enterprise firewalls. The security is essential for safe transaction of data between these two. This is very much normal in the hybrid cloud model as discussed earlier. Achieving secured connection is a mandatory requirement for cloud computing.

Service management means, as explained earlier, special services that are inevitable for cloud (SaaS) services such as BSS (billing the usage) and OSS (roll back of data).

10.2.2 Cloud Reference Architecture Derives Experience from SOA in Addressing these Aspects

Cloud RA will address these requirements as default for all cloud services solutions.

In all the above five classes of requirements identified, it becomes clear that those requirements that were optional in most of SOA-based solutions, it becomes inevitable and essential fundamental requirements in all cloud (SaaS) solutions.

Also in those SOA projects, service-based solutions have been developed but not idealized across industry, and hence across projects.

It also gives an idea that if one takes SOA RA and incorporates solutions to these requirements; probably, it can stand up for cloud computing (SaaS) solutions RA.

Cloud RA is going to derive its experience from those SOA-based architectures in providing solutions to these otherwise special requirements for SOA architectures.

It is better to look into SOA RA and apply all these essentials for cloud computing and thus derive the requisite architecture for cloud (SaaS) computing solutions.

In accordance to this, the open groups (TOGAF) SOA RA[27] have been provided appropriate hooks for cloud computing architecture:

(i) It has a domain architecture scope to service delivery and management principles.
(ii) Architectural principles and decisions are laid out to enable cloud computing architecture.
(iii) ABBs have also been identified for operational and business support.
(iv) Cloud service providers may provide well-defined and maybe even regularized management and security support and services.
(v) In addition, services that are specifically necessary for cloud computing have also been identified.
(vi) Since it is SOA-based service offerings from cloud, service consumers can easily adopt. The design and implementation for adopting or consuming services is also provided in SOA RA.

Therefore, it looks like that cloud only takes the experience gained from SOA to next higher levels.

10.3 A Quick Summary of the SOA RA

Figure 10.1 provides a visual idea of SOA RA as given in TOGAF[27]. It has five main functional concerns:

(i) Operational systems
(ii) Service components

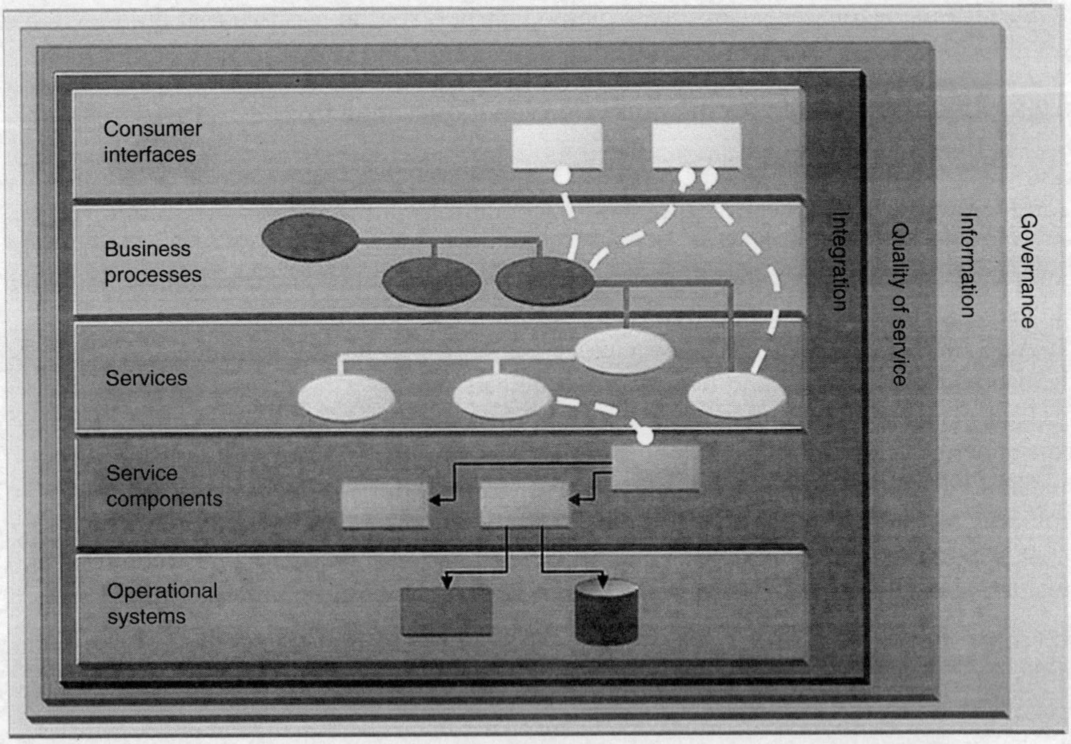

Figure 10.1 RA of 'Service Oriented Architecture'-SOA RA(TOGAF)[27]

(iii) Services
(iv) Business processes
(v) Consumer interface

In addition to the aforementioned layers, there are four 'cross-cutting' layers in SOA RA; contrast the term used for these layers as 'cross cutting' against the four layers discussed so far referred to as 'functional' layers.

The cross-cutting layers are marked on the sides of the SOA RA diagram; these are governance, information, quality of service (QoS) and integration layers.

These are referred to as 'cross cutting' since services in these layers are required for all the services exposed in the five 'functional' layers (as operational, service, business process and consumer layers).

Four cross-cutting concerns are as follows:

(a) Governance
(b) Information
(c) Quality of service (QoS)
(d) Integration

References [14, 15] provide a detailed discussion about enterprise SOA. Reference [16] provides detailed information about providing security in SOA environment.

Chapter 9 illustrates a practical use of these layers in cloud computing (SaaS) solution.

Reference [17] gives an idea of how to use these layers while architecting a solution, although the main aim of the reference is to indicate an agile architecting method.

The remaining review of the CCRA in this chapter will also provide some more details of these layers. Hence, we will proceed to review CCRA, which is the main objective of this chapter.

10.4 Using the SOA RA with the CCRA

Refer to Figure 10.2 for using SOA RA with CCRA.

The following provides a highlighted summary of additional focus points that are relevant for cloud architecture in each of the five functional layers of SOA:

(i) *Operational layer*: For providing cloud services, additional requirements are needed on infrastructure; they are to enable broadband access, resource pooling, rapid elasticity, virtualization and scalability.

This is very relevant to cloud IaaS providers. For cloud SaaS architect, one can assume the presence of these services and build the cloud SaaS on these as explained in Chapters 3 and 4. A cloud SaaS solution architect does not have to create IaaS platform for the purpose of providing SaaS solution.

CCRA is a generic architecture or providing any of cloud services including SaaS. In this chapter, we concentrate only on the points related to SaaS.

(ii) *Service layer*: All common cloud services are exposed or identified in this layer. Asset services namely SaaS are exposed in this layer.

This book prefers to use the term 'payload services' to refer to those set of services that are meant for customers who will pay a fees for using these services. These services are exposed in the 'services layer'. The term 'asset services' also refers to the same as per the specific document. The type of services exposed determines the flavour of cloud service being offered. In the context of this book, it will mostly be SaaS.

(iii) *Service components*:

All support services that will be consumed to provide this asset service can also be exposed in this layer (but need not be exposed to end-consumer).

(iv) *Business processes*: Business processes that participate as a part of cloud solutions can be provided here (as BPaaS); alternatively, business processes (that participate as a part of cloud solutions) can be consumer of business process services.

(v) *Consumer layer*: In CCRA consumer layer is strictly and carefully separated from service provider. This allows pooling and substitution of cloud services for providers themselves from those meant for consumers.

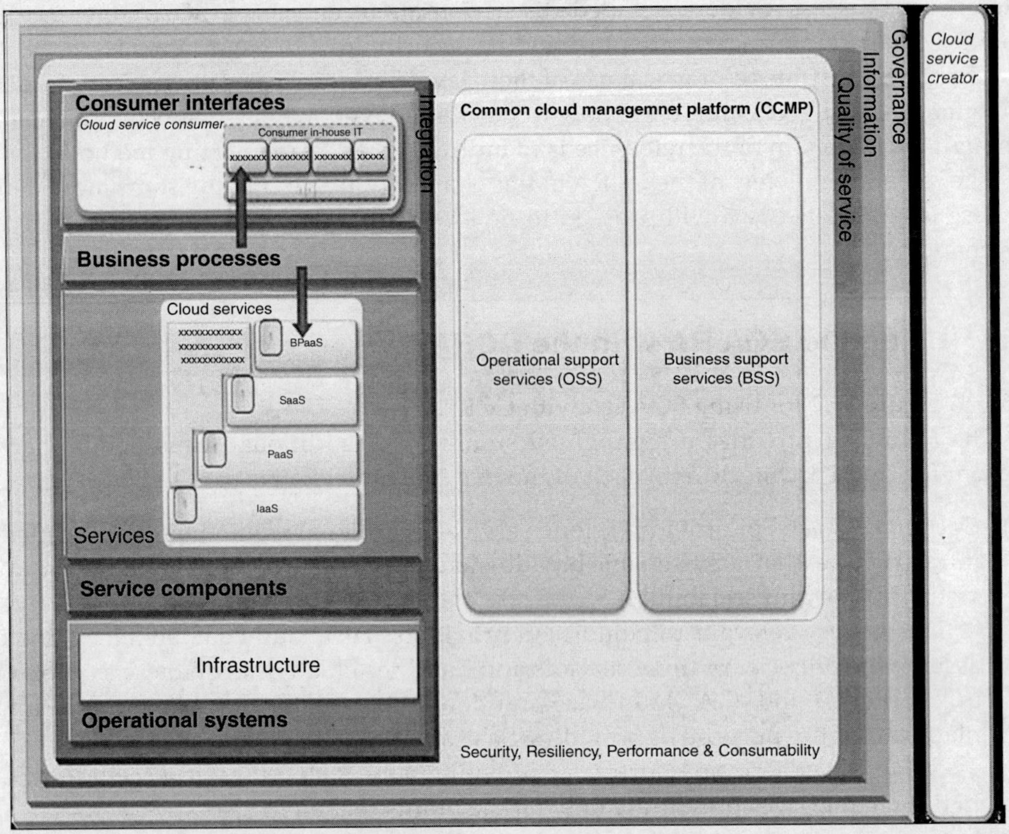

Figure 10.2 Using CCRA with SOA RA[24]

All the four cross-cutting concerns (services) in an SOA RA are very important concerns for all cloud architecture and solutions (see Figures 10.1 and 10.7). Hence, they become baseline for all cloud computing architectures. Subsequently, they find a detailed regularized best-practice incorporated as various architectural components in CCRA. Obviously, all the functional layers may have interactions with capabilities in these four cross-cutting layers in CCRA too.

The details of these four cross-cutting layers, and their relevance to cloud architecture and hence to CCRA is discussed below:

Special focus points for cloud architecture are as follows:

1. QoS layer: OSS and BSS are placed in this layer. They all collectively come under what is called common cloud management platform (CCMP) in CCRA. On-demand and self-service security is the cloud-specific requirements that are met through this layer.
2. Governance: Special governance support that is needed to support across organizational boundaries comes under this layer for cloud solutions.

So far, the above discussions gave a context of CCRA in relation to SOA and the gamut of solution architectures.

Remaining of this chapter will provide a formal abstracted review of core of the IBM's CCRA[24].

10.5 CCRA – Architecture Overview Diagram

Figure 10.3[24] gives AOD with highest level of abstraction of CCRA. Subsequent part of this chapter will provide a drill-down fine-granular details of this architecture.

10.5.1 Roles of CCRA

CCRA defines three major roles as follows:

1. Cloud service consumer
2. Cloud service provider
3. Cloud service creator

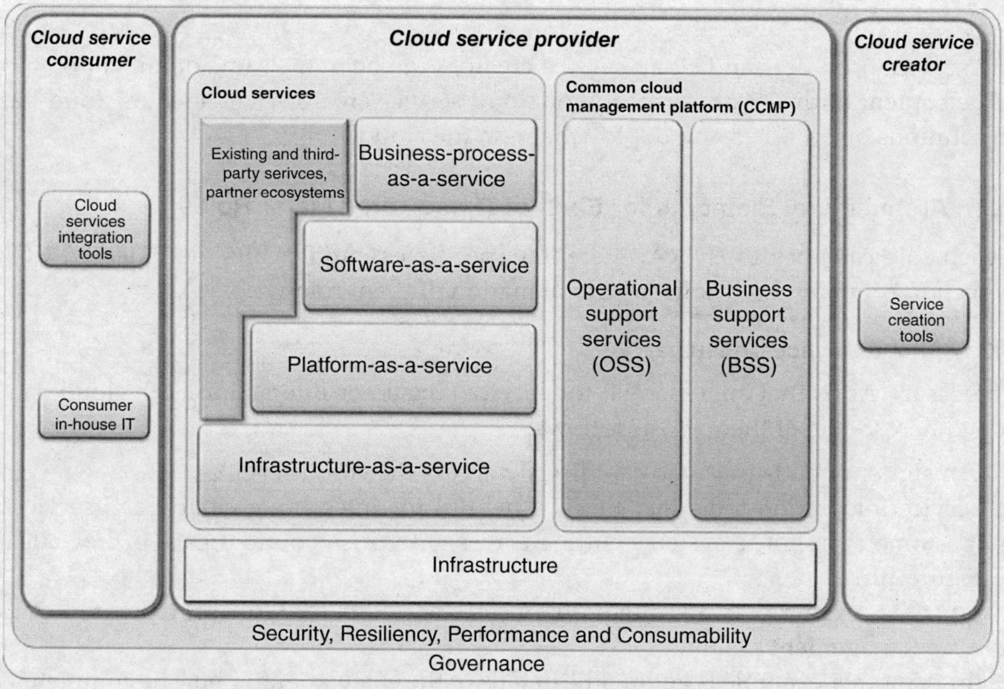

Figure 10.3 IBM™ CCRA overview[24]

10.5.1.1 Cloud Service Consumers

A cloud service consumer in a simplest term that refers to *an organization or a human being or an IT system* that

(i) Consumes cloud services (i.e. requests, uses and manages, e.g. changes quotas for users).
(ii) May be billed for all (or a subset of) its interactions with cloud service and the provisioned service instance(s).
(iii) Browses service offering catalog and triggers service instantiation and management from there.

10.5.1.2 Cloud Service Providers

(i) They have the responsibility of providing cloud services to cloud service consumers.
(ii) They own the responsibility of managing the cloud SaaS services (may be through a common cloud management platform or CCMP).

10.5.1.3 Cloud Service Creators

(i) They build cloud services by leveraging functionality (of various software) and that is exposed (as cloud SaaS) by a cloud service provider.
(ii) They design, implement and maintain (run-time and management) artefacts specific to a cloud service.

Cloud service providers and cloud service creators can be in the same organization too.

The content of this book is mainly for cloud service creators who creates cloud-based SaaS solutions or products and deploy them on the cloud.

10.5.2 Architectural Elements for Each of These Three Major Roles

For each role category in CCRA, there are specific essential ABBs identified in CCRA. This section provides a quick list and explanation of them role-wise.

10.5.2.1 Cloud Service Consumer

All necessary ABBs that are essential for service consumer interaction with cloud SaaS is grouped here. Some of them are as follows:

(i) Consumer or end-user who can directly access the cloud services.
(ii) Service integration tools that may be helpful for integrating cloud SaaS services to (customers) in-house systems cutting across enterprise boundaries and firewalls (see Figure 10.4).
   (a) One example is to integrate or interact with enterprise federated Access management system.
   (b) Another example is getting the details of the customer after he/she completed the formalities to open bank account. In this account-opening example, the account opening is provided as cloud SaaS service; small- and medium-sized banks that are typically cooperative banks or micro-banks avail this service.

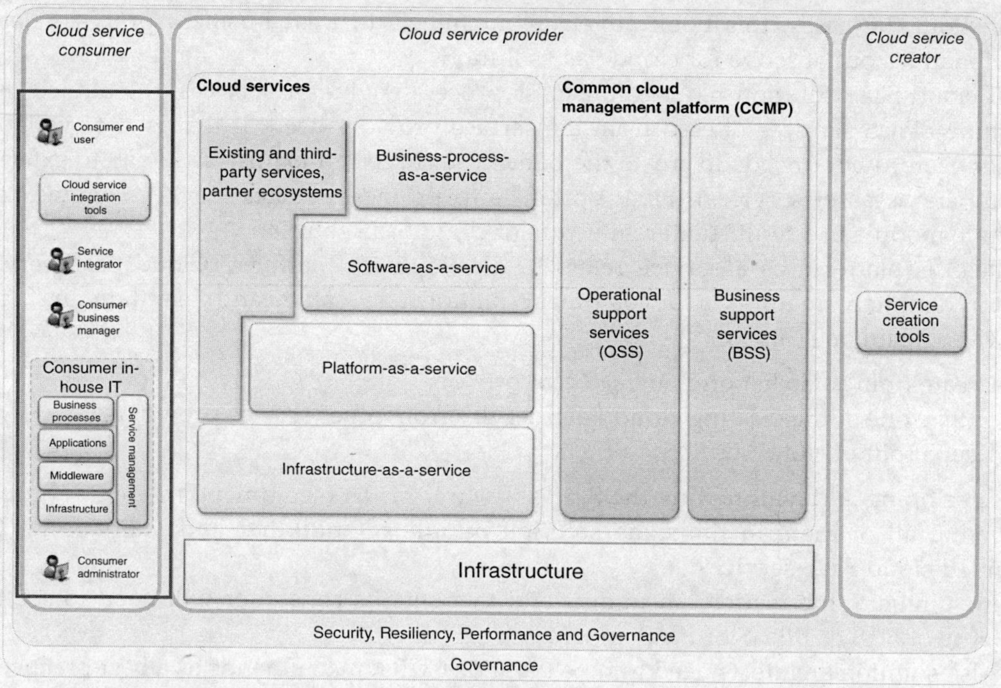

Figure 10.4 IBM™ CCRA – cloud service integration tools and consumer in-house IT[24]

(iii) Within enterprise, IT consumer may require a few more integration services such as to integrate offered cloud SaaS services to its, say, within-enterprise business processes.

(iv) As such, there is not much of need to integrate with within-enterprise other platforms such as middleware or infrastructure software.

(v) Consumer administrator is one of the key functionalities group: for example, from where each consumer IT administrator may provide user access management for their own users.

10.5.2.2 Cloud Service Provider

There are two major architectural elements within this 'cloud service provider' as shown in Figure 10.3.

(i) Cloud services model
(ii) CCMP - Common Cloud Management Platform

(The third not-so-major component is service provider portal as shown in Figure 10.6 and discussed in a section titled so).

SaaS is one of the four cloud service models. IaaS, PaaS and BPaaS are the other three models. Typically, cloud SaaS would be provided on *IaaS (Infrastructure as a Service)*; cloud SaaS software may also require business processes or cloud SaaS service may be consumed as part of a business process.

In both the cases, this book advocates architects to treat business process-related functionalities out of scope for cloud SaaS solutions.

If cloud SaaS solution requires business process engine or services, the advice is to consume BPaaS services offered from the service provider itself. If that is not available, the service provider needs to create the BPaaS (but need not expose as BPaaS to external consumers as asset services). Final option is to provide business process engine as a separate module in a multi-tier architecture of cloud SaaS solution.

PaaS is platform as a service refers to development platform. Cloud SaaS service creator definitely requires a development platform to create and maintain the SaaS software. Again one can

(a) Create from scratch a unique PaaS platform or
(b) Utilize one of the existing cloud PaaS service from other service providers or
(c) Keep it out of cloud services

For developing and maintaining the SaaS software, CCRA recommends an ideal solution of having all of them in the same solution bundle for building and maintaining the intended cloud SaaS services.

In summary, the reader can understand that service consumer will need to see the existence of IaaS or BPaaS or PaaS on which SaaS runs.

Also solution architects need to note that this CCRA recommends as a best practice to build cloud SaaS solutions on these three platforms. In other words, availability of these three platforms is a pre-requisite for building cloud SaaS (solutions).

But that is not the case always: also that may not be the quite practical way too. In practice, IaaS is inevitably required platform; using any public clouds (or setting up an in-house private cloud) will be quite advisable. However, for the other two (PaaS and BPaaS), solution architects can choose to consume from other cloud service providers or have non-cloud services too.

Salesforce.com™ exposed the SaaS first. It is not clear whether they had any IaaS at all at that time when they started their service. Later, they began exposing PaaS and BPaaS as asset services. It is not clear whether they really started creating the three service models before creating SaaS. But an intelligent guess is one need not. Later, these three might have been made to mature enough to expose them as asset services. But, they have not yet begin to offer IaaS, when the book was under print.

That is the path this book recommends to solution architects whoever encounters difficulties in creating cloud SaaS from scratch. Alternatively, as these services are available from various service providers, they can consume these services and build on.

This discussion is not part of CCRA specifications, and it is an analysis of its implications to solution architects.

Cloud Services Models

CCRA defines four cloud service models: IaaS, PaaS, BPaaS and SaaS in the document[24]. CCRA[24] defines Cloud SaaS as follows:

> The capability provided to the consumer is to use the provider's applications running on a cloud infrastructure and accessible from various client devices through a thin client interface such as a Web browser (e.g. Web-based email). The consumer does not manage or control the underlying cloud infrastructure, network, servers, operating systems, storage, or even individual application capabilities, with the possible exception of limited user-specific application configuration settings[24].

SaaS is also referred to as applications-as-a-service since SaaS is essentially about providing applications as a service.

The CCRA diagram (Figure 10.5) confirms that cloud SaaS provider can provide their application as SaaS over the three underlying cloud services: IaaS, PaaS and BPaaS.

For each of these four cloud services models, softwares are required for implementing cloud services specific to each of these models:

1. For IaaS, hypervisors are the software that need to be installed on the managed hardware infrastructure.
2. For PaaS, a multi-tenancy-enabled middleware development platform is required.
3. For SaaS, a (multi-tenancy-enabled) end-user application is required.
4. For BPaaS, a multi-tenancy-enabled business process engine software is required.

Each of the above four types of cloud service software exposes its functionalities as APIs towards cloud service consumer for programmatic use.

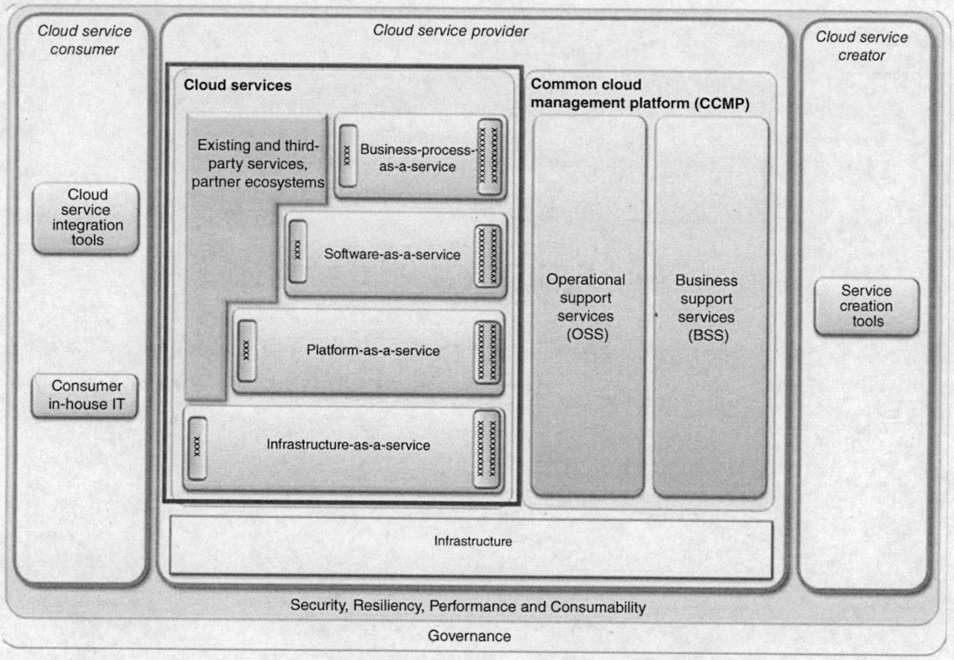

Figure 10.5 IBM™ CCRA – cloud service details[24]

It is imperative that cloud services need to be built on one another – for example, a cloud SaaS software service needs to be offered on IaaS. In such context, it is expected to use the same OSS/BSS structure by sharing them across various cloud services; in our example, they are SaaS and IaaS. However, the OSS and BSS need to independently provide services to each of the cloud services – here SaaS and IaaS. For example, if BSS is used to meter the usage of SaaS, BSS should measure SaaS used independently and the same OSS service can be used for IaaS to measure its usage but its measure should be independent.

In other words, OSS and BSS and all other components in CCMP is common to many of the cloud services provided – be it SaaS, or IaaS, or PaaS, etc. So all these cloud services can 'see' the existence of the common services in CCMP and use them for their purpose.

Common Cloud Management Platform (CCMP)

The CCMP (see Figure 10.6) exposes two important management focused services:

(i) BSS
(ii) OSS

A solution architect need to know and get himself or herself familiar with these functional building blocks. While architecting solutions, architects

(a) Need to identify matching solution building blocks and also
(b) Identify what is the subset of functionalities that are good enough for the particular solution being architected
(c) Explain how rest of the system can integrate or consume these services

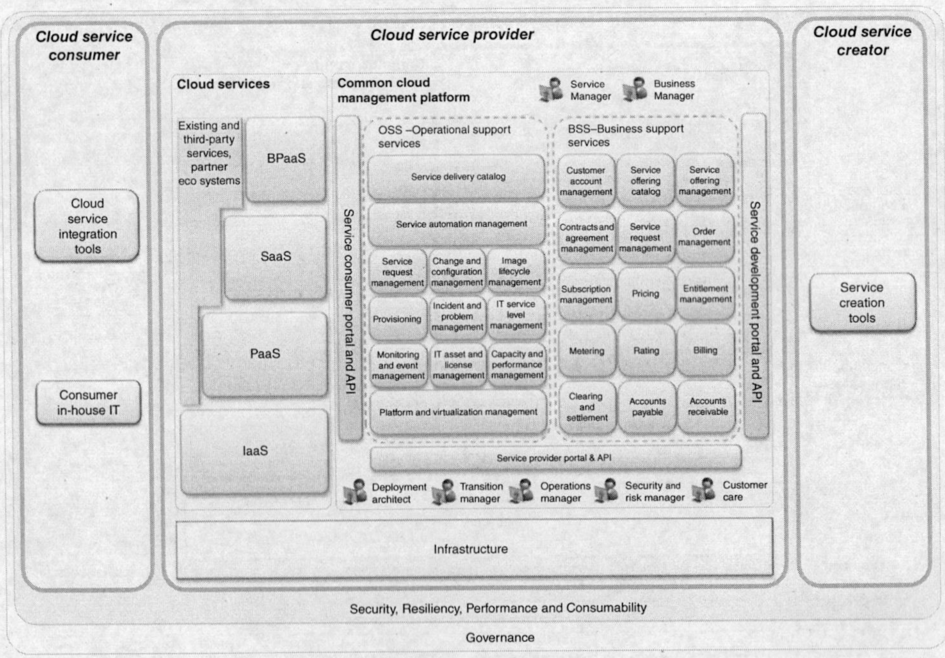

Figure 10.6 IBM™ CCRA – CCMP details[24]

Most of the time, it should be possible to locate a third-party services that can provide a complete CCMP functions; therefore, the job becomes simple for architects to integrate (consume these services) the same into their solutions.

The term OSS and BSS have been borrowed from Telco industry (telephone service providers) where this was used in a similar context.

BSS and OSS services are common accessible to all the four types of cloud service (IaaS, SaaS, BPaaS and PaaS).

Therefore, SaaS service creators should make use of this from the IaaS platform on which intended SaaS services will be delivered.

Thus, use only one single set of (BSS and OSS) services for both IaaS and SaaS (as against using one set of BSS and OSS for IaaS and a different set of BSS and OSS for SaaS although SaaS is also offered from the same IaaS). Such a practice is in conjunction with CCRA architecture principle (See also 'architecture principle' in Section 6 of this chapter) helping regularization; thus economy of scale and hence cost saving.

Cloud service creators and providers need to automate a lot of operational work: for example, automating data backup for all customers can be considered as part of this one; another example is to selectively isolate a customer whose usage tries to hang the system! Collections of those services, helpful for operational management as well as technical-related support services, are grouped in OSS in CCMP.

Supporting any level of virtualization is another role of CCMP. CCMP supports application-level virtualization (i.e. SaaS), platform level, operating system level and infrastructure hypervisor-level virtualizations. 'How to virtualize a software' is not discussed in this book. (Only 'how to virtualize a hardware' is discussed from solution architects perspective in Chapter 3.)

CCMP functionality is accessible via application program interfaces (APIs) exposed by the CCMP's internal components.

High modularization within CCMP helps service creators and providers to choose any appropriate tool or service vendors who can provide those CCMP functionalities or services that they specifically require.

The management services exposed by the CCMP are different from the services exposed by cloud SaaS which is developed and created. Normally the CCMP are purchased component and developed or created by Cloud SaaS developer themselves.

The Services from Cloud SaaS (which is the focus of this book) is the one for which customer signs-up for using this cloud service. Sometimes it is better to refer them as 'pay load' services to indicate these are the ones which generates revenue (and definitely not the CCMP services). The term pay load is borrowed from Aircraft design.

Since many cloud services – SaaS , IaaS or PaaS – which may stack up one over other can use the same CCMP service (for the sake of economy of scale/reuse) CCMP needs to be developed and exposed as 'Platform.' (How to render a software as a platform is something to be learnt outside this book)

Service Provider Portal

Besides CCMP, cloud service provider layer also includes three different portals – marked as service provider portal in Figure 10.6 for the three roles to access OSS and BSS.

(i) Service consumer portal is meant for cloud service consumers for self-service delivery and management (the actual cloud service instances are used via a cloud service-specific UI.
(ii) Service provider portal is meant for cloud service provider internal users and administrators for daily operations and
(iii) Service development portal is meant for cloud service creators.

While we refer to three different portals from an architectural perspective, all three portals could be realized by a single implementation with different access rights and presenting different capabilities depending on who logs in.

Security, Resiliency, Performance and Consumability

Security, Resiliency, Performance and Consumability are cross-cutting concerns and need to be treated as aspects running through and through of the entire cloud platform including the structure of CCMP by itself, the way the hardware infrastructure is set up (e.g. in terms of isolation, network zoning setup, data center setup for disaster recovery, etc.) and how the cloud services are implemented.

SaaS service providers are expected to choose this CCMP services for deploying their 'pay load' services.

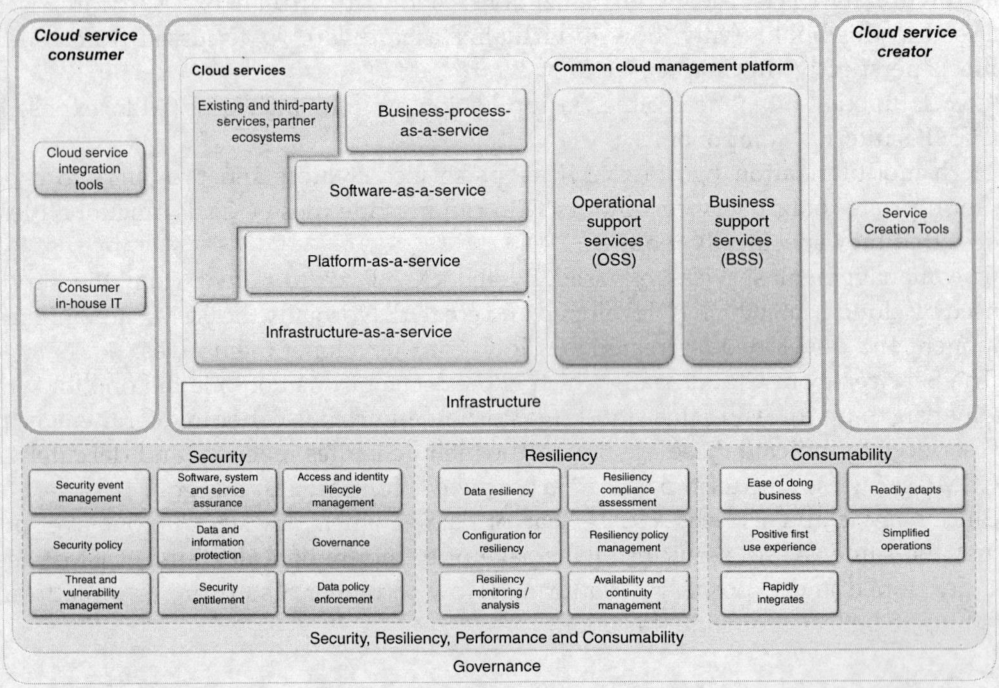

Figure 10.7 CCRA – security, resiliency, performance and consumability details[24]

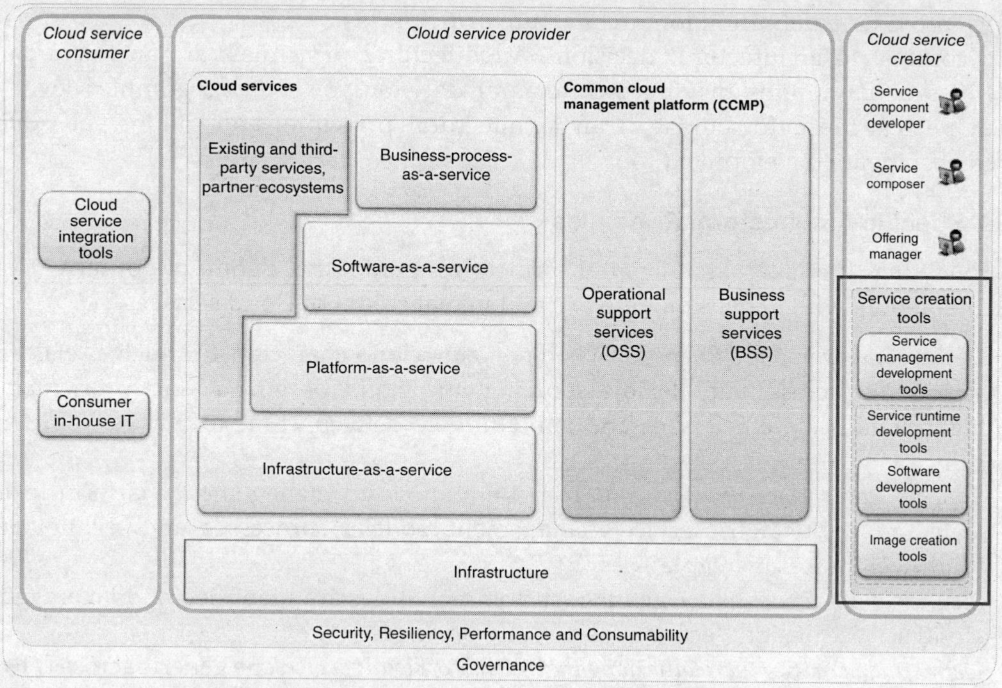

Figure 10.8 CCRA – service creation details[24]

10.5.2.3 Cloud Service Creator

Service Development Tools

Service Development Tools are used by the Cloud Service Creator to develop new cloud services. They refer to both development of runtime artefacts and management-related aspects (e.g. monitoring, metering, provisioning, etc.). "Runtime artefacts" refers to all capabilities needed for running what is delivered as-a-service by a cloud deployment or what this book refer as 'pay load' services. Some specific examples of 'runtime artefacts' are JEE enterprise applications, database schemas, analytics, *golden master virtual machine images*, etc.

10.6 Architectural Principles and Related Guidance

Any architecture is incomplete without specifying architectural principles. CCRA also identifies four important additional architectural principles.

This only means that general architectural principles can come from TOGAF's guidelines. Then a few more will come from TOGAF's SOA RA as that is the basis on which the CCRA is built. Then these four principles come from CCRA.

TOGAF provides a definition for 'architecture principle' as:

In contrast to architectural decisions, 'architectural principles' are an overarching guidelines or paradigms driving architectural decisions on a more granular level[4, 24] (which reflects the enforcement of an architectural principle) and guides subsequent phases of software development too.

CCRA-Specific Architectural Principles

The following top-level architectural principles guide the definition of any cloud implementation, with a focus on delivery and management of cloud services.

(i) *Design for cloud-scale efficiencies*: When realizing cloud characteristics such as elasticity, self-service access, and flexible sourcing, the cloud design is strictly oriented to high cloud scale efficiencies and short time-to-delivery/time-to-change ('efficiency principle')[24].
(ii) *Support lean service management*: The common cloud management platform fosters lean and lightweight service management policies, processes and technologies. ('lightweightness principle')[24].
(iii) *Identify and leverage commonalities*: All commonalities are identified and leveraged in cloud service design ('economies-of-scale principle')[24].
(iv) *Define and manage generically along the lifecycle of cloud services*: Be generic across I/P/S/BPaaS and provide 'exploitation' mechanism to support various cloud services using a shared, common management platform ('genericity')[24].

These principles can be summarized and abbreviated as ELEG (= Efficiency, Lightweightness, Economies-of-scale, Genericity).

This concludes a brief review of the proposed CCRA[24].

10.7 Comparison of CCRAs of IBM™, Microsoft™ and HP™[25]

If there are many CCRAs, it is a confusion as to which one should be used. That is why regularization helps. Until such a regularization occurs, architects should enjoy reading and comprehending as much as CCRAs as possible. Reading CCRA proposed by many in the industry will be beneficial in some of the following ways:

(i) A comparative or elaborate study of CCRAs in literature will help choose the right one for the right purpose; for example, if the project is to arrive at IaaS, may be understanding of Microsoft's[25] proposed CCRA may be beneficial.
(ii) Studying across the CCRAs will give a long list of many architectural components (such as ABBs); some of them might have been missed out in one or the other. The combined long list of ABBs will be handy to select the required ones for the project.
(iii) Architects should not be fancied by coming up with his or her own RA for the project and that will lead to non-regularization.

Table 10.1 The following table is based on Ref. [25]

	IBM™		HP™		Microsoft™
Service consumer in CCRA	A cloud service consumer can be an organization, a human being or an IT system that consumes services offered as service.	Cloud Service Consumer is represented in 'Demand' layer of CCRA. However the demand layer covers more than the consumer, but also service catalog, portal access for provision of services. 'Demand' Layer of CCRA includes the representation for Cloud Service Consumer. However the layer covers more than the Service consumer. It covers such as service catalog, (cloud service) portal access.			The customers' or tenants' or users' self-service layer provides an interface for Hyper-V cloud tenants or authorized users to request, manage, and access services, such as VMs, that are provided by the Hyper-V cloud architecture.
	Requests, uses and manages (e.g. changes quotas for users). The service consumer may be billed for all				
Service provider in CCRA	(Or a subset of) plays with cloud service(s) and any such provisioned service instance(s). Play their roles necessary to keep the up keeping of any provisioned services.	Service providers play their role in both 'Demand', 'Deliver' layers of CCRA. Service providers will have to touch and play their corresponding roles in both layers – 'Demand' and 'Deliver' – layers of CCRA.			Sharing the infrastructure provides economy of scale as explained in chapter 1.

(*continued*)

Table 10.1 The following table is based on Ref. [25] (Continued)

	IBM™		HP™		Microsoft™
Service creator in CCRA	Service creators are the ones who use service development tools to develop new cloud services. Service creators are the ones who use necessary development tools to create all cloud services. This includes both the development of runtime artefacts and management-related aspects (e.g. monitoring, metering, provisioning, etc.).	Service creator plays a role in 'Supply Layer' which functions as the dynamic resource governor that integrates a dynamic and mixed work load utility function. Supply layer has work load monitoring utilities to assess dynamic requirements of resources and also governs dynamic resource allocation. It is a place where service creator will only interact with.			the ability to design, test, implement, and monitor these IT workflows have to be provided by orchestration layer.
Infrastructure in CCRA	"Infrastructure" refers to all infrastructure elements needed to provide cloud services. Infrastructure element means only the hardware infrastructure. Infrastructure means all necessary infrastructure components required to provide cloud services.	"Infrastructure" layer is abstracted behind the 'Supply Layer' and consists of power & cooling, servers, storage, network, Software, information "Infrastructure" layer consists of power & cooling, servers, storage, network, Software, information. This layer is abstracted behind the 'Supply Layer'			"Infrastructure" layer covers all those items mentioned in the cells above which include, Servers, Storage, Networking, Virtualization.
		Demand layer	**Delivery layer**	**Supply layer**	
Management platform in CCRA	Business Support Services that are needed by Cloud Service Creators to implement a cloud service. Some of them being: Customer Account Management Service Catalog Offering Pricing/Billing/Metering Accounts Receivable and Payable Payable, Accounts Receivable, Pricing/Billing/Metering, Service Catalog Offering, Customer Account Management	User Access Management Service Offer Management	Billing and Rating Request Processing & Activation	Usage Metering Dynamic Work Load Management	The Cloud service management layer consists of all the necessary tools and systems that are used to deploy and operate the cloud infrastructure.

	IBM™		HP™		Microsoft™
	The set of operational management / technical-related services that Cloud Service Creators needed to implement any cloud service is considered as Operational Support Services. Some of them being: Provisioning Incident and Problem Management Image Life Cycle Management Platform and Virtualization Management				
QoS (Quality of Service) in CCRA	Security, Resiliency, Performance & Consumability are cross-cutting aspects on QoS	Quality of Experience SLA Compliance	Quality of Service	Resource Monitoring and Dynamic allocation	The service management layer helps in automating cloud service management. It also helps in adapting best practices too.
	Also the major aspects of QoS being Threat and Vulnerability Management Data Protection Availability & Continuity Management Ease of doing business Simplified Operations				

10.8 Summary

- This chapter reviews one of the proposed CCRA.
- This reference architecture is a logical extension of SOA reference architecture (under approval of SOA RA with TOGAF).
- This chapter discusses the cloud specific SaaS-related extensions that make up the CCRA, although the proposed CCRA is meant to address all types of cloud computing services.
- CCRA identifies three major roles: service consumer, service provider and service creator.
- With respect to these major roles, this chapter gives architectural elements and their positions in the reference architecture.
- The discussion of common cloud management platform is something very specific to cloud computing and important for readers to understand mastering solution architecting in this space.
- Architectural principles and guidance that come from the reference architecture is summarized; this needs to be applied in addition to what TOGAF provides for all architectural projects.
- Finally, a comparison of three reference architectures are summarized in a table from Ref. [25].

Chapter 11

Architecting for Security in Cloud SaaS Software

11.1 Introduction

A book on cloud computing is never complete without a chapter on security. Many readers of this book may be more aware of the security threats for cloud computing rather than the exact technical knowledge about cloud computing itself! ☺ That speaks of the word-of-mouth or adverse publicity that has gained roots about fear of insecurity in cloud. An enormous amount of body of knowledge is available on this subject area of secured cloud computing.

11.2 Segments of Security

When one refers to security in cloud computing, it may mean anything. Two important aspects of security in cloud computing are given below:

(i) To develop a secured software as a service (SaaS) solution or product
(ii) To securely
  (a) Deploy SaaS in public cloud
  (b) Provide SaaS through public cloud
  (c) Access SaaS services through public cloud
  (d) Keep the data in the SaaS environment

Out of the two important points mentioned earlier, the second one is treated as out of scope of this book. That comes under deploying software in cloud environment and maintaining and providing services. In this book, the subject is centred around architecting cloud compatible SaaS software. Therefore, this chapter will give a brief treatment to the first one – how to write a very secured code and models for the cloud.

The volume of knowledge may be so huge that it will require a separate book (see Ref. [16]). A single chapter may not be adequate to cover the same or do justice to this topic.

Maybe in the subsequent editions of this book, a reasonable justice will be done to cover this topic. Some basic cursory pointers for security will be provided in this chapter.

Obviously, one cannot develop a solution or product and then infuse security into it. Therefore, architecting security right from the beginning is a must.

11.3 Security Architecture for Cloud SaaS

Just like starting with Cloud Computing Reference Architecture (CCRA) for architecting cloud SaaS software, one need to start with appropriate security reference architecture for the same.

(i) Security for service-oriented architecture (SOA) is very basic knowledge that an architect needs. Reading the book[16] will serve a good base for starting the security planning or architecting for cloud SaaS software architecture too.

(ii) Security architecture of the open group architecture framework (TOGAF) and security architecture and the architecture development method (ADM) of TOGAF are very relevant and applicable materials. However, the current versions of these are in general nature, in the sense, oriented towards areas such as enterprise security architecture or specific software systems development architecture. Architects need to master these subject areas and bring relevance to cloud SaaS software architecture too as TOGAF and its ADM will always give a robust methodology for architecting security in the cloud SaaS software.

(iii) Anything specific such as cloud SaaS security reference architecture may emerge in the near future, or may be a general Cloud Security Reference Architecture (CSRA) may emerge, which can be customized to cloud SaaS. (Security reference architecture is different from the other reference architectures such as SOA RA or CCRA mentioned in this book). Refer to Figures 10.2 and 10.7 and relevant discussions for an understanding of how the above points take specific realization in architecture.

(iv) The CCRA has clearly given a place for security in the overall architecture. It has also clearly defined security as a cross-cutting aspect just like security is treated in a similar way in SOA RA.

Therefore, this implies that security should be available uniformly for all services in the cloud SaaS.

Architecting for security in cloud SaaS starts right from selecting reference architecture and following it through to the specific SaaS software: architecting security at every level of the architecture.

Accessing through service and the architecture being service-oriented itself is highly vulnerable to security failures.

The very nature of the fact that SaaS software are hosted in a cloud environment itself brings a lot of security vulnerable points. This is what is referred to as point (2) under Section 11.2.

An intruder can get into any one of the area permitted for him or her and get into any other area which is forbidden for the intruder. These aspects are more elaborately discussed in Refs. [16, 38].

11.4 Security as an Aspect

Aspect is contrast to a function; a functional feature can be programmed and contained within a module or sub-program or a procedure whereas the aspect is a cross cutting in nature and it will run through several modules or sometimes several tiers of the software too. Thus it even violates the principle of 'separation of concern.' It may run parallel to execution thread of a functionality.

Security is an aspect, and its nature is to run along with functions of the software rather than being separated out as a functionality.

If a user logs into a cloud SaaS software and invokes a specific service (function) in it, then until the service is completed, the security aspect should run in parallel to it.

(i) One specific service may be implemented as a collection of functions.
(ii) Each function can run across several tires of a specific architecture.
(iii) Even in each tire, it can invoke various modules.

The inter-tier, inter-module interfaces are expected to be service oriented. A user who logs in for using a specific service should not inject a code in the middle and call a different tire and module to get an axis to a forbidden functionality or service.

Thus, security has to run in parallel and while the service is served using functionalities. This is one way of visualizing the service. Figure 11.1 schematically illustrates this best.

Here, security is an 'aspect' to the 'service'. A good knowledge of aspect-oriented architecture (AOA) as well as aspect-oriented programming (AOP) is essential to implement security as an aspect along with each service.

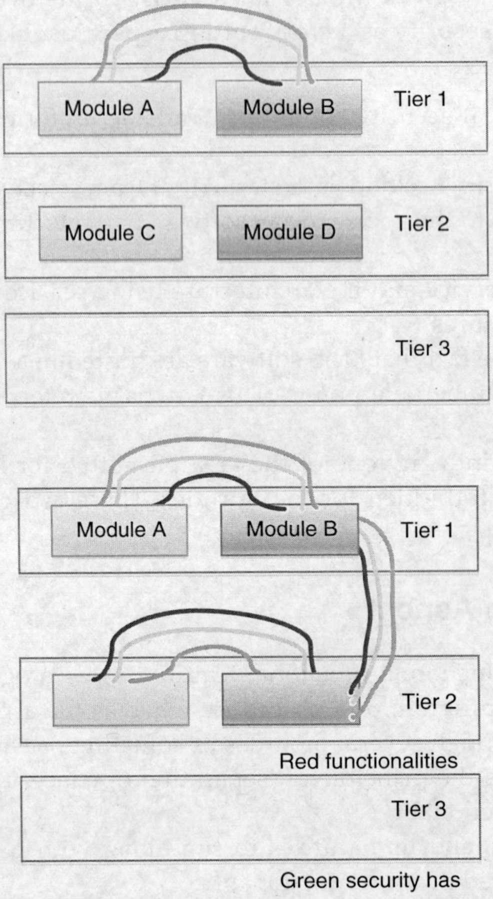

Figure 11.1 Schematic illustration of security is provided as 'aspect' protecting access of every module

11.5 Building Security within SaaS Software: Some Implementation Tips

AOP or simply aspect programming is the way to go for implementing security.

Aspect programming is a lot different from programming to implement a functionality.

To prevent security breach, user's credentials have to be checked before entering into any module be it on the same tier or service in different tire.

On the one hand, it is apparently a huge over head; on the other hand, modern-day computing power being available at a lower cost, this additional computing power needed can be brought in to provide this security aspect.

Spring™ framework[38–40] provides a convenient and easy way of programming aspects such as security. AOP is lot different compared with conventional structured programming or now mostly practised object-oriented programming (OOP).

This framework is available both for Java as well as for .Net programmers.

The following gives a conceptual description of how Spring™ framework can be used to implement security as an aspect along with service.

(i) Spring™ framework allows module dependency to be injected into the framework.

(ii) That means when module A calls module B, it does not call module B directly; instead,

  (a) It calls the Spring™ framework.

  (b) Also the module A need not know the syntax of the interface of module B.

(iii) The Spring™ framework, before calling module B, can be programed to check the login credentials of the user who invoked module A.

  (a) A logic can be put in that place whether the login user has adequate credentials to make use of the module B functionalities.

  (b) Normally, this kind of security check is put around each functionality usage.

(iv) In a similar way, anybody who tries to access any module or functionality bypassing the Spring™ framework or this security check can be rejected or denied access before executing the module.

(v) This way of providing security in a software can be implemented to any extent of fine granularity. Fine granularity means or implies that

  (a) It can be at a functional level that can run through and through all the modules and tires.

  (b) It can be at the entry of every object irrespective of the functionality. If it is too fine grind as mentioned above, the overhead of checking for security shoots up like anything. One main reason is that the software designer has to envisage a table for each of these individual fine-granular objects, that are the types of login users allowed or denied, and this table has to be accessed and verified for breach of security before entry of every small object.

The above explanation will make more sense now along with the Figure 11.1. Before entering into any module, the user credentials are checked. It is also ensured that no intruders can directly access any module. Thus, security is running in parallel and along with the execution of any functionality or *realization* of service.

This is one of the main ways of providing security to functionalities execution. There are many more ways of doing the same thing.

Providing thread level security while execution is another aspect that has to be taken care at design and implementation level. The industry practice has mastered this art, and there are plenty of literatures available. Such security has been implemented for all multi-user multi-tasking systems even before cloud arrived. It is not anything specifically new for cloud SaaS software alone. Hence, it is treated as out of scope for this book.

Providing secured way of accessing or storing data from database is another important architecting consideration.

11.6 Summary

- This chapter introduces the security needs for any cloud SaaS software.
- This chapter has also acknowledged that this is a separate subject calling for may be a separate book itself.
- This chapter has provided in schematic an idea of how to treat security as aspect and implement it within the cloud SaaS software.
- Spring™ framework is used to illustrate the implementation of security within a software.

Abbreviations

ABB	Architectural Building Blocks
ACL	Access Control List
ADM	Architecture Development Method
AOA	Aspect Oriented Architecture
AOD	Architecture Overview Diagram
AOP	Aspect Oriented Programming
API	Application Programming Interface
AWS	Advanced Wireless Services
B2B	Business to Business
BPM	Business Process Management
BSS	Business Support Systems
CCMP	Common Cloud Management Platform
CCRA	Cloud Computing Reference Architecture
CECM	Computer Enhanced Curriculum Motivators
CMS	Content Management Server
CNC	Cloud Non Compatible
COTS	Commercial off the Shelf
CPU	Central Processing Unit
CRM	Customer Relationship Management
CSRA	Cloud Security Reference Architecture
DAO	Data Access Objects
DB	Databases
EA	Enterprise Architecture
ECM	Enterprise Content Management
ELEG	Efficiency, Lightweightness, Economies of Scale, Genericity
ERP	Enterprise Resource Planning
FAX	Facsimile Automatic Xerox
FIFA	Federation of International Football Association
FTP	File Transfer Protocol
GB	Giga Byte
Ghz	GigaHertz
HP	Hewlett Packard
HRM	Human Resource Management
HTML	Hypertext Markup Language
HTTP	HyperText Transfer Protocol
HTTPS	HyperText Transfer Protocol Secure
I/O	Input/Output
IaaS	Infrastructure as a Service
IAM	Identity and Access Management
IBM	International Business Machines
ID	Identification
IIS	Internet Information Services
IM	Instant Messaging
ISO	International Standards Organization
IT	Information Technology
LAN	Local Area Network
LDAP	Lightweight Directory Access Protocol
MB	MegaBytes
MP3	MPEG Layer-3 Sound File

MP4	MPEG-4 Part 14
NGOSS	New Generation Operations Systems and Software
NLB	Network Load Balancers
O/S	Operating System
OLE DB	Object Linking and Embedding Data Base
OOP	Object Oriented Programming
OSP	Open Source Product
OSS	Operation Support Services
PaaS	Platform as a Service
PCB	Printed Circuit Board
PDF	Portable Document Format
QoS	Quality of Service
RA	Reference Architecture
RDBMS	Relational database management system
REST	Representational State Transfer
ROI	Return On Information
RSS	Really Simple Syndication
SaaS	Software as a Service
SAN	Storage Area Network
SBBs	Solution Building Blocks
SDLC	Software Development Life Cycle
SEO	Search Engine Optimized
SME	Small or Medium Enterprises
SMS	Short Message Service
SOA	Service Oriented Architecture
SOAP	Simple Object Access Protocol
SQL	Structured Query Language
TELCO	Telecom
TOGAF	The Open Group Architecture Framework
UI	User Interface
UML	Unified Modeling Language
URL	Uniform Resource Locator
VoIP	Voice over Internet Protocol
VPN	Virtual Private Network
WAN	Wide Area Network
WURFL	Wireless Universal Resource FiLe
XML	Extensible Markup Language

References

1. Small Business Enterprises Could Prove to Be the Big Opportunity for Indian IT, Business World-January 2010, http://www.businessworld.in/bw/2010_01_16_A_Small_Success_Story.html, Venkatesan Ravi, ex-Chairman, Microsoft, India.
2. Cross Dissolve Method for EA Implementation, Sankaran Prithviraj, Open Group TOGAF EA practioners Conference, 4–6 June 2008, Johannesburg, http://www.opengroup.org/johannesburg2008/prithviraj.html, Prithviraj, Sankaran.
3. Componentized EA Development, Sankaran Prithviraj, Open Group TOGAF EA Practitioners Conference – Munich, 22 October 2008, http://www.opengroup.org/Munich 2008/prithviraj.html, Prithviraj, Sankaran.
4. Version 9, TOGAF's Enterprise Edition, 2009, www.opengroup.org/TOGAF,2009.
5. Building Distributed Applications, Architecture Strategies for Catching the Long Tail – MS Arch. Journal, April 2006. Frederick Chong and Gianpaolo Carraro, Microsoft Corporation. http://msdn.microsoft.com/en-us/library/aa479069.aspx
6. ISO-IEC-WD3-42010 Systems and Software Engineering – Architectural Description – ISO standards (ISO 2008).
7. Jeanne W. Ross, Peter Weill and David Robertson, 2011, 'Enterprise Architecture As Strategy: Creating a Foundation for Business Execution', Harvard Business School Press.
8. http://www.devx.com/architect/Article/33059/0/page/2
9. http://www.wfmc.org/standards/docs/TC-1011_term_glossary_v3.pdf
10. 5 Things to Consider When Integrating Your CMS and Portal Products: http://www.cmswire.com/cms/enterprise-cms/5-things-to-consider-when-integrating-your-content-management-system-and-portal-006789.php
11. Architectural Pattern in integrating BPM and ECM: http://www.cmswire.com/cms/enterprise-cms/integrating-an-enterprise-cms-with-bpm-a-strategy-for-bridging-the-gap-008073.php
12. Part 2: Architectural Pattern: http://www.cmswire.com/cms/enterprise-cms/integrating-an-enterprise-cms-with-bpm-a-strategy-for-bridging-the-gap-part-2-008098.php
13. Engineering well formed Services, Sankaran Prithviraj, Hi-PC Conference, December 2008, www.hipc.org/hipc2008/documents/hipc2008-workshops-dec9.pdf; http://www.hpl.hp.com/india/senopt08/papers/senopt08104.pdf

14. Shankar Kambhampaty, 'Service Oriented Architecture for Enterprise Applications', Wiley India Pvt Ltd., New Delhi, ISBN13: 978-81-265-1989-7.

15. Shankar Kambhampaty, 'Service-Oriented Architecture for Enterprise and Cloud Applications', Wiley India Pvt Ltd., New Delhi, ISBN 9788126519897.

16. Ramarao Kanneganti and Prasad Chodavarapu, December 15, 2007, 'SOA Security' Manning Publications, ISBN: 1932394680.

17. 'Agile Architecting Method' Enterprise Architecture Practitioners' Conference (EAPC) – TOGAF – The Open Group Architecture Forum, accepted for publication, To be published in TOGAF Conference.

18. BPM or CMS Platform? Design Principles to Manage Your Business Processes 'Cms wire' an online magazine, March 2011 (**a**) http://www.cmswire.com/cms/enterprise-cms/bpm-or-cms-platform-design-principles-to-manage-your-business-processes-009828.php

19. Cloud Based SaaS Solution Architecture for SMBs (EAPC), Sankaran Prithviraj, October 2010 – Amsterdam – TOGAF EAPC.

20. How Cloud Pushed Frontiers of Software Architecture, Webinar to Architects in Chennai, Sankaran Prithviraj, 9 December 2010; yet to be published in media as of Sep 2014.

21. Len Bass, Paul Clements and Rick Kazman, 2003, 'Software Architecture in Practice', Peason, New Delhi.

22. Paul Clements, Rick Kazman and Mark Klein, 2002, 'Evaluating Software Architectures', Pearson Education, ISBN 978-81-317-1592-5.

23. Allen Dreibelbis, Eberhard Hechler, Ivan Milman, Martin Oberhofer, Paul van Run and Dan Wolfson, 'Enterprise Master Data Management: An SOA Approach to Managing Core Information', IBM Corporation.

24. https://www.opengroup.org/cloudcomputing/uploads/40/23840/CCRA_IBM Submission. 02282011.doc. IBM cloud computing Reference Architecture 2.0 (CC RA).

25. Sysop Cloud Computing Journal, Cloud Computing.sys.con.com/ node/1752894, Cloud computing reference architecture. – Review of the BIG Three (IBM, HP, Microsoft).

26. TOGAF, SOA definition, http://www.opengroup.org/soa/soa/def.htm

27. HP CCRA, also *HP Cloud Reference Architecture – HP Software Universe 2010 – Presentation on Slide Share*, http://h18006.www1.hp.com/storage/pdfs/4AA3-4548ENW.pdf

28. [togaf AND soa ra] 'Using TOGAF to Define & Govern SOAs' Chapter 22 of TOGAF v9.1 http://pubs.opengroup.org/architecture/togaf9-doc/arch/chap22.html

29. '20. Applying the ADM across the Architecture Landscape' http://pubs.opengroup.org/architecture/togaf9-doc/arch/chap20.html#tagfcjh_27

30. Enterprise Continuum, http://pubs.opengroup.org/architecture/togaf9-doc/arch/chap39.html#tag_39_04_01

31. CMS wire: 'RIP to Your Web site', Digital Communication Platform.

32. Part 1: http://www.cmswire.com/cms/customer-experience/a-new-avatar-for-web sites-digital-communication-and-collaboration-platform-015549.php

33. Part 2: http://www.cmswire.com/cms/customer-experience/rip-to-your-corporate-websites-015798.php?pageNum = 2

34. C.K. Prahalad, 2005, 'The Fortune at the Bottom of the Pyramid', Wharton School Publishing, Pearson, New Delhi, ISBN: 81-297-0712-8.

35. Zaachmaan, 'Frame work-Enterpize Architecture Model', http://en.wikipedia.org/wiki/Zachman_Framework

36. Long Tail, http://www.wired.com/wired/archive/12.10/tail.html

37. SaaS Architecture by, Progress Software, http://www.greenemotion-project.eu/upload/pdf/deliverables/D3_2-ICT-Reference-Architecture-V1_2-submitted.pdf

38. Rod Jhonson, Juergen Hoeller, Alef Arendsen, Thomas Risberg and Colin Sampaleanu, 2006, 'Java Development with the Spring frame work', Wiley India, New Delhi, ISBN: 81-265-0610-5.

39. http://docs.spring.io/spring/docs/2.0.x/reference/introduction.html, referred on 12 December 2013.

40. http://docs.spring.io/spring/docs/3.2.4.RELEASE/spring-framework-reference/html/, last referred on 12 December 2013.

Keyword Taxonomy Through Semantic Tree

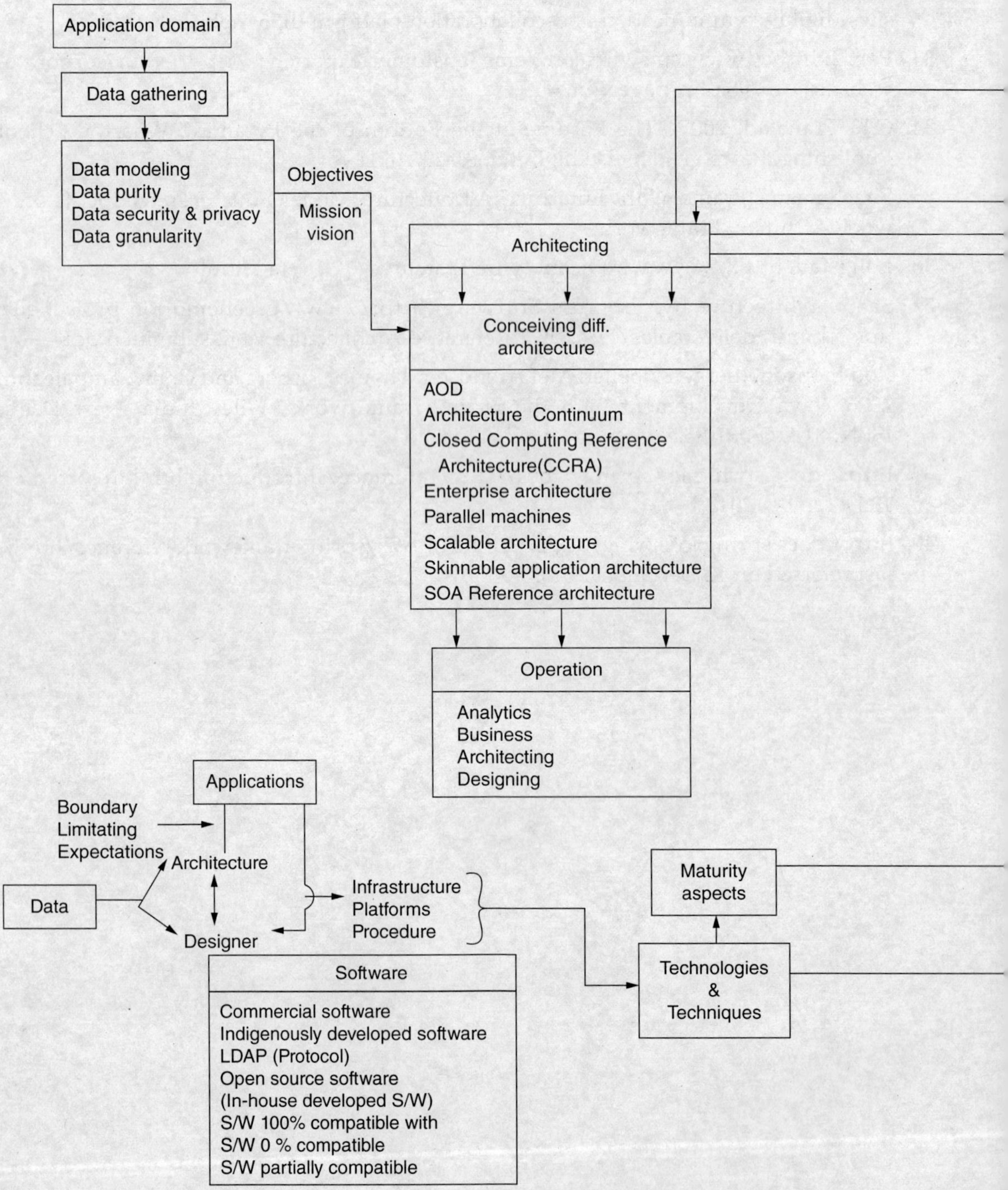

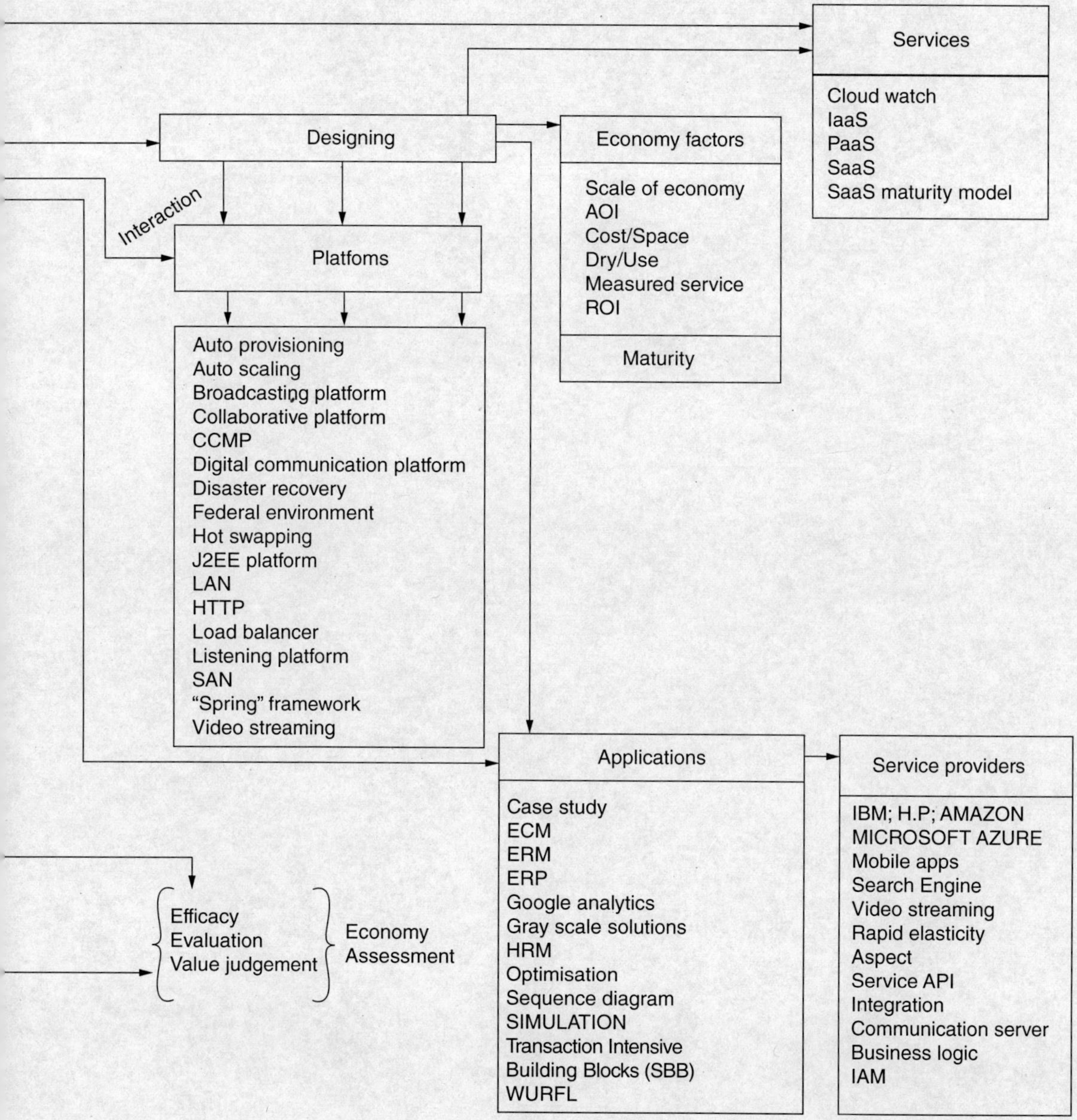

Services
Cloud watch
IaaS
PaaS
SaaS
SaaS maturity model
Designing
Economy factors
Scale of economy
AOI
Cost/Space
Dry/Use
Measured service
ROI
Maturity
Interaction
Platfoms
Auto provisioning
Auto scaling
Broadcasting platform
Collaborative platform
CCMP
Digital communication platform
Disaster recovery
Federal environment
Hot swapping
J2EE platform
LAN
HTTP
Load balancer
Listening platform
SAN
"Spring" framework
Video streaming
Applications
Case study
ECM
ERM
ERP
Google analytics
Gray scale solutions
HRM
Optimisation
Sequence diagram
SIMULATION
Transaction Intensive
Building Blocks (SBB)
WURFL
Service providers
IBM; H.P; AMAZON
MICROSOFT AZURE
Mobile apps
Search Engine
Video streaming
Rapid elasticity
Aspect
Service API
Integration
Communication server
Business logic
IAM
Efficacy
Evaluation
Value judgement
Economy
Assessment

Key Words Taxonomy

Process
- Analytics
- Architecting
- Business
- Designing

Data
- Data modeling
- Data purity
- Data security & privacy
- Data granularity

Architecture
- AOD
- Architecture continuum
- Closed architecture
- Cloud Computing Reference Architecture (CCRA)
- Enterprise architecture
- Parallel machines
- Scalable architecture
- 'Skinnable' application architecture
- SOA Reference architecture

SAN
- Hardware virtualization
- Horizontal/Vertical scaling
- Hypervisor
- IAM server

Platforms
- Auto provisioning
- Auto scaling
- Broadcasting platform
- Collaborative platform
- CCMP
- Digital communication platform
- Disaster recovery
- Federal environment
- Hot swapping
- J2EE platform
- LAN
- HTTP
- Load balancer
- Listening platform
- SAN
- "Spring" framework
- Video streaming

Economy Factors
- Scale of economy
- AOI
- Cost/Space
- Dry/Use
- Measured service
- ROI

Services
- Cloud watch
- IaaS
- PaaS
- SaaS
- Saas maturity model

Rapid Elasticity
- Agile Era
- "Bare metal" in Computing parlance
- Cloud Compatibility Measure (CCM)
- Radian – 6

Applications
- Building Blocks (SBB)
- Case study
- ECM
- ERM
- ERP
- Google analytics
- Gray scale solutions

HRM
Optimisation
Sequence diagram
WURFL
Simulation
Transaction Intensive
UML

Service Providers
Aspect
Business logic
Communication server
IAM
IBM; HP; Amazon
Integration
Microsoft Azure
Mobile apps
Rapid elasticity
Search Engine
Service API
Video streaming

Software
Commercial software
Indigenously developed software (In-house developed S/W)
LDAP (Protocol)
Open source software
S/W 100% compatible with cloud solutions
S/W 0% compatible
S/W partially compatible

Index